The Conquest of Society

The Conquest of Society

Snell Putney

*sociological observations for the autonomous revolt
against the autosystems which turn
humanity into servo-men*

Focus Books
Published by
Wadsworth Publishing Company, Inc.

Acknowledgments:

Excerpt from "Prescription of Painful Ends" by Robinson Jeffers. Copyright 1939 by Robinson Jeffers. Reprinted from Selected Poems, *by Robinson Jeffers, by permission of Random House, Inc.*

Excerpt from "Howl" by Allen Ginsberg. Copyright © 1956, 1959 by Allen Ginsberg. Reprinted by permission of City Lights Books.

Cartoon by Jules Feiffer. Copyright © Jules Feiffer 1960. Reprinted by permission of Publishers-Hall Syndicate and Jules Feiffer.

ISBN-0-534-00168-8
L. C. Cat. Card No. 71-187498
Printed in the United States of America

1 2 3 4 5 6 7 8 9 10—76 75 74 73 72

Pay no attention to Caesar.
Caesar doesn't have the slightest idea what's *really* going on.*

---

* Kurt Vonnegut, Jr., *The Books of Bokonon,* in *Cat's Cradle* (New York: Dell, 1965), p. 73.

Preface

This is not a book against society. One might as well be against respiration; men require society and its systems to become human. Neither is it an attack on America, whose faults have long been documented. This book is an analysis and protest of the ascendance of the social system over men.

Sociologists study men in society and especially the interaction between men and society. Such interaction can be studied with a focus on people or with a focus on society. In *The Adjusted American*,* Gail Putney Fullerton and I focused on people, on normally neurotic Americans and on the way in which American society generates their neuroses and in turn is shaped by these neuroses. We wanted to show that despite deficiencies in the social system, the individual who learns to understand himself and his needs can find fulfillment. The book was a manual to help Americans go beyond their society and become autonomous.

That manual left largely unexamined the question of why human society should become so incongenial that men have to go beyond it to find fulfillment. So, *The Conquest of Society* focuses on society. Social systems have a kind of separate existence apart from men and are capable of a surprising degree of selfish self-direction. This results in a conflict of interests between men and society which underlies most modern problems, although it is obscured by the protestations of the systems as they seek to domesticate humanity into servo-men. By understanding this conflict of interests, men could find the means to conquer their society and establish the primacy of people; they could maintain an environment truly conducive to the fulfillment of human needs. This book is a primer for the revolt of the autonomous against the autosystems.

My debts to others are too complex to explain neatly. Annotations indicate quotations and paraphrases, but such debts are not the

---

* Snell Putney and Gail J. Putney (Fullerton), *The Adjusted American* (New York: Harper & Row, Publishers, 1966).

major ones. The ghosts of Freud and Marx are never far away, and Gail's unique mind continues to be a companion and foil. Mervyn Cadwallader taught me to take systems themselves as a unit of study, and exemplified the uphill educational reformer. Bonnie Doran and Patricia Crespi provided secretarial expertise, and Susan Shirley was research assistant and friendly critic. But my greatest debt is to several thousand students whose smiles, scowls, and challenges have forced me to develop, justify, and revise these observations over the years.

Snell Putney
Yacht Troika
Mazatlan, Mexico

Contents

Prologue

Up and Down

Historically, men have hoped that things might stay the same instead of getting worse. The idea that things were going to get better and better was born in the eighteenth century, developed in the nineteenth, and seems to be dying in the twentieth as changes accumulate and people don't seem to be any happier. But then again, maybe they were just the wrong changes.

According to the poem and the song, Richard Cory was the man who had everything other men dreamed of having, and who was everything other men dreamed of being. And yet he went home one night and put a bullet through his head. In a similar way, America has achieved so much of so many dreams—from social security to a national superhighway system—and yet now seems to be floundering and wondering if any of it was worthwhile. The question scurries across the corner of our minds: how can we *have* so much, and *get* so little?

As individuals, we worry about how to overcome our shyness at parties, or how to pay the dentist. And collectively, we worry about how we can stop pumping excrement into our rivers or how we can reconcile blacks and whites. But whereas we used to feel that it was only a matter of time until things worked out, we now begin to wonder if they will. Is it *possible* to create a happy society, or had we better just accept trouble as our lot and cope as best we can? Where did we ever get the idea that there is a solution to every problem, or that things should get better all the time?

Throughout history men have generally accepted life as they found it, without hope for general improvement. They only hoped that it wouldn't get worse—at least for them. In Egypt thousands of years before Christ, a priest of Heliopolis wrote:

Transformations go on, it is not like last year, one year is more burdensome than the next.... Righteousness is cast out, iniquity is in the midst of the council halls. . . . Nobody is free from evil; all men alike do it. . . . There is none so wise that he perceives, and none so angry that he speaks.[1]

We can learn much about men's expectations of social change by looking at the theories they use to understand it. Perhaps the most ancient is golden age theory. It posits a time in the past when the gods had created a perfect world and then explains the troubles of the present as the consequences of imperfect management by men. Golden age theory holds out no hope for improvement, but merely offers an explanation for present suffering. A simple example of golden age theory is the biblical story of the fall of man from the Garden of Eden.*

Another ancient theory of social change is cyclic theory. It holds that history is repetitive, like a great wheel revolving or like plants sprouting, growing, dying, and leaving seeds to repeat the cycle. Golden age theory can be transformed into cyclic theory by merely adding some sort of rescue apparatus to restore things to perfection when the decline has reached the bottom. The Greeks called such a rescuing apparatus a "Deus ex machina" after the miraculous stage tricks by which some of their dramatists rescued heroes from hopeless situations.† Although neither cyclic theory nor

---

* The first historian to write history (as opposed to the simple recording of stories and legends) was probably Herodotus. In the fifth century BC he developed a theory of history which postulated a golden age in the past, which inevitably had degenerated into a less perfect silver age. The silver age, in turn, had been followed by the sorry bronze age in which he found himself. But he predicted that an even more unhappy iron age was to follow.

† A familiar example of such a cyclic theory is found in Plato's *Republic*. He presents aristocracy as the ideal state, but predicts that it would inevitably degenerate. Aristocracy was government by the best, but how were the best to be determined? In time, the rule would pass to the most honored, who would not necessarily be the best. Thus aristocracy would degenerate into timocracy, rule by the most honored. But the timocracy would also degenerate as the rulers found means of passing power along to their children. Such children would not be the most honored members of their society, but merely the most powerful, so their rule would become merely an oligarchy. Yet the oligarchy would also degenerate because the oligarchs would become so oppressive that the people would take power into their own hands and establish a democracy. Such a democracy, in Plato's view, would be a worse government than an oligarchy, and in fact would create such disaster that the people would call for a tyrant to rescue them from their own rule. At this point the degeneration of the state would be complete, since tyranny was the worst form of government; but also at this point the cycle could begin again. For a wise tyrant (especially if trained and guided by a philosopher) would use his power to establish the best form of government—an aristocracy. Yet that aristocracy, too, would degenerate, and the cycle would repeat. See *The Republic*, Book 8.

golden age theory provides any grounds for optimism about the future, these theories of social change have dominated man's thinking through the ages.

The Invention of Progress

The idea that things might be getting better does not seem to have been seriously entertained until the eighteenth century, and then only in Europe. A unique combination of events at that time and place resulted in the infinitely exciting idea of progress. It is difficult today to understand the innocence and exhilaration of that era—but it is important to try.

Emerging from the Middle Ages, Europe had passed through the Renaissance and the Enlightenment. The writings of the ancient Greeks and Romans, preserved in monasteries and in Byzantium, had been rediscovered. The oceans had been crossed, and the Western Hemisphere poured forth its curiosities and its riches. Trade routes to the Orient had been reestablished. New ideas poured into Europe.

Tremendous strides occurred in that branch of man's intellectual life which we now call science. Newtonian physics, in particular, seized the imagination of Europe to a degree that is hard to understand today. It seemed to show that man's mind could explain the universe. Planetary orbits were no longer divine whims, but the products of simple and definite laws. It was soon proposed that no further discoveries would be possible in physics because everything would be known. Only a few details remained to be settled.* Suddenly it seemed that man's reason was the most important and powerful force in the world, and that man was destined to discover all the secrets of nature.

The idea of developing knowledge set the stage for the idea of progress. The first real glimmer of the idea came in a rather curious way. Certain young writers rebelled against the traditional view that the greatest works had all been written, and that the modern writer could only try to imitate them more skillfully than others had done. The young writers contended that although they might not be as gifted as the ancients had been, they could begin where the

---

* Now, of course, we look back and see how Einstein pulled on those "few little details" like loose threads on a sweater until the whole of Newtonian physics unraveled. But there was no hint of that possibility in the eighteenth century.

ancients had left off, and go on beyond them. Thus, they contended, literature could progress ever further.[2]

In the general climate of enthusiasm, this revolutionary idea of progress was generalized into a vision that man was capable of endless intellectual and spiritual development. In sharp contrast to the earlier concepts of the depravity of man and the futility of his reason, the perfectibility of man and the limitless capacity of his mind became the credo of the day.

In the nineteenth century, Darwin combined the idea of progressive development with Malthus' pessimistic concept of competition for a limited food supply and emerged with the theory of evolution. This theory could be interpreted as showing that biology itself had progressed because it had finally produced man, the reasoning animal.

Darwin's theory launched a great wave of enthusiasm for tracing the evolutionary stages of other forms of development. Social scientists developed theories about the stages through which societies evolved and (by regarding their own society as the highest and best to date) were able to speak of society as a whole evolving toward ever higher forms.

By this time the industrial revolution was well under way; new technological developments were occurring at accelerating rates. Intellectuals, enjoying the benefits of the new technology, felt they discerned yet another dimension of progress.* Up to this time, progress had been conceived primarily in terms of moral and intellectual development. But now progress came to include material and technological development; man would progress until he was able to build anything, go anywhere, do whatever he wished.

Marx was perhaps the greatest theorist of progress. It was he who tied all these ideas to the Hegelian concept that there was an inherent upward pattern in history. Marx attempted to prove that, through technological change, society would inevitably progress toward a utopia in which there would be no more exploitation of man by man and in which human potential would be forever carried to higher levels of development.

---

* For the working masses of Europe and England, of course, the early days of the industrial revolution were a disaster. But the masses were not the ones who wrote the books or who believed in the idea of progress.

And thus dawned the twentieth century—with the belief in progress full-blown. One of the most eloquent statements of the vision came from Leon Trotsky. Standing at the pinnacle of power, when the victory of the first scientific revolution made everything seem possible, he wrote:

> Mankind will educate itself plastically, it will become accustomed to look at the world as submissive clay for sculpting the most perfect forms of life. . . . The present distribution of mountains and rivers, of fields, of meadows, of steppes, of forests, and of seashores, cannot be considered final. . . . In the end [man] will have rebuilt the earth, if not in his own image, at least according to his own taste.[3]

The End of Innocence

For a time, the idea of progress came to be a nearly universal article of faith in Europe and America. The common man came to accept the idea that everything was going to get better just as un-reflectively as his ancestors had accepted the idea that things would stay as they were or deteriorate. Those of us who were adolescents in the 1940s were perhaps the last generation to believe in progress in this innocent manner.

We never doubted that the future would be bright. Once the war against Germany and Japan was won, there would be an end to war. The United Nations would keep the peace, and the postwar world would be full of miracles. Mankind was really going somewhere, and we were part of the most advanced and exciting part of mankind—America! It seemed to us that in every realm, from the creation of free institutions to the development of technological know-how, we were blazing the path that the rest of humanity would someday follow.

In post-war America it seemed that we would all be engineers or the wives of engineers; we would live in new and beautiful plastic houses full of surprising gadgets. We would fly to and from work in helicopters, and would watch new movies every night on our own television sets. And all the while our laboratories would keep unlocking secrets of nature and making new advances possible. Someday we would even travel to the moon—and beyond.

---

* Trotsky added that he had complete confidence that man would rebuild the world in good taste.

It never crossed our minds that technological advances might not automatically result in greater happiness—at least not until Hiroshima and Nagasaki. And then things were suddenly different. Moreover, the post-war world in those early years was a bit disappointing: the helicopters and plastic houses didn't materialize, and the television often showed only wrestlers. And instead of peace, we got the cold war.

The innocence was ending, and the dream was tarnishing. I read with fascination how the poet Robinson Jeffers compared our destiny with that of past civilizations:

> Lucretius felt the change of the world in his time, the
>   great republic riding to the height
> Whence every road leads downward; Plato in his time
>   watched Athens
> Dance the down path. The future is a misted landscape,
>   no man sees clearly, but at cyclic turns
> There is a change felt in the rhythm of events, as when an
>   exhausted horse
> Falters and recovers, then the rhythm of the running hoof-
>   beats is changed: he will run miles yet,
> But he must fall: we have felt it again in our own life time,
>   slip, shift and speed-up
> In the gallop of the world; and now perceive that, come
>   peace or war, the progress of Europe and
>   America
> Becomes a long process of deterioration—starred with
>   famous Byzantiums and Alexandrias,
> Surely—but downward. . . .[4]

My generation became increasingly discouraged and disillusioned —beat. Allen Ginsberg caught the mood of many of us when he wrote:

> I saw the best minds of my generation destroyed by madness, starving
>   hysterical naked,
> dragging themselves through the negro streets at dawn looking for an
>   angry fix. . .
> who passed through universities with radiant cool eyes hallucinating
>   Arkansas and Blake-light tragedy among the scholars of war,
> who were expelled from the academies for crazy & publishing obscene
>   odes on the windows of the skull,

who cowered in unshaven rooms in underwear, burning their money
in wastebaskets and listening to the Terror through the wall. . .
who demanded sanity trials accusing the radio of hypnotism & were
left with their insanity & their hands & a hung jury,
who threw potato salad at CCNY lecturers on Dadaism and subse-
quently presented themselves on the granite steps of the mad-
house with shaven heads and harlequin speech of suicide, demanding instantaneous lobotomy,
and who were given instead the concrete void of insulin metrasol
electricity hydrotherapy psychotherapy occupational therapy
pingpong & amnesia. . . .[5]

Meanwhile a new generation had been born to a life of affluence—
and continual crisis. From infancy they accepted the threat of nuclear annihilation, the cold war, and the growing domestic unrest.
Also from infancy they took for granted the possibility of attaining
the version of utopia their Depression-reared parents had struggled
so hard to achieve: the good house, the steady job, the new car, the
suburban life style. They grew up in this utopia, so secure and yet
so insecure, but it did not always make them happy. And when
their parents thought they were asleep, the children heard the quarreling from behind the closed door of the master bedroom. And daily,
the television reminded them of the disparities between the ideals
they learned in school and the realities of the American scene.

Their poet was Bob Dylan; he blazed a trail for them which
began with protest over America's violation of her own ideals,
plunged through a psychedelic nightmare which pulverized the
American Way of Thought, and finally emerged into a pastoral
reaffirmation of the timelessness of warmth and simplicity. But in
this *tour de force,* any thought of progress was utterly lacking.

There arose what Roszak termed the "counter culture," a sub-
culture characterized by its fundamental repudiation of the basic
values of technocratic America and its dream of progress.[6] And the
counter culture spread from the colleges and city streets to the high
schools and the junior high schools, and even found many fellow
travelers among older intellectuals. Such divergent men as Herbert
Marcuse, Benjamin Spock, and Timothy Leary made a common
cause with the youthful rebellion. Of course, the counter culture
was diluted as it spread, but skepticism concerning progress seemed
to be one of its most persistent elements.

Today, the idea of progress seems to be almost dead among the young, and to be dying in bewildered, defensive, middle America.* For a little while there was an automatic and unreflective faith that things were getting better and that man was going somewhere. But as wars continue despite ideals and good intentions, as poverty remains amid affluence, as ennui afflicts the affluent, the perfectibility of man and society seems problematic. And the bitter experience of littered, gaudy America casts doubt on Trotsky's faith in man's taste.

The Baby or the Bath

And yet ... and yet.... The idea of progress was a good one. There need not be an inherent reason why society could not offer men ever increasing opportunities for fulfillment. There is nothing stupid about the idea that life might be made progressively more rewarding. Was it the idea of progress which was wrong or the way we went about seeking it?

So we return to the question with which we began: can a happy society exist? This question is really the crucial one. In *Civilization and Its Discontents,* Freud summarized his theory that a happy society was inherently impossible. He argued that man must develop a social order in order to survive, but that in order to live within a social order man had to curb some of his most basic urges. To live in a society a man had to be psychologically maimed, and therefore unhappy. The details of the social order did not matter, and no amount of social reform could change things very much. Freud's theory goes directly to the heart of the matter, for he recognized that there was a fundamental conflict between the interests of men and the interests of society. Moreover, he was able to show how certain specific problems such as family conflicts derived from the more basic conflict between human interests and societal interests.

But many have felt that Freud's pessimism was excessive. For example, Herbert Marcuse, while a Freudian, has argued that although living in any society will produce a certain degree of misery, modern societies produce a much greater degree of misery than they

* Paradoxically, it seems to be alive and well in the Orient, especially in China.

need to. Marcuse speaks of *surplus repression*—of constraint of human impulses far beyond the necessary minimum to render social cohabitation and cooperation possible.[7] Marcuse has not held out much hope, however, that modern societies will relinquish their demands for surplus repression.

If Marcuse is right, then some progress is at least theoretically possible. The problem then becomes one of trying to discover why societies impose surplus repression, and why men tolerate it. And what can be done about it.

Part One: The Nature of Systems

1   Autosystems and Servo-Men

Men need society to survive, and through it almost everything becomes possible to them. But the larger and more complex the social order becomes, the more it tends to become an autosystem and to pursue its own objectives at the expense of human welfare. Worst of all, the autosystem creates servo-men whom it has convinced the system is right after all. The problem of man and society is strictly who is to be the servant, and who is to be the master.

The fundamental reason why there is an inherent conflict between men and society is not, as Freud believed, that society imposes restraints on man's instinctual nature. The whole thrust of modern social and psychological science has been toward the recognition of the social (rather than the antisocial) nature of man. The human soul looks less demoniacal to those who were spared the Victorian repressions of Freud's childhood.

Instead, the basic problem is that large systems over a period of time take on objectives of their own, distinct from the objectives of the men who created the systems in the first place. It isn't the generals who are running America, nor the stockbrokers, nor the politicians. To a surprising degree, American society is running itself—and running amuck.

Meet the Autosystem

An autosystem is a social system which comes to pursue its own objectives by its own means and ceases to be under the effective control of men. An autosystem becomes a sort of juggernaut which rolls relentlessly on over the bodies of its adherents. Thus—in order to carry out the procedures defined in the Handbook of Operations which it has evolved over the years—a welfare department may operate in ways which actively contribute to the destruction of the clients which it is supposed to aid. And thus the Department of

Defense has pursued its interests and objectives in ways which could very well have resulted in the annihilation of the American people.

Any social system has a tendency to become an autosystem, and the tendency seems to increase more or less exponentially as the system becomes larger and more complex. In large societies, therefore, it may be more or less expected that the social institutions will be pursuing objectives very different from those for which they were presumably established. Small wonder, then, if the interests of men go begging.

Meet the Servo-Man

The problem is vastly complicated by the fact that autosystems persuade their participants that there is no possible conflict of interest between man and system. Because men live their lives within the social system, most of their information comes from the system. Because they labor within the system, most of their energy and attention are concentrated within it. Their consciousness (and unconsciousness) becomes inextricably linked with the system. It is not an idle phrase to say they develop the "corporate point of view," become a "fixture in the company," or a "member of the team." They become effective components within the system. But in so doing, the system comes more and more to be their reality. The very goals they seek are goals the system has taught them to desire: wealth, higher status, or power. They seek these goals within the system by means the system defines for them. Their very definition of the meaning and purpose of life is fundamentally shaped by the system. Inevitably the by-product of all this integration into the system is that their capacity for autonomous thought is greatly reduced. Conversely, their uncritical support of the system, which has become the central organizing principle in their lives, is virtually guaranteed.

The problem is further complicated by what Erich Fromm called "the escape from freedom," [1] or what I like to term "existential copping-out." Existentialists have long described the anguish that man experiences when he confronts the ambiguities of the human condition. Man finds himself existing, but needs to generate his own definition of what his existence means. There is a terrible insecurity in the necessity to make choices for which he will hold himself responsible, because choices are always made without full knowledge of their long-range results or implications. Yet out of such uncertain choices man creates the self which he must then learn to accept. It is painful to face the fact of individual autonomous existence, and men retreat from this fact in a variety of ways. The social system rewards with praise or power the individual who makes an existential cop-out—who abdicates to the system and says, "I don't make the rules; I don't break the rules; I just do my job as well as I can."

A servo-mechanism is a device by which some aspect of a system is regulated. It receives information on conditions inside or outside the system and performs some switching operation in order to carry out the objectives of the system. The toilet tank valve is a very simple and purely mechanical servo-mechanism; its task is to open and close the water inlet valve in order to keep the tank full. It is entirely uninvolved in whether the tank should be full or in the possible consequences of its operations. Modern electronics has made possible the development of vastly more complex and flexible servo-mechanisms. But men still do most of the regulation and adjustment required by the social systems.

A servo-man is a man whose consciousness is fundamentally determined by an autosystem and who therefore functions merely as a servo-mechanism within it. This does not necessarily mean that his role is a menial one, or that he does not display creativity in playing it. The consciousness of the president of the corporation may be more completely controlled by the autosystem than the consciousness of the file clerk. The president may perform brilliantly as a servo-man, and the file clerk may retain a sullen sense of his own autonomy.

The servo-man is likely to be rewarded by the system in terms of its own values (which he has accepted as his own); his real needs may remain unfulfilled. But the essential point is that his being a servo-man leaves the system out of control.

The servo-man is beautifully illustrated in the cartoon by Jules Feiffer on the next page.[2]

The influence of an autosystem is insidious. Even those who actively resist becoming servo-men may be more dominated than they realize. Thus individuals who seek to prevent the system from abandoning its intended purposes, or who try to shield those below them from its full rigidity, usually do so on the system's own terms.

THE COMPANY'S BEEN VERY GOOD TO ME SINCE I GOT OUT OF SCHOOL.

FIRST THEY ENROLLED ME IN THEIR EXECUTIVE TRAINING SQUAD — LEARNING ALL PARTS OF THE FIELD AND GETTING PAID FOR IT AS WELL.

THEN THEY HELPED EVELYN AND ME FIND A HOUSE CONVENIENTLY LOCATED IN A SECTION WHERE **OTHER** YOUNG EXECUTIVES LIVE —

AND WHEN EVELYN BECAME ILL SMACK DAB IN THE MIDDLE OF HER TWENTY FIRST BIRTHDAY PARTY THEY ALLOWED US FULL BENEFIT OF THE COMPANY'S HOSPITALIZATION PLAN EVEN **THOUGH** I WAS A MONTH SHORT ON ELIGIBILITY —

— AND IN SPITE OF MY LOW SCORE ON THE MONTHLY PROMOTIONAL EMOTIONAL QUIZ AND SUBSEQUENT DAILY MAKE-UP SESSIONS WITH THE MORALE DEPARTMENT'S PSYCHOANALYST.

THEN WHEN, BECAUSE OF EVELYN'S DRINKING PROBLEM, IT LOOKED LIKE I MIGHT BE CASHIERED, THE EMERGENCY AID COMMITTEE OF THE COMPANY'S FAMILY COUNSELING PLAN PLUS THE WIVES' AUXILIARY'S "BE A PAL" SERVICE HELPED PULL US THROUGH.

NOW THE LITTLE WOMAN AND I ARE BACK IN STEP HERE I AM ONLY TWENTY-FOUR AND ALREADY A SECOND CONSULTATION ASSISTANT. AND JUST YESTERDAY EVELYN ENROLLED OUR THREE-YEAR-OLD IN THE EXECUTIVE JUNIORS TRAINING SQUAD.

I COULD DIE FOR THE COMPANY.

The Hall Syndicate, Inc.

The professor uses loopholes and personal contacts to get a worthy student into classes which he cannot get into through the registration system; the social worker finds regulations which can be twisted to allow giving aid to a nonqualifying family who really needs it. But these actions, however meritorious, are not effective restraints on the autosystem. It can tolerate and assimilate them without really retreating an inch from the path it is pursuing.

The opposite of an autosystem is a *controlled* system, and the key to control is vigilance. The tendency to become an autosystem is inherent in the very nature of social structures (as we shall see later); it can be checked, but never eliminated. Robert Townsend's book, *Up the Organization,*[3] is largely a handbook for the executive who wants to control his corporation's natural tendency to become an autosystem.

The opposite of the servo-man is the *autonomous man*—the man who is able to base his actions and decisions on a real understanding of himself and his needs, on a real acceptance of his existential ambiguity. The controlled system is controlled because autonomous men compel the system to continue serving human ends defined by criteria external to the system.

This is not to say that the autonomous man exists in some sort of social and cultural vacuum. All men's consciousness begins and develops in association with others, and all thinking is shaped by the linguistic and normative context within which it occurs. The autonomous man is quite as much a product of socialization as is the servo-man; the essential difference is that the autonomous man has a strong sense of his individual identity, of his needs, and of how to fulfill them. He is conscious of the process by which he assembles his identity from the cultural heritage available to him, and of his capacity for choice.[4] The servo-man passively accepts an identity defined for him by the autosystem, and he accepts its description of his needs and of the method of their fulfillment.*

Are There Really Autosystems?

Some people will challenge the existence of autosystems. They will argue that while systems *do* become very large and complex, there are still men at the top who are making the decisions, and that the systems are therefore not autonomous but merely oligarchic. This challenge seems to overlook several important considerations.

First of all, no man created the systems. Who created the American economy, or, for that matter, the San Francisco Police Force? They grew up over a considerable period of time as a result of the activities of a large number of people coordinated and directed through the system. These systems, like the product of any committee, in the long run are a product of no one. After a while, a committee's traditions and procedures may have more effect on its actions than the personalities and intentions of its members.

But more important than this, the system will accept only certain directives, even from the top. Consider the following fantasy: the president of the United States has for years been a secret, practicing nudist. Indeed, his whole motivation for seeking the presidency has been to use the power and prestige of the office to promote nudism. One day he decides that the time has come, and announces to his advisers that he is going on television the following night to remove his clothes and proclaim National Nudism Week. His advisers are unlikely to take him seriously, but if he does convince them that he is not joking, they will probably arrange for him to be taken to some quiet sanitarium where highly placed people can

---

* Obviously the concepts "servo-man" and "autonomous man" are used here as ideal types, or limiting cases. Actual individuals will probably show traces of both tendencies, although one or the other is likely to predominate. And some individuals will show a tendency much more strongly than others.

indulge their eccentricities in private until they recover their "rationality." The system, in other words, simply will not accept some kinds of directives from anyone. Any leader can in fact make only certain types of decisions—those that the system is prepared to accept.

Further, the man who rises to a position of great power and high status within a system has necessarily played the game for many years, functioning well and effectively. In this process he has inevitably been heavily influenced by the system; in all probability, he has become a servo-man. To return to the example, somewhere along the line this president would probably have lost his passion for nudism, or at least would have shelved any immediate intentions of acting on it.

But what about the truly great leader? Are there not some men who seize the times, who confront the system directly and force it to change? I believe there are, but with qualifications. Such great leaders are probably always around, but they are able to overturn systems only when the system is already deeply in trouble. The opportunity to topple the system is at least as much a product of the system's weakness as it is of the greatness of the leader. And, sad to relate, thus far in history, the next thing great leaders have done after toppling an autosystem has been to reorganize it into something larger and more complex. Naturally, the new system comes to be even more uncontrollable than its predecessor. It was Lenin's genius to overthrow moribund Czarist Russia and to reorganize its pieces into a new and viable whole. But the modern Soviet bureaucracy, which equals or exceeds the American in complexity and inflexibility, is the present product of Lenin's revolution.

Science fiction writers have perhaps recognized the potential of autosystems far more clearly than most sociologists. For example, many science fiction tales involve the limiting case wherein the entire social structure, from government to manufacturing, has been turned over to machines and computers, and mankind is either forced to submit utterly, or to destroy the entire apparatus in order to regain control over its own life and destiny. But an autosystem need not exclude humans from its operations to proceed autonomously. It is sufficient that most of the humans within it are servo-men.

Although they can operate autonomously, it is important not to reify autosystems. They are not a thing in the sense that a table is a thing; instead, they are a structure of relationships. It is also important not to anthropomorphize them; they are not living things and have no conscious volition. But they are real.

We cannot destroy the autosystems without destroying ourselves, for we live within them; and merely to exchange one autosystem for another does not reach the heart of the problem. But if these systems were brought under control and forced to serve human ends, most of our problems would disappear. War, pollution, waste, and alienation are not inevitable problems of mankind. They are the result of autosystems pursuing objectives essentially alien to real human interests.

---

2   On-Going Stuck-Togetherness

A system is a kind of self-perpetuating happening; it's a lot the same whether it is happening in an engine, a snail, a candleflame, the Department of Defense—or you. The first step toward house-breaking the autosystems is to understand how systems survive and grow.

An autosystem is first of all a system. It is therefore to systems theory that we must turn first. There are certain basic characteristics of systems in general which are fundamental to the understanding of any specific type of system.

In any mode of thought, the most basic concepts are also the most difficult to define. The fact that systems are comprised of relationships—not a concrete entity such as a mountain or a cloud—creates an additional difficulty.

A system can be defined accurately, if rather fancifully, as *that kind of a stuck-togetherness which results in an on-goingness.* The system consists of parts; but it is not the parts nor the sum of the parts. It is the result of the parts being assembled in a particular way so that a continuing process results. This continuing process is sometimes called a *steady state,* a pattern of relationships which tends to be self-maintaining.[1]

Candleflame

A candleflame is a system. It is an open system; that is, it interacts with its environment.* The candleflame consists of parts— paraffin, a wick, and air—together with certain properties of all three, such as the capillary action of the wick, the capacity of the paraffin to oxidize and produce heat, and the tendency of hot gases to expand. But these parts and properties do not make the flame; the system is not the parts nor the sum of the parts. The flame exists when a process is established as a steady state. The heat of the flame melts the wax, which is drawn upward by capillary action to where it is vaporized and oxidized producing heat to melt more wax; meanwhile, the by-products of the oxidization—water vapor and carbon dioxide—expand and are carried away from the flame, drawing fresh air in their wake. Once ignited by a match, the system tends to assume a steady state, although sooner or later the flame will be unable to maintain itself and will go out. The parts may still all be there, but the system will have perished.†

Note that in its interaction with its environment the candleflame produces by-products which are toxic to itself, such as carbon dioxide, and that it depends on its environment to absorb and remove these substances as well as to provide it with fresh needed supplies, such as oxygen. Such consumption and pollution of the environment is characteristic of open systems. When yeast is introduced into grape juice, it consumes the sugar and excretes ethyl alcohol. This alcohol is toxic to the yeast, and when it reaches a concentration of approximately 12 percent the yeast dies. Of course, one system's excretions

---

* Closed systems are sealed off from their environment and are usually artificial or even hypothetical.

† Part of the difficulty in talking about systems in general is finding words which can refer with equal ease to the same event as it occurs in very different entities—for example lizards, candleflames, and corporations. Thus, when the togetherness comes unstuck and the on-goingness stops, it seems appropriate to speak of death in the case of the lizard, but inappropriate to speak of the death of the candleflame (although we do speak of an automobile engine dying). The abstract process, however, is the same in all cases.

may be another system's food; after the yeast has died, other organisms consume the alcohol and excrete acetic acid, making vinegar.

The Reality of Systems

It is sometimes argued that systems are not "real," that they do not have an independent existence apart from their components. Ultimately, this is a philosophical question which can perhaps be sidestepped here; it may be sufficient to point out that systems are real in the same sense and to the same degree that people are real.

What are people? When we speak of a person, we speak of a "personality," an on-goingness which endures over the period of time that his body remains appropriately stuck together. That is to say, people are systems; they are made up of parts, but they are not those parts, nor the sum of those parts. Every person has a pancreas, a liver, a heart, and a brain; but dead bodies may also have all of these parts. The personality, the life, was the manifestation of the steady state of the system.

Gauges

Any open system requires certain conditions to survive. It must obtain certain things and get rid of certain things. It must maintain certain inner relationships and certain conditions which those relationships require. It must have an external environment which allows its particular type of functioning. In principle, one could list all of the necessary conditions for the survival of any particular system.

An automobile, especially a sports car, has an instrument panel which contains various gauges. These gauges display the state of various factors important to the functioning of the engine. There is a gas gauge which shows the available fuel and defines a lower limit below which the system will stop. An ammeter, an oil gauge, a tachometer, and so on, show the state of some of the most important requirements of the system. It would be possible to expand the instrument panel to include a gauge for everything necessary for the continued operation of the engine. The probabilities of various changes, problems, or breakdowns could then be readily estimated.

In theory, such an instrument panel could be constructed for any system. One could be made for a candleflame, to display such data as wind velocity, the depth of the melted wax, the length of the wick, and so forth. Even a human being may be monitored this way; the astronauts had extensive instrumentation connecting them to gauges which indicated the state of their functioning.

Normally a gauge will define a green zone within which the system can function easily, a yellow zone within which the system can function only with difficulty or danger, and a red zone within which the system cannot function at all. To study the gauges—whether in a literal or in a figurative sense—is the best way to understand what is really happening within a system and to predict its future.

To maintain its steady state and survive, a system must have a tendency to manipulate itself and its environment in order to keep its gauges out of the red. In the case of a candleflame, such manipulation is primarily mechanical—too large a flame deepens the wax pool reducing the exposed wick area and producing a smaller flame. In the case of a human being, much of the process is chemical (hormonal balance) or electrical (heart function), but some of it is consciously determined (crossing a street). But in every case the system is organized to struggle to survive. It "notices" its own gauges, refers to a basic pattern to evaluate what it "saw," and undertakes what actions it can to keep the needles of its gauges in the green. It is extremely important to understand the way in which systems are programmed to exhibit these survival mechanisms. As we will see later, survival mechanisms are one of the fundamental factors which lead social systems to get out of control and become autosystems.

Development and Decisions

Most systems are programmed not only to survive, but to attempt to grow and develop in specific ways. For example, a corporation is programmed to struggle to survive by avoiding bankruptcy, but also to attempt to increase sales volumes and profit margins. Complex systems such as animals or corporations *innovate;* that is, they begin doing new things on an experimental basis. A corporation may introduce a new line of products in the effort to increase profits.

Such innovation requires complex evaluative and decision-making operations. Animals and social systems depend on securing, storing, retrieving, and evaluating large amounts of information. Such data processing is never completely efficient. A person always perceives things imperfectly, forgets some things, and makes some errors of judgment. In a social system, the original information is never totally accurate; it may be changed in the process of storing; it may be lost, altered in retrieval, or inaccurately evaluated. Filters may be installed at any point in the process to screen out certain types of information—for example, items which contradict the preconceptions of the boss. Analysis of how persons or corporations process their data is a basic tool in predicting their future decisions.

Another aspect of complex systems is feedback—the capacity of a system to utilize part of its energy to "notice" the effect of its own behavior. Feedback can be purely mechanical, as in the toilet tank valve, or it may be complex, as in the kitten learning to hunt or the Defense Department evaluating public response to a proposal for a new weapons system. In complex cases, feedback provides the data by which the system "learns," or decides whether its innovations are worth continuing.

These fundamental concepts of systems theory are the necessary foundation for a specific examination of social systems and their maverick cousins, autosystems.

---

3   Pieces of Social Systems

Man's lack of instincts makes human society much more flexible and much more error-prone than the anthill. Men learn how to behave in order to occupy the sockets which make them function as components within the social system. But who's in charge? The transistor asked the television set to tell it the purpose of television. The set didn't answer; it just kept on showing reruns.

Why Are There Social Systems?

Not all animals create social systems; sharks have gotten along without them for millions of years. But some animals have come to depend on them, especially certain insects and mammals. All of their societies are structurally similar, but the operating principles are different.

The social insects have developed such specialized types within the species that they are absolutely dependent on social cooperation for survival. Among bees, for example, the queen, the drone, and the worker are distinct biological types. Not only their bodies but also their behavior is specialized; each type has different instincts.* These instincts give the beehive tremendous stability since they can be changed only through the slow process of evolution. Error is thus unlikely, but rapid or deliberate adaptation to change is impossible.

In human societies there is no biological specialization of members, except sexual; hunters and shamans are not biologically different. But humans specialize within their societies, just as do ants or bees. This is called the division of labor, and it presumably developed because it resulted in an increase in efficiency over unspecialized life styles. In all societies, somewhat different tasks are assigned to males and females and to the young and old, but most go much further in specialization.

Human societies, however, base their specialized tasks on learned rather than instinctive behavior. The difference here is analogous to the difference between an adding machine and a computer. An adding machine adds because it is hooked together inside in such a way that it *has* to add, but a computer cannot add at all until it is programmed. The advantage of the adding machine is that it does not have to be taught, and it is very unlikely to make a mistake. The computer requires programming for each task and is error-prone, but it is vastly more flexible and adaptable. Like the computer, a man has to be programmed for each task, but he can easily be taught to perform a different one.

A computer can be programmed very rapidly, but the information inputs of a human child are so slow as to require a number of years in a stable social grouping. Perhaps as a by-product of this long period of socialization, men have also come to develop emotional needs for association with each other.

To effect the division of labor, to socialize the young, and to fulfill emotional needs, men must come together in societies. Because

---

* Instinct is simply an unlearned behavior pattern, something which the organism can do without learning. We do not fully understand how this is achieved, but it is analogous to the way a washing machine washes clothes. It does not know how; it is simply constructed in such a way that a certain stimulus (a button pressed) results in certain behavior (the washing cycle). When certain stimuli are presented to the insect, it engages in certain behaviors just as blindly and as automatically as the washing machine.

men need society, some have argued that no man has a right to oppose society. This argument is a version of what political scientists term social contract theory. In other words, if you don't want to play by the rules, then go out and live alone in the desert; there is no in-between because if everyone claimed the right to make exceptions, there could be no rules at all, and hence no society. There is a grain of truth in this. But there is also a danger in this use of social contract theory. In the end it can justify autosystems riding roughshod over all human values. If the only alternatives are to love it or leave it, there is no way of dealing with a system which ceases to serve the functions men created it to serve.

Man needs society, but he also needs to keep his eye on it.

What Are Social Systems Made Of?

The first and most basic part of a society is a *role*. A role is a behavioral specialization. The individual learns, out of the vast range of possible behaviors, to do some particular thing in some particular situation. Without roles, human behavior becomes unpredictable and cooperation difficult. In large societies, it is only through roles that strangers are able to interact, and large societies require that strangers interact continuously. By knowing each other's roles, people know what to expect even though they do not know each other—the motorist and the pedestrian, the customer and the waitress. If a stranger does not play a known role, chaos may result.* Roles are also the means by which specialization is learned and carried out: doctor, lawyer, merchant, chief. To learn a role is essentially a process of programming.

After role, the next building block of a social structure is *prestige*. In any human group some people tend to initiate more of the decision making than others. Some people tend to play the role of leader

---

* For example, walk into a restaurant and go stand in the corner. The waitress will probably come by and ask "May I help you?" Answer "No" and continue standing in the corner. She will become acutely uncomfortable, and will probably ultimately call the police—not because you are standing in the corner, but because you are not playing a recognizable role and she is frightened because she cannot predict your behavior. But if you do this every day, she will become accustomed to it; you will then have created a new role which she will recognize, and your behavior will no longer be a threat. You may hear her explain to another waitress, "Oh, he *always* goes and stands in the corner!"

while others play the role of follower. Particularly in small, free-forming groups, such leadership seems to be an essentially democratic process. For example, if a group of six people are engaged in a task without an assigned leader, as they get to know each other they will select a leader. This may or may not be stated in so many words, but it will be obvious from the way the group operates; they will come to him for advice and willingly follow his suggestions. Such a leader has prestige—the respect or admiration that a group concentrates on particular individuals.

The simplest form of social organization is based on a small group with such a prestige leader. This is an *informal* social structure consisting of networks of attitudes, information flows, directives, and so forth. The familiar "sociogram" is a graphic technique for displaying such an informal social structure. Each girl has been asked to name her best friend:

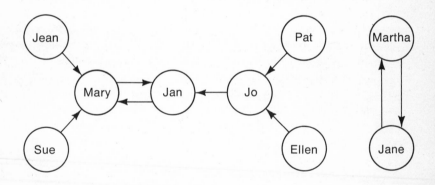

In groups that exceed the number of people an individual can know intimately, informal social structure becomes fragmentary. It still exists, but some more formal structure is necessary if the group is to function as a whole. Such formal structures are often represented by organizational charts such as the one on the next page. Such a chart attempts to portray the parts of a *formal* system. The lines symbolize quite a complex set of relationships: downward flow of directives, upward flow of information, coordination, supervision, and so forth. They also imply various material paraphernalia such as telephone lines, mail deliveries, and memo distributions. Formal

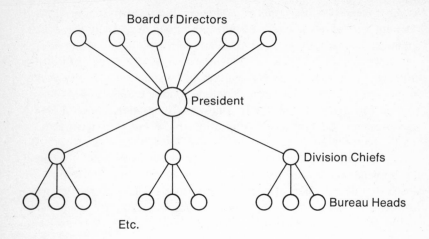

structures in literate societies are usually defined in documents such as constitutions, by-laws, charters, and articles of incorporation.

The circles on such charts symbolize *statuses*. A status is perhaps the most important element in social structures, and it is very unfortunate that the word "status" is so frequently used incorrectly as a synonym for "prestige." Properly defined, *a status is a position within a social system with defined rights and duties*. But it may be more easily understood as a "socket" into which an individual is plugged in order that he may function as a component within the system. The analogy to a socket in an electronic system is very close: it is through the status that the individual connects into the on-goingness of the system; moreover, he may be replaced by another component without fundamentally altering the functioning of the system, and he is likely to be replaced if his functioning is somehow defective. The system does not use all his potentialities, but only those that are relevant to the status into which he is plugged.

Unlike simple electronic equipment, however, the individual does not function automatically when he is plugged into a status. He must be programmed; he must learn the role that he is expected to play when occupying the status. At the lower levels of an organization, this programming may be very simple—a clerk may learn to open incoming mail, to respond to it with the most appropriate of five printed form letters, and to recognize exceptional letters which must be forwarded to a higher level for disposition. At the higher levels the programming is much more complex and much more subtle. It cannot be taught so directly.

Today, there are many instances when statuses may be fulfilled either by human or electronic components. In the large corporation, many statuses once filled by clerks are now filled by computers plugged into essentially the same sockets. Presumably this trend will continue and accelerate.

A social system begins, then, with roles and prestige—interpersonal relationships and behaviors which make up an informal structure. Superimposed over this, and to some degree uniting it, is a formal structure intercoupling statuses into an elaborate network connected by channels of information and directives. The formal and the informal structures may complement each other; if individuals who are assigned to cooperate are close friends, efficiency will be increased. Or they may contradict each other, as when an unpopular section head is bypassed as his underlings go directly to his more popular superior.

Material inputs and outputs are established to fulfill the purposes of the system, and complex flows of information (including extensive feedback) connect the system to the environmental field in which it functions. Some of the data gathered are stored in human minds, some on paper in files and cabinets, and some on magnetic tape or computer cores.* The gauges are monitored, and the "controls" are constantly manipulated in order to keep all of them in the green. But a social system is so complex and the feedback it receives is so ambiguous, that no one understands all that is happening. The president seeking reelection desperately studies all the economic gauges and fiddles with the controls to bring prosperity at election time. But no man really controls the American economy.

It is all very complex; but it is real. We live our lives within it.

---

* In this regard modern societies differ considerably from preliterate societies where all data are necessarily stored in human memories.

4   Segments of the Orange

The different sectors of society have unequal influence. There are tens of millions of American families, but only one government and one military. It isn't hard to see which sectors can get it together most easily. Or which ones are most likely to get out of control.

What Is a Society?

An ant society is the complete anthill: all of the on-goingness that maintains its steady state together with the material equipment— the hole in the ground, the food, the waste products, and so forth. In the same way, a human society is the on-goingness, the steady state, which results from the complex interactions of a group of people living together. The human society is a little harder to de-lineate than the anthill because human societies interrelate with each other more than anthills do.

Societies can be pulled apart into pieces which we can call *institutional sectors.** The division into sectors is somewhat arbi-trary; after all, the society is a whole which is divided into segments only to facilitate its analysis.

Institutional sectors differ in their *degree of centralization.* This is a point which the sociological literature has generally failed to em-phasize, but it is very important. At a high degree of centralization, an institutional sector will consist of a single, large, complex system; at a low degree of centralization the sector will consist of a large number of small, simple, and relatively independent units doing similar things but not connected with each other. Between these

---

* The word *institution* might be more familiar than *institutional sector;* but the former sounds like something that is separate and distinct, whereas *sector* implies that a whole has somehow been divided up.

extreme cases, of course, there can be any intermediate degree of centralization.

In American society, the family is an example of an institutional sector at a very low degree of centralization. The things that families do are carried out by tens of millions of small units which are largely independent of each other. In contrast, the military in American society is at a very high level of centralization; the entire military apparatus is integrated into one enormous, complex system. Army platoons may be somewhat analogous to families—they are relatively small, stable units. But army platoons are connected together into companies, the companies into divisions, the divisions into armies, and so on. Families remain independent.* Our school system is at an intermediate level of centralization; there are fewer school boards than families, but more school boards than armies.

The degree of centralization of an institutional sector has a number of consequences. For example, a great deal of sloppy sociological thinking has resulted from talking about the American family as if it existed in the same way that the American military does. When we speak of the military, we are talking about a single system; it is meaningful to say that the military has decided to do something. But when we speak of the American family, we are referring to an enormous number of separate systems, and it is meaningless to say that the American family has decided to do anything. The *American family* is an abstraction which presumably refers to certain common characteristics shared by many or most American families, while the *American military* is not an abstraction.

One of the consequences of this difference is the type of change which can occur within the sector. An institutional sector at a high level of centralization is capable of deliberately initiating change from within the sector, whereas an institutional sector at a low level of centralization is not. Thus the military can decide to make

---

* In a more primitive society, the family may be at a higher level of centralization than it is in the United States because families are collected into clans. The clans are a structure over the family, somewhat as the company is the structure over the platoon. The clan has regulations which all families within that clan must follow, placing the family at a higher degree of centralization than in our society. In the Israeli kibbutzim, the family is also at a higher level of centralization because the kibbutz unites families into a larger structure.

specific changes: a number of years ago the armed services decided to abolish overt segregation of the races in its ranks. That is to say, at the highest decision-making levels of the system, the commander-in-chief and his joint chiefs of staff made a decision which was then sent through the formal structure of the military system. But there are no joint chiefs of the American family who could sit down at a conference table to plan changes in the family system. The family does change, surely, but because it is at a low degree of centralization it is not capable of planning the changes it will make. Individual families may make deliberate changes, and if external conditions stimulate numerous families to make the same changes, the cumulative effect may be apparent on the American family system. But the sector is not capable of making planned changes as a unit.*

Most of the changes which occur within a sector at a low level of centralization are the result of influences from the highly centralized sectors. Thus the state, by changing divorce laws, effects basic changes in the family. Or the economic sector, by extending into every home a tendril in the form of a television set, alters the way in which children are socialized. When television replaced grandmother as the baby sitter, for better or worse the socialization of American children became more uniform.

Leading Sectors

The institutional sectors that are most centralized tend to be the *leading sectors*. A leading sector is one which initiates more of the changes which occur in the society than other sectors do. The term is not generally used, but a trailing sector would be one in which very few changes originate. Simply because the more highly centralized sectors have a centralized apparatus and are capable of deliberate, internal innovation, they largely determine what happens in the less highly centralized sectors.

---

* Thus it is the sectors at a low level of centralization which are the more change resistant and tend to stabilize society. Such sectors are therefore favored by conservatives, and disliked by radicals. For example, some radicals, who would like to end racism in America, become impatient with the socialization of children in the family. Because they would like to see the content of socialization changed, they tend to dream of an American Child Rearing System. In such organized nurseries the content of socialization could be changed uniformly as fast as the administrative arrangements could be made. Similarly, conservatives who like things the way they are want to keep socialization of children in the home as a means of resisting social changes.

Throughout history, sectors have changed in their level of centralization. For example, religion was a more highly centralized sector in Europe during the Middle Ages than it is today. In the Middle Ages there was basically one church (or at the most two, if the peasants' Black Mass is treated as a separate church), but today there is a considerable number of separate churches. In contrast, the economy was much less centralized when the basic economic activity was subsistence farming. Each little farm tended to be a miniature economy, in contrast to the nationwide economies of today. The changes which occur in the degree of centralization of the sectors are thus important clues to shifts in the leading sectors.

A change anywhere in a society tends to produce changes everywhere else. Changes usually originate in the leading sectors and precipitate changes in the other sectors. The changes in the leading sectors may be termed primary changes; resulting changes in the other sectors, secondary changes. However, the secondary changes lead to tertiary changes back in the leading sectors. David Riesman illustrated this very well in *The Lonely Crowd*.[1] He showed how the primary economic change of industrialization produced secondary changes in the socialization of children within the family. Thus arose the other-directed personality type. And other-directed people bought products for different reasons than their inner-directed parents, which forced a tertiary change in the selling practices of the economy: instead of telling them that the product was good for them it became necessary to tell them that the product would make them less unpopular.

Obviously it is very difficult to foresee the long-range effects of a primary change. When Henry Ford set up his assembly line for the Model T, it never crossed his mind that he was preparing a revolution in the courtship customs of America, and he could not have conceived of the drive-in churches of southern California. And now changes in climate are beginning to result from automobile emissions. The more rapid the rate of social change becomes, the greater the risk of unanticipated and undesired consequences.

One final complexity results from the linkages between human societies. For example, the American military sector is so closely linked to the Soviet that any change in one produces a change in the other, and in fact the actions of neither can be understood without reference to the actions of the other. In the economic sector, there is a marked trend toward systems which extend through several societies. The European Common Market—a single economy linked to several separate governmental sectors—raises complex questions about just where one society begins and another ends. The trend toward institutional sectors which span the globe will presumably continue, especially in the economic sector, if we refrain from blowing ourselves up.

Sectors of America

American society can be divided into seven institutional sectors. There is the *family* at a low level of centralization, consisting of some 30 to 40 million small units, each containing several statuses (father, mother, siblings) and possessing both formal and informal structures. At a medium level of centralization there are the *educational sector* and the *religious sector*—the Catholic and Lutheran churches resemble the California and New York school systems in centralization, and there are isolated store-front churches corresponding to the small private colleges.

Two large interrelated sectors which are rarely differentiated from one another are the *technology* and the *economy*. The technology is the system which produces material things, while the economy is the system which arranges their distribution and ownership. There is the *political sector*—operating at city, county, state, and national levels, all of which are integrated into a single immense system. And then there is the *military sector*. In theory the military is simply a part of the political sector, and historically this was true in America. During its frequent wars, America would expand its military apparatus, and then largely disband it after the war; the sector never had time to achieve leadership. But since 1950, the military sector has become a permanent giant and has achieved partial independence of the political sector. The Pentagon does not necessarily tell the White House what it is doing nor do what the White House tells it to do.*

---

* There may be another bud beginning to split off from the political sector. I believe I notice in the police a certain tendency toward becoming a sector separate from the political sector of which they have hitherto been a part. Police forces already operate somewhat independently of the courts and legislatures. If the police forces are considerably expanded, as seems likely, they may become a definably separate sector as they were in Russia during the final years of Beria.

The four highly centralized sectors—technological, economic, governmental, and military—form the leading sectors of the society. It is in these sectors that most social changes originate.

It is in these four leading sectors that the trend toward becoming autosystems is most alarmingly evident. Although nominally they exist simply to serve the needs of the American people, they have become ends and forces in themselves. They pursue policies aimed at their own survival and expansion without regard to welfare of human beings, who become merely components. Although it is true that men occupy the central and powerful statuses within the leading sectors, most such men are servo-men who have been programmed to regard the system's welfare as identical with their own, and with the welfare of humanity.

The time seems overripe for a change in trend. But to make changes effectively we need to understand the process by which changes occur. We need a theory of change to guide us.

---

5   Change in the Changes

Change isn't too hard to cope with until the kinds of change start changing. Then things can get bewildering unless you learn to look for the causes of the change in the changes. To understand those causes is to be able to put your weight where it counts—at the pivot points of your era.

The Place To Begin

The point, Marx said, is not just to understand the world, but to change it.[1] To change the world, however, it is necessary to understand how it changes—as Marx well knew. Society can be like a Chinese puzzle—amazingly resistant to all attempts at manipulation, yet falling open to a tap at just the right point. He who would battle the autosystems must arm himself with a theory of how and why such systems change. If his theory is good, he will know where and how to tap. If his theory is bad, or if he abjures theory, he will have only blind luck to guide him.

There are two fundamental types of change: linear (quantitative) and nonlinear (qualitative). Linear changes occur within a steady state; they tend to be gradual and readily predictable. Getting older, getting poorer, and getting drunker are all linear changes. Nonlinear changes disrupt a steady state; they tend to be abrupt and difficult to predict. Dying, going bankrupt, and passing out are nonlinear changes.

Most theories of social change have tended to view stability as normal. Since they have taken stability for granted, they have not attempted to explain what underlies stability. With no explanation of what underlies stability, they are at a loss to explain why it sometimes breaks down. Such breakdowns have to be passed off as unique events, accidental happenings, or catastrophes. In other words, most theories of social change have concentrated on explaining the linear changes that occur within the steady state of a social system. They have not dealt with the reasons why these steady states are disrupted from time to time by nonlinear changes which leave the system fundamentally altered and result in a new steady state.

There is some justification for this neglect of nonlinear change. Since linear changes tend to be common and continuous and nonlinear changes tend to be sporadic, men naturally focus their attention on the linear changes. They can easily generalize their experience with linear changes; on the basis of yesterday and the day before, they can predict tomorrow. But nonlinear changes tend to be unexpected and relatively unique events which admit of no easy generalization.

But for the social theorist, to neglect the analysis of nonlinear change is to neglect learning to understand and predict the really basic changes which occur in society. And for those who seek to encourage basic changes in society, an understanding of the sources of nonlinear change is the point to begin.

A Theory of Nonlinear Changes

The theory we will use in our analysis of the American autosystems begins with the assumption that change is normal and natural, and that stability—a steady state—is the result of particular conditions. Basically the conditions for a steady state are a balance of the forces which are acting on it and within it. Two men of comparable strength may create a stable system in an Indian wrestling match—for a time. Their locked hands remain stationary as their forces balance. But inevitably there will be linear change in the forces which underlie the steady state. The muscles of both men fatigue, but at unequal rates. These linear changes continue until the balance collapses; then a nonlinear change occurs in the very nature of the system. One of the men rapidly forces the hand of the other down onto the table.[2]

Or take the analogy of a planet rotating around the sun in a constant orbit—a steady state. The orbit is the result of a balance of forces, the two most important being the centrifugal force pulling the planet outward and the gravitational attraction pulling it inward. The balance of the forces explains the stability. However, linear changes are occurring; there is friction in the planet's rotation which reduces its velocity so that the orbit must move inward and become shorter. But there is a critical point at which an orbit can no longer be maintained at all, and then the planet will spiral rapidly into the sun.

In social systems the collapse of a steady state is less likely to result in complete destruction of the system than it is to result in the transformation of the system into a new form based on a new balance of forces. Examples include reorganization of bankrupt corporations, revolutions, and remarriages. Of course the new balance ultimately undergoes the same process.*

Sources of Disruption

The linear changes which lead to the disruption of steady states in social systems can be grouped into a few categories.

External changes. Changes in the environmental field may affect the inputs of the system. *Competition* may restrict the access of the system to raw materials. A fishing tribe may be driven from its villages on the salmon run and be forced to reorganize itself as a nomadic hunting tribe. A corporation may be forced to enter a

---

* This approach to the analysis of change is fundamentally the Marxist–Hegelian dialectic in modern terminology. Unfortunately the terminology of German romantic philosophy in which it is usually expressed has tended to obscure its significance and utility outside orthodox Marxist circles, whereas within these circles doctrinaire ritualism has often impaired its application.

new field when a competitor is able to appropriate its major customers. Or the *exhaustion of resources* may render the continuation of a particular system impossible. The collapse of a mining region when the ores run out is an obvious example. A more unusual one is a problem that Alcoholics Anonymous has encountered in small communities. This organization's cure depends on the zeal to cure other alcoholics it instills in its members. But in towns with a limited number of alcoholics, the system can exhaust its resource of potential converts, whereupon it tends to fall apart, and its members frequently return to the bottle.

Linear environment changes may also interfere with the outputs of the system. A *rejection* may occur whereby the environmental field increasingly resists the necessary outputs of the system. Changes in consumer taste may make a product line increasingly difficult to sell. More commonly, *pollution* may increasingly threaten the system with its own toxins. A confidence game in a small town produces toxins in the form of previous victims, making the game increasingly difficult to play as word gets around.

Institutional sectors, of course, form major elements of each other's environments. Therefore it is important to see how the changes in other sectors affect the inputs and outputs of the sector under examination. Especially if a leading sector has recently undergone a nonlinear transformation, this single factor is likely to be the most basic influence on changes in other sectors until the process of secondary adjustment is well advanced.

The response of a social system to external changes is to meet them with internal linear changes. A corporation will resist transforming itself for as long as possible despite a disappearing market for its present type of products. Only when the gauges are in the yellow and collapse of the steady state is clearly at hand will the average social system undergo fundamental modifications in its structure. Such fundamental changes destroy the old steady state and are therefore resisted. In some cases the system will allow its gauges to go into the red and perish rather than accept fundamental change; or it may simply be unable to discover a way of achieving a new steady state.

Internal changes. Two internal changes of particular importance are growth and decay. *Growth* or development is an objective and sometimes a necessity in the program of many social systems. The social organization seeks new members and the family seeks a higher standard of living. But the linear process of growth and development places strains on the structure of the system. As the organization becomes larger, the old, informal procedures become increasingly inadequate. Correspondence, for example, may become an increasing burden on the officers until they are forced either to let the organization collapse or to make a nonlinear leap into a bureaucratic structure complete with secretaries, form letters, and mailing rooms. A family whose standard of living is rising reaches a point where its old life style is no longer possible; it must either stop rising, or the family must remold itself into a new style of life.

Decay is a linear process by which the system becomes increasingly inept, inefficient, and inflexible. The process seems to be universal in social systems and is roughly comparable to the effects of aging on the living organism.* In the end, the system becomes unable to maintain its steady state, and the gauges go into the yellow—or the red. In the end, the old dictatorship cannot be maintained, and a revolution revitalizes the state. The process by which social systems decay is so important that we will devote the next chapter to examining it in detail.

Checking the List

The major advantage of the theory of change outlined above is that, unlike most others, it makes nonlinear changes predictable—at least in principle. In fact, the steps can be listed:

1. Determine the forces that must be balanced (the contradictions) to maintain the steady state.
2. Conceptualize the gauges which would portray the conditions essential for the steady state.
3. Explore the changes which the gauges reveal. Look for:
   a. Exhaustion of resources or competition, which may be affecting the inputs of the system.
   b. Pollution or rejections, which may be affecting the outputs of the system.

---

* We take it for granted that living creatures will age, and that death by old age is "natural." But we really do not understand the process, and it does not occur in all organisms. Single-celled creatures which reproduce by fission do not age; in a certain sense the original amoeba is still alive.

    c. Changes, especially nonlinear changes, in other systems to which the system under study is intercoupled.

    d. Processes of internal growth which are straining the structure of the system.

    e. Processes of decay which are destroying the ability of the system to adapt.

4. Note the linear changes which the system is making in an effort to maintain the steady state.

5. Estimate when such linear changes will become inadequate to sustain the steady state. That is when the gauges will go into the yellow and nonlinear change will be imminent.

6. Try to predict the various new balances which could result in steady states.

The activist will want to add one final step:

7. Pick the best of these possibilities and act to increase its probability. *Tap the social structure at that point.*

---

6   Systematic Stupidity

The vitals of a social system are its decision-making centers. Over a period of time these centers become ossified, and the system ceases to adapt and begins to blunder. Ultimately its gauges go into the red, and drastic change becomes inevitable. That is the pivot point at which dreams may be levered into reality.

Ossification

Social systems are surprisingly adaptable structures. As internal and external changes weaken the balance underlying their steady state, they are able to modify their structure to achieve new balances. Thus the capitalist economic system has shown an impressive and unexpected capacity to adapt to changes which might have been expected to destroy it.*

Adaptation, however, is dependent on the decision-making centers of the social structure. Over a period of time these centers tend to lose their capacity to adapt, leaving the system rigid in a changing environment. The system then begins to make stupid blunders.

For example, during a period when the use of big cars as prestige symbols was declining and small car sales were rising, the Ford Motor Company produced the Edsel. It was a disaster. Yet how could Ford—with all its talent, experience, and research facilities—do something so stupid?

The CIA invaded Cuba at the Bay of Pigs in the conviction that the landing of a small force of exiles would lead the Cuban people to rise against Castro. The Cuban people did rise, but it was to push the exiles into the sea. The CIA is a multi-billion dollar secret organization. No means are forbidden to it; information can be obtained by bribery, espionage, or torture. How could the CIA do something that any knowledgeable American could have told them would fail?

Probably many people in the Ford Motor Company and the Central Intelligence Agency knew better. But Ford and the CIA did not; they were stupid.

Systems decay and become stupid through *ossification:* the process by which the decision-making centers of a system come to derive their decisions independently of the information inputs and feedback. The decisions become increasingly unrelated to what is happening within and without the system. There are a variety of reasons why this happens.

Sources of Trouble

1. *Reinforcement.*   One of the reasons is that any social system is programmed to repeat successful responses and to drop

---

* The capacity to adapt is not unlimited, however. Conditions sometimes arise in which a particular kind of steady state simply cannot be maintained, no matter how much it may be modified. There comes a point when the system can no longer be made to work; it must be replaced. As we shall see later, capitalism may be nearing such a point today. Social history is thus divided into eras—during which the social system is able to adapt its steady state to the inevitable changes. The eras are separated by crises—which entail the replacement of one system with another.

out unsuccessful ones; that is, to learn from experience. Learning theory explains that behavior which is reinforced by success tends to be repeated, and behavior which is not tends to be extinguished. The problem is that previous learning may prevent adaptation. Skinner found that if a pigeon had always been reinforced for some behavior, the behavior would soon be extinguished when the reward was terminated. But if the reward had been intermittent, the behavior persisted much longer after the reward ceased.[1] Having endured periods of no reward before, the pigeon kept hoping. The successes of a social system are almost always intermittent. So the system will keep trying long after its behavior has become obsolete. Meanwhile disasters may multiply.

2. *Human Bias.*   Freud taught us that a man's opinions are determined by internal as well as external factors. Religious concepts, for example, are heavily influenced by the earliest images the individual had of his parents; these images—and the associated attitudes—are irrelevantly applied by the adult to the supernatural. Other attitudes have similar origins. The internal determination of the attitudes of its human components may thus lead a system to make decisions which have little to do with what is currently going on. Over a period of time, a system may increasingly absorb into itself the biases of highly placed individuals. In fact, the biases may long survive the individuals who introduced them.

3. *Inertia.*   Another factor is inertia—the tendency of things in motion to continue in motion. Within a social system, inertia causes information consistent with prevailing conclusions to be taken more seriously than contrary information. Decisions which follow the on-going trend tend to be almost automatically approved and implemented, even if they are wrong. Unfamiliar information and decisions tend to be rejected, even if they are right. Some of the people in the system may realize mistakes are being made; but the system is set up and moving in a particular direction, and the individual incurs no risk in contributing to this direction. But the system may punish him for unfamiliar information or decisions.

4. *Crackpot Realism.*   Another source of ossification is what C. Wright Mills called "crackpot realism" [2]—that kind of thinking which picks the best alternative within a certain set of assumptions, but steadfastly refuses to consider any alternatives which lie outside the original assumptions.

The U.S. war in Vietnam is a very apropos example. One of the Pentagon's fundamental assumptions is that there are military solutions to problems. Operating within that framework, it showed incredible ingenuity trying to find the military solution to Vietnam and Southeast Asia.* To most observers outside the Pentagon it became apparent that there was no military solution to the problem, and that the answer would have to be sought in other ways.† No doubt many people within the Pentagon knew this; but the Pentagon didn't know it.

Crackpot realism sounds convincing because the arguments are logically developed within familiar assumptions. Concerning Vietnam, it was argued: "We don't like fighting and killing any better than you do, but we are involved in a war, and until that war is won we won't be able to straighten out the rest of the mess." Such an argument merely reiterates the assumption that a military solution is possible and desirable. But it reiterates it in such a way as to imply than any other way of thinking is sentimental, unrealistic, or feebleminded. Crackpot realism is the means by which a system justifies its inertia by discrediting any arguments which go beyond its assumptions.

5. *Identity Crises.*   Yet another factor in ossification is an identity crisis. A system generates certain images of itself: a corporation has by-laws, procedures, and brochures which display its formal image and various traditions and customs which contribute to its informal image. The overall conception—the image by which the system recognizes itself and establishes its identity—tends to come under the protection of the basic survival directive. Adaptations which violate this image come to be viewed as a threat to survival and are resisted accordingly.

6. *Filters.*   Partly because of the tendencies described above, systems tend to install filters in their information inputs. Such installation may be a conscious action on the part of human components: "If the boss sees this report he'll fire every one of us." In

---

* Including a proposal to orbit a huge mirror so there would never be darkness in Vietnam for the guerillas to hide in. See "Giant Sky Mirror Alarms Scientists," *San Francisco Chronicle,* May 31, 1967, p. 9.

† Such as buying the land for a fraction of what it cost to destroy it (thus giving the landlords money to retire on), giving the land to the peasants, and emerging as everyone's friend.

other cases it may be an unconscious result of the programming the individuals have received from the system. They have learned to use the system's concepts in thinking, and therefore they mold information so it will fit the system's preconceptions. This may be done in easy stages. Imagine an information flow across the desks of ten people. Suppose that none of them deliberately changes the information, but merely condenses and interprets it. As it passes each desk it will become a little more in line with the prevailing views; if it is changed as little as ten percent at each desk, it could be entirely reversed by the tenth desk.

It is said that when the Johnson administration was in bad trouble over Vietnam in 1967, one could enter the White House and find at the very first desk a little less gloom than in the world outside. As one went from desk to desk, moving closer to Johnson, things gradually got happier and brighter. Tragic facts disappeared, and hopeful wishes become possibilities, probabilities, and finally certainties. By the time one entered the President's office the world was basically rosy, and the few problems which existed were on the way toward solution. It is because of filters that leaders so often know less about what it really happening than the people on the outside.

All Together Now

In the production of the Edsel all of these sources of ossification were probably involved. Reinforcement: Ford had been intermittently successful in marketing larger cars, but there had been a recent shift in the market which the system did not recognize. Human bias: Henry Ford II liked big cars, and he liked the Edsel. Inertia: any trend toward larger and more expensive cars was reasonable, rational, and routine; whereas the idea of small cars was strange and seemingly dangerous. Crackpot Realism: small cars just weren't practical on American highways; the Crosley and Bantam had failed. Besides, the car has always been a basic prestige symbol; the bigger the better. Identity Crisis: Ford wanted its line to parallel General Motors' line; it did not want to become known as a builder of small cars. Filtering: the filtering of information seems to have been very complete. One of the arguments which was apparently used to filter out the statistics about Volkswagen sales was that VWs were only bought by "kooks," and most of the kooks already had a VW. Therefore, Volkswagen sales would soon decline.

Transformation

The result of ossification is that sooner or later the system gets into a situation where it cannot maintain its steady state and the gauges go into the yellow and the red. Then, one of two things must happen: the system will simply disintegrate, or it will be transformed into another system. Such transformation is a very interesting process.

Fundamentally, the system is taken apart and reassembled to function under different conditions. Unable to get the needle out of the red, the system is reorganized so completely that the red range is moved away from the needle. It can now function under conditions in which in its previous state it could not.

Complex social systems are capable of such basic changes in their steady states, but by the time such changes become necessary, they are usually so ossified that they have great difficulty in using this capacity. Moreover, the threat of being torn apart so completely triggers survival behaviors, and the system resists furiously.* Successful transformations are usually achieved through coercion by the next higher level in the total structure. It was not the Edsel division which abandoned the Edsel and turned to the successful Falcon, but rather Ford Motor Company. When ossification occurs at the highest levels, usually only insurgent forces from outside can effect the transformation.

There seems to be no way of preventing ossification. It is a natural process in social systems, yet it can be dealt with. Perhaps the best way is to periodically tear up the internal structure of the system and reassemble it—sometime before it becomes completely ossified. Good results can even be obtained by using the same personnel in different positions: a person hopelessly biased in one status may

---

* For example, a committee structure may be so ossified that the decisions produced by the committees are worthless. But while the organization is collapsing and the gauges dip into the red, the committee system will defend itself desperately. "Now is not the time to start messing around with established, workable procedures. These committees may have faults, but there is a lot of experience embodied in them. Wait until the crisis is over."

be able to function flexibly in a new one. But quite apart from the resistance of the system and its servo-men, such reorganization has a heavy cost as working procedures are disrupted and inexperienced men replace experienced ones. In the long run, however, much more is usually gained than lost.*

At the time of a transformation, an autosystem tends to be temporarily returned to human control. New faces replace the servo-men in powerful statuses, idealism and enthusiasm run high, and the new order is flexible and receptive.

Thus, although American society is currently dominated by the autosystems in the leading institutional sectors, there are grounds for cautious optimism. The next period of transformation in a leading sector might well provide the opportunity to regain control and humanize the system. An analysis is needed of each of the institutional sectors, their defects, and their potential for change. In each sector we need to decide what we would like to have, and the kind of system that would provide it.

We can begin with the simplest and the oldest of the sectors— the family.

---

* The cultural revolution in China seems to have been precisely such an effort to stave off ossification through drastic reorganization. Mao Tse-tung deliberately tore apart the structure of China, enduring a tremendous loss in efficiency, morale, trained personnel, and so forth, in an effort to recapture flexibility and rekindle enthusiasm. It was a colossal experiment in fighting ossification, and its outcome deserves the most careful study.

7   In the Beginning There Was the Family

Man's earliest societies consisted simply of a family. There were problems aplenty, but no autosystems. Over the millennia, new institutional sectors have formed and taken over the old functions of the family. These sectors have become the autosystems, and the main function of the family is now to provide the individual with a place to hide.

Miniature Societies

The earliest men almost certainly lived in very small groups within which there was basic biological kinship.* Small groups here imply something on the order of 5 to 30 individuals depending on the terrain, but with the lower numbers the more probable. Groups had to be small so that the food supply would not be exhausted more rapidly than the group could move on.† Each of these groups was presumably a separate entity with no continuing relationship with other groups. Thus each group was a *social microcosm,* a miniature society within itself. The family and society were synonymous.

These small groups gathered, prepared, and distributed everything they ate and made every possession they had. All their rules, and their enforcement, came from within the group; so did recreation, magic or ritual, and care (if any) of the sick and old. This way of

---

* In an evolutionary sense, it is arbitrary to speak of a specific point at which man appeared. Uniquely human characteristics seem to be the use of abstract language and the use of tools. Although some of the cetaceans (whales and porpoises; see John Cunningham Lilly, *The Mind of the Dolphin* [Garden City, N.Y.: Doubleday & Co., 1967]) seem to use complex language and some other mammals such as sea otters use very simple tools, the combination of language and tools is apparently uniquely human. If the emergence of a language- *and* tool-using animal is taken to signal the origins of man, then he was undoubtedly already living in family groupings when he emerged.

† Very little is known about this period, as man was then a rare animal and his remaining fossils and artifacts are few. Guesses can be based on the situations in which he lived and on analogies to other animals and more recent human groups.

life has evident limitations,* but the social structure is certainly not impersonal, remote, or capricious. In such groups, society is personal, visible, and comprehensible.

This type of life is described in the novel *Top of the World* by Hans Ruesch.[1] In vivid and accurate detail, he describes two generations in the life of a family of polar Eskimos living as a social microcosm. Their independence probably resembles that of very early human groups although, lacking the elaborate Stone-Age technology of the Eskimos, the earliest men could not have inhabited the Arctic.

On Toward Rome

The history of society from perhaps a million years ago until today can be characterized by the emergence of systems external to the family to fulfill functions formerly served by the family. The exact details of the early stages of this process are not known. The process of interrelating primordial family groups into more centralized social systems may well have begun in the economic realm. Migratory groups in adjacent territories may have developed a fondness or a need for things which were more abundant in each other's territory, and simple trade relations may have resulted.† Ultimately, formal trade customs would be established—the price of a squirrel perhaps being established at three clams—which transcended the original families. Neither family could change the system without the agreement (through negotiation or coercion) of the other.

The trend toward an ever more complex economic system external to the family continues to the present day. In fact, the family today has almost no economic role left, and the economic sector is so complex that even nations are not in complete control of their own economic affairs.

Probably government also passed very early from the family to a separate sector. Perhaps to implement the development of economic

---

* For example, with the food available to them, the diet of such groups is likely to result in the teeth being worn to the gum by the age of twenty, or at the most, thirty. Those who have not already died by that time are thus condemned to starvation.

† The simplest known trade relations in modern societies involve one group carrying something into the territory of another group, laying it down, and fleeing. The other group then comes and picks up the commodity, leaves something else, and also flees. This process occurs without any clearly defined exchange rates and with no direct contact between the groups. Such might have been the beginnings of trade among very early men.

interrelations, families were persuaded to surrender some of their sovereignty to a larger, more remote unit—presumably the clan. And, although benefits accrued in the prevention or resolution of certain types of disputes, in hindsight the path from clan leader to Caesar is clearly discernible.*

As it was with economic and governing activities, so it was with religion. It may be that the clan leader achieved his ascendancy by apparent efficiency in supernatural matters; almost certainly he claimed such efficiency. But whether the chief became priest, the priest became chief, or the two were merely cohorts, families found themselves involved in rituals, taboos, and credos not entirely of their own making, and not entirely under their control. What was good for the gods was not necessarily good for the godly, even though it was rationalized in terms of subsequent rewards for good behavior and long service. The priests chanting by the fire had the potential to become a vast Church which could kill thousands for heresy and can still condemn contraception in an overpopulated world.

Education remained a function of the family for a longer period than most of the original functions. In a simple society where an adjustment to existing conditions has been worked out over hundreds of generations, everyone knows what he needs to know. Children learn naturally and automatically as they copy their parents. It is only when children need to learn what their parents do not know (or are unable to teach them) that schools as a distinct institutional sector emerge. Initiation into priestly and magical rituals was probably the first hint of an educational system.† But for the majority of the population, training remained a largely unconscious by-product of family life until the Industrial Revolution.

There has probably always been some violence within and between families. But a separate military institution does not emerge

---

* The motivation for the development of these larger institutions was probably efficiency. By specialization and exchange, a greater variety and abundance of goods became available. Larger governing units made possible more complex activities and undertakings. The necessity for efficiency presumably arose from what Malthus called pressure against food supplies. In a sense, then, it can be argued that the development of society apart from the family was the consequence of uncontrolled reproduction.

† The first formal schools, however, came after the invention of civilization in the Middle East between 6000 and 3000 BC. In these schools children were taught to read and write (skills which their parents lacked) in order that they could become the clerks and record keepers of the Pharaoh. But only a minute fraction of the population attended these schools.

until the society undertakes organized violence for objectives defined by the leaders. The appearance of the military as a separate institution marks the end of the family's control over the use of violence; henceforth one system is pitted against another with individuals serving merely as agents of the systems. Warfare began with nomadic raiders, and by the time Egypt had become a great civilization, armies were a standard feature of civilized life.

The Man in the Hut

Since the development of agriculture, most men have lived in small huts, trying to wrest a living from uncooperative plots of land. Indeed, much of humanity still lives this way. For the man in the hut, civilization has usually meant exploitation, tyranny, or death. He has found little benefit from the development of complex societies. From time to time some army has swept across his little plot, raped his daughters and killed his sons, stolen his crops, eaten his animals, knocked down his hut—and then demanded tribute of him as he attempted to assemble the wreckage of his life. After a decade or a century, the process repeated itself; the only difference being the conqueror's language. It matters little to the man in the hut whether the army is Genghis Khan's, is rescuing him from Genghis Khan, is bringing him Islam, returning him to Christ, representing the Kaiser or the Czar, or acting in the name of democracy or communism. He has no delusions as to his fate. When we write of the glories of Egypt, Athens, and Rome, we tend to forget the man in the hut from whom everything was ultimately extracted. Nor is his suffering over; the Vietnamese peasant has had a recent course in civilization.

Near the End

Despite all its loss of functions, the family remained the basic producing unit of the technology until the Industrial Revolution. With the factory system, the organization of production moved from the home to the larger society. Little was then left of the family's role. It was no longer in charge of distributing goods, governing itself, practicing religion, or educating its members. It no longer determined the use of violence. And it no longer created the things which men use. The family which was once everything became basically a haven in which the individual could seek temporary respite from the elaborate and impersonal social structure which had absorbed the former functions of the family.

---

8   The Family as a People Wrecker

It is emotional fulfillment that Americans want from the family. But the existing family system evolved as a means of operating small farms. Small wonder there are problems. The autosystems enforce the present family system, teaching people that it is their own fault that their marriages fail. And people believe it.

Once everyone had to belong to a family. The apprentice became a member of the master craftsman's household because there was no place for him in society as an employee living separately. The Eskimo who had no wife had a mother or sister living with him, or he lived with another man who had a wife.

Today the laundromat, prepackaged foods, sexual liberalism, and employment outside the home have removed the necessity for marriage. Yet marriage remains popular; most Americans marry, and many marry more than once. Those unmarried past the usual age of marriage are a small and persecuted minority. The married do missionary work among them; the bachelor learns not to be surprised to find a young lady present when a married couple asks him to dinner.

Why Marry?

Why did you get married? An Eskimo would have found the question absurd; for him marriage was an aspect of survival. But the American marries by choice, and has usually pondered the reasons for his action. He may give a variety of explanations, but almost always they involve the fulfillment of emotional needs. He may say

he married to escape loneliness, or because he found someone warm
and rewarding, because he wanted to live with the one he loved, or
because he found someone who seemed to lack the faults of his
previous spouse. All of these reasons are based on the expectation
that marriage will contribute to the fulfillment of emotional needs.

Emotional fulfillment has always occurred in the family; probably more so in the past than is usual today. But it was never before
seen as the primary *function* of the family. It was the lucky by-
product.

Australia was first colonized by male convicts. On their release,
they were encouraged to go into the outback and establish farms.
They were forbidden to return to England. Quite a traffic in mail-order
brides resulted. Some men wrote to relatives in England asking for a
girl who would come to Australia to marry them. Commercial enter-
prises arose which brought young women to Australia where they met
their prospective husbands. Most of these marriages seem to have
been successful for the simple reason that the prospective husband
and wife expected things of each other that the other could provide.
The man needed the assistance and companionship of a woman in the
arduous task of making a farm, and he wanted sons to help him. He
expected certain skills in his wife, but all girls raised in rural England
were likely to have them. Her expectations were similarly pragmatic.
She expected him to know farming, to work hard, and to protect her.
Neither thought of the other as a happiness machine. If they found
happiness together more often than American couples do, it may
have been because they were not looking so hard for it. They fulfilled
each other *because* they shared a life; they did not share a life in the
hope of being fulfilled.

The modern American lives much of his life within the sockets of
the giant autosystems where his needs for intimacy, meaning, and un-
complicated enjoyment are difficult to fulfill. It is not surprising that
he turns to the smaller world of the family for fulfillment. He *is* looking for a happiness machine.*

---

* The family also is used to provide a perverse form of fulfillment by
serving as an existential cop-out. The male, by encumbering himself with a
wife, ex-wives, children, and child support, may sufficiently complicate his
economic situation to conceal from himself the necessity of choosing his life.
Similarly, the female may retreat into traditional sex roles and evade the painful task of choosing for herself. She becomes "what her husband wants and
needs" or "lives for her children." Either partner may then play the game of
"If it weren't for you. . . ."

Sex and Children

There are a few other functions remaining to the family. Approved sexual relations remain a monopoly of the family (although the strength of disapproval of nonmarital sex seems to be weakening). Similarly, the bearing and socialization of children remain a presumed monopoly of the family (although the diminishing importance of children and the intrusion of other agencies of socialization, such as television and the nursery school, affect this).

There is an interesting tendency to group the sexual and child-rearing functions together under the general and pervasive quest for emotional fulfillment. In the past, a man had children in order to claim the labor of the child and to perpetuate his lineage. These two reasons have largely disappeared. Children now constitute one of the greatest economic liabilities that can be undertaken, and they do not effectively continue lineage when they depart to far corners of the country and pursue lives incomprehensible to their parents.

Today, people have children for different reasons. Of course some people, having grown up expecting to have children, have them without thinking much about it (perhaps to their later regret). Those who *decide* to have children usually do so for about the same reasons they got married: to enhance their opportunity to fulfill emotional needs. The specific reasons may be as healthy as liking to watch children develop or as pathological as wanting to relive their lives vicariously. But all of them are emotional.

In a similar way, sex is incorporated into the idea of emotional fulfillment. Americans see the goal of the family as "togetherness," and sex is viewed as the ultimate form of togetherness. This is a very limited theory of sexuality. It is true that people who are fond of each other within a stable and monogamous relationship can enjoy sex—if they work at reducing the inevitable boredom. But it is also true that people can enjoy sex in very different situations.*

An indication of the degree to which sex and children are

---

* For example, two competent and enthusiastic strangers can find great sexual enjoyment, part of which derives from the fact that they are strangers. Literature repeatedly suggests that individuals who passionately hate each other may find great fulfillment in bed. And many friendships can happily be taken to bed that would never survive cohabitation. Human sexuality is complex, and the simplistic view that sex is worthwhile only when it expresses a sustained and monogamous love is an attempt to find secular justification for taboos which originally had religious justifications.

subsumed under the pervasive goal of emotional fulfillment is the fact that when the family ceases to fulfill emotional needs for the spouses, sexual relations are generally terminated, and it is assumed that the children might be better off if the marriage were dissolved. All of the eggs are in one basket, and when it drops, all of them break. The wife of the outback farmer may not have "loved" her husband, but she did not think much about it, and she certainly did not contemplate taking the children and leaving because she was not emotionally fulfilled. She had too many other things to do.

The Family versus Its Functions

The system of the family as we know it evolved gradually over a long period of time. It was presumably well suited to the functions which the family served on the subsistence farms where most people lived. But it would be amazing if this same system were well adapted to fulfill the different functions expected of it in modern urban society.

Once things are viewed in this light, a number of questions arise. For example, the demand that marriage should entail sexual monogamy may have made sense in an era when contraception was largely impossible and questions of lineage and inheritance were of considerable moment. And in any case, long hours of hard labor used to restrict sexual energies. But it is by no means certain that the demand for monogamy contributes to marital success under present conditions. American society constantly suggests the delights of sexual variety, and forbids the enjoyment of it. It teaches people to experience intense sexual jealousy, and provides innumerable opportunities for sexual infidelity. A vast amount of energy is unhappily consumed in repression, fantasy, scheming, guilt, and quarreling over sexual matters. There is bound to be a better way of arranging things!

The present family system encourages viewing spouses and children as property—marriage confers rights of ownership. Such attitudes may have had some utility in days when brides were purchased, and wives and children were largely regarded as instruments of production, but these attitudes are grossly inappropriate to marriages among individualistic Americans. They have enough problems without a system which encourages them to think of each other as chattels.

The family system insists that children belong in the home of their biological parents. Yet this is hardly easy to achieve as people change partners looking for the greatest emotional fulfillment. Countless people find themselves living stunted lives because it is financially impractical for them to escape each other, or because they have separated and the burdens of separate households and child support ruin them financially. Nor is the picture necessarily brighter from the child's viewpoint. Parents may insist on their inalienable right to produce children and then drive them neurotic, but where is the child's right to a mentally healthy childhood in an uncrowded world? It is interesting that we require barbers to be licensed to protect people from getting poor haircuts, but allow anyone at all to attempt to shape and rear another human being.

The present family system holds up the ideal of a lifetime relationship—which made a great deal of sense in the Australian outback or in the English village. But it is not at all clear that such an expectation makes sense under present circumstances. Probably one marriage in three ends in divorce, and another one in three becomes a protracted struggle to destroy one another. If the function of the family is to help the individual find fulfillment, it is only logical to encourage him to experiment until he finds a situation to his liking. But even in the one marriage in three which might be termed amiable, it is unclear just why there should necessarily be a lifetime commitment. The man who leaves a successful career in the middle of his life to seek new experiences in another field is applauded, yet it seems shocking to think of someone leaving a happy marriage in order to experience other intimate and rewarding relationships. But why not?

The Hand of the Autosystems

The family system did not evolve to do what we now expect of it, and yet we seem bewildered that it does not work. The family system itself is at such a low level of centralization that it does not become a formidable autosystem. But the highly centralized institutional sectors—especially the state—undertake to enforce the existing family structure. Legislation is directed against experimentation which might uncover family forms—for example, communes—more propitious to yielding what we want from the family. And the church, school, and advertising join the state in teaching people to believe that there is something unalterable about the present system.

The autosystems thus force people to fit an arbitrary family system, rather than let people create a system which will fit them. The family as it exists is a people-wrecking machine of awesome effectiveness. It hardly seems excessive to estimate that two-thirds of the unhappiness which Americans experience derives from the family—if not from marital conflict, then from parent–child conflict. But Americans are massively programmed to assume that the system is all right, and that their unhappiness is the result of their own deficiencies or those of their spouses and children.

I recall talking to a young bride who told me that her entire evaluation of herself as a person would depend on the success of her marriage. She defined success as finding happiness herself, and in making her husband happy. I shuddered and said nothing, but I felt a real sense of tragedy that this young lady was so willing to play the system's game against the odds, and with her ego at stake. A few months later, I heard that she and her husband had separated.

It is long past time to reexamine the whole question of the family from the *human* point of view, and to withdraw the misplaced loyalty we have been taught to render unto the present system.

---

9   Humane Alternatives

Since the only real function for the family is to make people happy, why not just encourage them to work out whatever kind of family arrangements suit them best? Why let the autosystems surround us with rules and preconceptions?

One of the advantages of the vast institutional structure of modern society is that it does provide for the maintenance of the individual. He could, therefore, be left free to organize his personal life to his liking. It has become practical to examine alternatives to the present family system.

Traveling Light

First of all, we should reexamine singleness as a way of life. For the Eskimo or the outback farmer, remaining single was not a practical alternative, but for the modern American, it is. Being unmarried no longer imposes serious material inconveniences. Nor does it entail isolation; the single individual may have more opportunity to cultivate friendships than his married counterpart. Nor need the single state impose sexual deprivation. At least in metropolitan areas, the unmarried find many others in the same situation with the same needs. Actually, in terms of the variety and competence of his sexual partners the single individual may have the better sexual opportunity.

The advantage of singleness is freedom and flexibility—the opportunity to live as one wants and to do what one wants when one wants to do it. The price of these advantages is occasional loneliness—the lack of some particular individual to bore, exploit, and monopolize in exchange for reciprocal privileges. The single individual lacks an automatic audience for his rambling thoughts, and someone to do the laundry when he doesn't feel like it, or to hold his hand when he is sick. Whether the advantages of flexibility outweigh the advantages of convenience is a matter of individual choice. But such a choice should certainly not be coerced by the blind assumption that marriage is an intrinsic goal in life, or that remaining single reflects some sort of failure.

Serial Polygamy

Like singleness, serial polygamy is already a part of the system —although we attach a negative value to it. We regard divorce as failure, and several divorces as a series of failures. Yet the practice of having several spouses one after another deserves examination as a potentially desirable alternative.

We would think someone insane who was willing to sign a contract at age 22 to keep a given job for the rest of his life. But we expect him to be prepared to sign a lifetime marriage contract. If a shift in jobs can be desirable, or add depth and variety to life as one changes and develops, why not a shift in marriage partners? As people pass through life, do not the qualities they most desire in a spouse change? And should someone who goes through life knowing only one extended intimate relationship be admired or pitied?

Margaret Mead has made proposals to facilitate serial polygamy. One is the renewable marriage license. Instead of a lifetime contract, marriages would be arranged to run for a given period of years. The contract could then be renewed with the consent of both parties. This would not actually change what people do, but it might greatly change their attitudes toward separating. In a similar vein, Mead has suggested that there might be two stages of marriage: the first a simple childless relationship which was easily entered and easily terminated, and the second a more binding relationship intended primarily for those who decided to have children.[1]

A serious argument for serial polygamy derives from the observation that the same marriage may be congenial during some stages of life, and bitterly unhappy during other stages. In fact such variations within a given marriage are probably greater than those between one couple's marriage and another's. The stage of life which one is in may have much more to do with determining marital success than to whom one is married. Under these circumstances it would seem very sensible to be married during the stages of life when marriages are most likely to be happy and to be single during the stages of life when most marriages become acutely painful.

Marriages seem most likely to be happy among the young and the old. Many people seem to need marriage in the early years of adulthood. They need to leave the parental home, but are not yet sufficiently mature and secure to operate happily as single individuals.* A marriage at this stage in life is usually very close as the couple sustain each other through the transition. Yet in a few years when they are ready to stand alone, they find less and less in common, and want to experiment with their potential as separate individuals. Would it not be much better to call such marriages—which readied the individuals to live alone or with someone else—a success? Instead, we pressure such couples to remain together and call their marriage a failure if they separate.

Marriages in the teens and twenties also profit from the novelty of cohabitation, sex, and creating a household. In contrast, the late thirties and forties are usually the low spots in marriage. The novelty is gone, and—quite suddenly—so is half of life. Individuals become restless and eager for new experience. Would it not be wise to help

---

* After all, American culture is extreme both in the degree of emotional dependence which it encourages the child to place on the parents and in the degree of emotional independence which it demands that the adult show from his parents. Other societies have allowed the child more adults to spread his dependence among, and also have allowed him to retain more of his dependence in adult life. Traditional Chinese society is an excellent example. For the American, then, the transition from childhood dependence to adult independence is necessarily turbulent.

people to go it alone for awhile rather than to encourage a sense of personal failure about a nearly universal experience?

In the sixties and seventies there seem to be few *unhappy* marriages (however unhappy some of these same marriages were earlier). The convenience and stability of marriage tend to take on an increased appeal. Under serial polygamy these years would seem an excellent time for remarriage.

Living Arrangements

Cohabitation without marriage is increasingly practiced in our urban centers. For some individuals at least, such nonmarital pairing avoids stresses which derive from the contractual nature of marriage. In many cases individuals live happily together for several years and then get married, only to find that their relationship deteriorates within a few months. Obviously the presumption of a lifetime contract precipitated problems which simply living together did not.

Cohabitation need not necessarily be sexually monogamous; some unmarried couples live together but practice sexual freedom. In principle, such relationships combine the advantages of freedom with those of deep and continuous association. Unfortunately, for those socialized in America, these relationships pose particular difficulties. Even those who believe completely in sexual freedom can find it difficult to accept the practice of such freedom by their partner. As one girl explained, "When I sleep with someone else I *know* it means nothing to our relationship, but when he sleeps with someone else I can't help thinking that it might." *

Another possible arrangement is pairing without living together. This may seem strange, but it has advantages. In a society where living standards are high enough to provide each individual with his own house or apartment, everyone can have a place that is truly his

---

* People who have experimented along these lines report that one of the hardest things is to sit alone at home when the other half of the relationship is out with someone else. And yet dates cannot always be arranged to fall on the same nights. Perhaps this is why couple swaps seem to be rather popular. By its very nature, swapping involves both partners at the same time leaving neither partner with a lonely period to brood about what the other is doing. The difficulty in couple swaps is that they severely limit choice, since the other couple must be taken as a unit. In each swap, therefore, one party is likely to be considerably less interested in the arrangement than the other.

own (even though he shares it almost continuously with another person). When a couple can ask each other "Shall we spend the night at my place or yours?" squabbles over taste, tidiness, and life style are vastly reduced. Moreover, each has a place to which he can retreat.

Such relationships are not necessarily monogamous. A friend explained to me that he and his girl friend had a "permanent part-time relationship." Part-time relationships can deal with the problem of jealousy more easily than full-time ones. Some couples have worked out mutual agreements whereby each shields the other from information about outside sexual activities, unless such information is specifically requested. They agree: "If you ask a question you get an honest answer, but be sure you want the answer before you ask the question." Meanwhile, each can assume that there is nothing to be jealous of if he chooses; since they do not live together full time, it is not necessarily obvious when one partner has another date. Other couples prefer complete honesty, and derive vicarious enjoyment from accounts of each other's activities. Unfortunately, there is a middle situation in which couples attempt to reveal everything to each other, but in fact are unable to enjoy such revelations, or even to avoid bitter jealousy over them. But however things are arranged, and regardless of the individuals, nonmonogamous relationships will cause some jealousy among people who were socialized to think of other people as private property. Many find the advantages of freedom worth enduring the occasional jealousy. As one friend told me when I asked him how he had combined freedom with a twenty-year relationship: "We didn't. Sometimes the freedom suffered, and sometimes the relationship. But we have had both, and it was worth it."

Individuals might maintain more than one "permanent part-time relationship," although the finite nature of the individual's time and attention would limit the number. But whether one or several, relationships which are both permanent and part-time would seem to combine intimacy with freedom, and autonomy with sharing.*

In the discussion thus far, there has been the implicit assumption that the pairings would be heterosexual. Yet there is no reason to expect that this would necessarily be the case, nor should it be. Man-

---

* They may, however, require a relatively high level of self-assurance and self-acceptance. Moreover, over a period of time, it may take real effort to keep them *both* permanent and part-time. There is a tendency for the relationship to drift either apart or into full-time cohabitation.

kind is merely sexual; both heterosexuality and homosexuality are learned behaviors. It is quite possible that the cultural demand for exclusive heterosexuality is the major causative factor of exclusive homosexuality.* If people were raised without pressure one way or the other, they might very well choose their partners primarily in terms of personality and only secondarily in terms of sex.

Group Marriage

There is considerable current discussion of the possibility of group marriage, and a limited amount of experimentation. One form of group marriage emerges when two or three couples undertake to create a larger unit in which they will share income, expenses, household activities, and recreation, but maintain monogamous sexual relationships among the original couples.

Somewhat more radical are the group marriages which involve nonmonogamous couples. This pattern is being tried in some of the current communes. Within the larger group, couples form lasting ties, but they are not sexually exclusive. The group as a whole attempts to maintain very strong ties among all its members.

The most extreme form of group marriage would be one without any stable pairing into couples. All of the possible ties within the group would be kept as equal as possible, although in the short run, particular pairings would inevitably come and go. Under this concept, stable pairing is seen as a threat to the unity of the group. Such group marriage is rather close to what Huxley envisioned in *Brave New World,* and it is interesting to note that he assumed the need for moral strictures against monogamous pairing.

Group marriage in any form offers variety and diversity. It could be more stable than smaller groupings because the spreading of ties among more people could reduce the traumatizing effect of particular conflicts. In some ways, however, it might place more restrictions on the individual than conventional marriage; there are just that many more people to take into consideration. Imagine, for example, making a decision to move a group marriage to another town. There is

---

* Thus in societies which allow homosexual experimentation, there seems to be a very low incidence of exclusive homosexuality. See William Davenport, "Sexual Patterns in a Southwest Pacific Society," in Ruth and Edward Brecher, eds., *An Analysis of Human Sexual Response* (New York: The New American Library, 1966), pp. 198–200.

also a serious problem in defining and maintaining the stability necessary to sustain a sense of family. Communes where people come and
go too readily cease to be a family and become merely an unstable
conglomeration of individuals.

Free Form

An alternative to the present family is leaving everyone free to
remain single, or to join with other people in whatever way seems most
congenial to his desires and needs. Let individuals form families of
two, three, four, five, or any number, and in any combination of sexes
they choose: three men, two men and four women, one woman and
three men, two women—or one man and one woman. Within these
families let them play whatever roles they choose without regard to
traditional sex roles: let the cooking, wage earning, faucet fixing, and
child care (if any) fall where they may according to people's personalities and not according to their sex.*

Such a proposal flies in the face of traditional regulating of
family behavior, but whereas past societies may have needed to control the family, our society can afford to allow people to do what they
want.

Necessary Changes

To establish a free-form family system would require various
changes. First, the interference of the autosystems in family relations
would have to cease. Legislation regulating family groupings would
have to be repealed, and pressures to maintain the present family
system eliminated.

Fortunately there seems to be a trend in this direction. We are
seeing the gradual repeal of various types of legislation relating to the
traditional family. Changes in divorce and abortion laws are a case in
point.

---

* I know a couple who lived relatively unhappy lives for more than two
decades largely because she hated housework and wanted a career, and he
hated business and loved to putter about the house. The cultural expectations
were too much for them to overcome, until he was stricken and became unable
to work. Then they switched roles with social approval—"Isn't it nice that he
takes care of the house now that she has to work." Under this arrangement they
spent their final years quite happily.

A second necessary change would be the institution of some form of guaranteed annual wage so that everyone could live apart from a family if he chose. To a degree the family is still a means of economic distribution: the wife may live by her husband's wage or pension, having none of her own. For economic reasons unrelated to the family, it is probable that at least a minimal guaranteed annual wage will be established.*

An alternative child-rearing system would also have to be provided. If people were allowed to choose their family forms freely, it seems inevitable that only some of these forms would provide the continuity necessary to raise children. Of course with adequate contraception and a free-form family system, many people would probably decide not to have children. Certainly many people who have them today do so more in response to the pressures and expectations of society than out of a deep desire for children.

But children must be produced and reared if the race is to continue, and if the family is no longer to take full responsibility, other agencies must be provided. And, in fact, we are seeing a trend toward child-care centers wherein children of working mothers can receive day care; it is only another step to allow (as they do in Russia) the children to spend most of their time in these centers if the child or the parent desires it. Our present state-supervised foster homes are another beginning of a child-care system external to the family.

Professional child rearing outside the home could have advantages from the viewpoint of the child. He could receive care from people who had elected child rearing as a profession because they were interested in children, rather than fallen into it because they forgot to take their pill. Each child could also be given a guaranteed annual income independent of the family. The child could then (as some children of divorced parents can do now) take his child support and move from one situation to another according to his wishes and preference instead of being sentenced to a particular situation by his parents or the state. It is appealing to think of a child having the option of staying in a child center, with his biological parents, with other families, or even going on his own without financial or legal barriers. It is now recognized that a child can determine what he needs to eat; he may also be capable of determining where he should live.

---

* See Chapter 17.

Perhaps the biggest change necessary to implement a free-form family system is in the programming of people. Rather extensive change in attitudes would be essential. People would have to stop claiming the right to regulate other people's personal lives. The insistence on traditional sex roles would have to be abandoned, both in the family and in the economy. The prejudice against homosexuality would have to be eradicated. The concept of sexual monogamy as a precious aspect of human relationships would also have to be relinquished.* And it would be necessary to cease regarding other people as personal property; we would have to become secure enough to stop demanding that society coerce our lovers and children to remain with us.

There is evidence that all these changes in attitudes are slowly coming to pass. The interest in the liberation movements—women's lib, gay lib, and others—are evidence of a trend toward greater flexibility. And there is a general liberalization of attitudes. The hand of the autosystem is weakening, and it is about time. Now we need to study the situation very carefully and decide what it is that *we* want to do.

---

* It is curious just how much emphasis we lay on *sexual* monogamy. The wife who suspects that her husband is out with another woman feels relieved if she discovers that the other woman is a business associate—despite the fact that her husband could easily have a more meaningful relationship with a business associate than with some woman whom he bedded and passed by. The wife will accept a deep relationship with someone else, provided it is not sexual, and she will become jealous of the most superficial and passing sexual affair. And American men are even more jealous than American women. Many males have terminated otherwise acceptable relationships because they discovered evidence of infidelity—sometimes as long as ten years before.

Part Three: The Technological Base

_____

10   Behind the Scenes

Technology stakes out the boundaries within which the society develops, and when the type of technology changes, the stakes get yanked up and moved. Changes in other institutions which used to be impossible come to be inevitable. To grasp social change, therefore, study technology.

Technological Determinism

With nothing but a description of its technology, we know an amazing amount about a society. If the geographic setting in which the technology operates is also known, one can be very specific. For example, if all you know of a society is that it uses a hunting technology, you can nevertheless conclude that it will be migratory, since it will have to move to follow the game. It will also tend to be cooperative, since hunters must share in order to average their luck; the less favorable the terrain, the more highly cooperative it is likely to be. The groups will be small, lest they exhaust the food faster than they can move, and they will have few possessions, because everything must be carried with them. Apart from articles of personal use or adornment, there will be little private property, for there is no way the hunting territory can be divided and privately owned. There will be no slavery, for slaves are useless in hunting. And there will be little specialization, because the energy and attention of everyone will be directed to subsistence.

There are exceptions to these rules, but there are technological reasons for the exceptions. There were hunting people in the Pacific Northwest who did not migrate, who had slaves, who laid great emphasis on private property, and so forth. But these were peoples who had evaded the fundamental limitation of a hunting technology by locating themselves on salmon runs. There the food travels to the hunter while he remains in one place. He can therefore accumulate property, control slaves, and even lay personal claim to the best fishing spot along the river bank. Thus these exceptions also support the generalization that the technology determines the basic structure of society.

In Contrast to Marx

Obviously, theories of technological determinism derive from Marx. His theory of economic determinism was an effort to explain why periods of social stability alternated with periods of profound social change. Like any great thinker, his genius lay more in the question he asked than in the answer he gave; it is the sign of a truly creative thinker to ask a question so that a problem, heretofore murky, becomes clear. The answer which the great thinker provides to his question is usually less valuable than the question itself. Once the question is defined the real creative leap has been made, and the answer can be doggedly pursued by lesser minds.*

Marx's answer was not all bad; in the world today it is still the most widely accepted theory of social change (although some of its acceptance derives from political rather than theoretical considerations). It provides an excellent starting point, and given the experience of an additional century, it does not require another Marx to suggest refinements.

It seems to me that the errors Marx made derive primarily from his failure to distinguish adequately between the various institutional sectors of society. It is altogether logical that he did not do so, for in the period of history with which he was primarily concerned, the distinctions were not prominent.

Marx studied the transition from feudalism to capitalism in order to discover a pattern by which to predict the transition from capitalism to the next stage of development. This transition from feudalism to capitalism was marked by three parallel events. There was a *political* revolution. In some countries violently, and in some countries peacefully, the bourgeoisie gained control of the state apparatus from the aristocracy. There was also an *economic* revolution. The feudal

---

* The great thinker, however, usually misjudges his contribution. It is for his answer that he wants to be remembered, not for the question. Thus Marx seems to have felt that his greatest insight was his contention that class conflict was the fundamental mechanism of social change. Yet this contention is precisely the source of some of his massive errors in predicting the situation of the twentieth century.

system of ownership and distribution (a decentralized, agrarian, master–serf pattern, based on tribute and barter) was transformed into the mercantilist–capitalist system (an increasingly centralized, urban, merchant–laborer pattern, based on wages and the operation of the means of production for profit). Finally, toward the end of the period, there was a *technological* revolution which resulted in the rise of the mechanized factory as the basic means of production.

These three types of revolution occurred in the same process of upheaval, and were not particularly differentiated by Marx; one looks in vain in his writings for a clear distinction between them. At best, he speaks of economic developments paving the way for a new class to come to power and transforming the means of production. But he viewed the entire process as an inevitable whole, thereby projecting forward and backward in history the relatively unique events of his era. Such an error is only human, but today these three types of revolution are occurring separately, and it is both easier and crucial for us to distinguish them.

A political revolution occurs when a new group or class takes control of the state (a coup d'état occurs when the control shifts *within* a group or class). Political revolution can occur without technological revolution (without a new type of technology) and without economic revolution (without a new form of ownership and distribution). Thus Perón in Argentina conducted a political revolution by mobilizing an unlikely coalition of the working and military classes to seize power from the traditionally rural aristocracy. But his revolution was not accompanied by either a new technology or a new economy.

Similarly, an economic revolution means that the way goods are owned and distributed is fundamentally altered. Such a revolution took place early in the twentieth century in Sweden, without being accompanied by either a political or technological revolution. And a technological revolution can occur without either a political revolution or an immediate economic revolution. Indeed, as we shall see, it is now occurring this way in the highly industrialized countries.

When the three types of systems are distinguished, it becomes easier to describe and understand the similarities and differences between the United States and the Soviet Union. The two nations have the same technological system (advanced industrialization), but somewhat different economic and political systems. A communist revolution is a political revolution, ideologically committed to certain economic and technological changes. Communism is not the successor to capitalism (as Marx believed it would be), but an alternative framework within which to make certain technological changes.

In the United States today a technological revolution is instituting automated production. This is difficult to conceive in Marx's terms because the technology is being transformed without a new class seizing the state and without the establishment of a new distribution system. But the process is clear enough if it is recognized that the three areas of change are separable.

I am arguing that the real basis of society, in the sense that Marx discussed base and superstructure, is the technology. On top of this technology rises an economic system which controls the means of production, distributes the goods, and regulates their ownership. The same technology may underlie more than one type of economy. And on top of the economic system rises the political system which regulates and enforces the economic order.*

Leading versus Dominant Sectors

By definition, the leading institutional sectors of the society are where most of the primary changes originate. The technology is usually one of the leading sectors today, but this was by no means universally true in the past. Industrial societies have a highly centralized technological system, but where subsistence farming predominates (as in traditional China) the technology is at too low a level of centralization to initiate basic changes.

But whether or not the technology is a leading sector, it is still the dominant sector—the sector which most influences the overall form of the society. The type of technology defines what is and is not possible for the leading sectors to do. Thus in China today, the state is the leading sector, and it has been pressing very hard for technological change. But there are changes which are still impossible within the present technological framework, as some of the failures of the Great Leap Forward revealed. For this reason the Chinese leaders are now consciously stimulating those technological changes which will

---

* The man who started me thinking along these lines, although he does not make these points explicitly, was V. Gordon Childe in his book *Man Makes Himself* (New York: Mentor, 1951). Childe called himself a Marxist, but he ended up talking much more about technological revolutions than about class conflict.

consummate the industrial revolution and thereby produce fundamental transformations of the entire social system.

Technological Revolutions

What causes a technological revolution to be relatively abrupt? Why do these changes not occur in a gradual, linear way? The answer seems to lie partly in the fact that there is usually a point of no return at which involvement in the new technology necessitates the abandonment of the old, and partly in the fact that the new technology is usually so much more efficient that it crowds the old out of operation.

For example, a hunting group can make clearings or scatter seeds to increase their harvest of fruits or berries. But they can do this only insofar as it does not interfere with mobility. As soon as they become involved in protecting the plants from small animals and in weeding and watering, they are forced to remain in one spot and can no longer follow the game. And in their forced choice between the two systems, they are likely to be heavily influenced by the vastly greater yields of agriculture.

Once a group makes the leap to agriculture, the rest of the society must be rapidly transformed. For example, private property becomes important; a field can be owned in a way that ten square miles of hunting territory cannot, and it is necessary to invent a system of property and inheritance rights.[1] In every area of the social system, adaptations to the new system of production must be devised.

The first major technological revolution for which we have written records was the Urban Revolution which occurred around 5000–3000 BC in Egypt and Mesopotamia. With the possible exception of the last two centuries, this revolution was probably the most significant era in human history. The revolution began when agricultural groups moved down into the alluvial valleys—a difficult process due to floods, massive underbrush, and minimal rainfall. Very large-scale public works had to be completed before these valleys could be cultivated successfully. However, the rewards were extremely rich bcause the floods made the valleys immune to the problem of soil exhaustion which plagued early agriculture in other areas.

Accompanying this technological change was a total shift in the rest of the society. Civilization as we know it was quickly created. A strong central government was developed as a means of collecting, conserving, and distributing the agricultural surplus. Written language was developed out of the urgent necessity of keeping records of vast and complicated operations. Mathematics was developed to survey land, to calculate volumes of grain storage areas, and do other practical tasks. Astronomical research of a very high order was carried out in order to predict the timing of the floods. The army was developed as a means of collecting the surplus (by violence if necessary) and of protecting the surplus from outside raiders. Bureaucracy, including legal codes and courts, developed as a means of administering daily affairs. Organized religion arose to rationalize and justify the whole.[2]

In a word, in this era and in these valleys, the first true auto-systems were born as the result of a technological revolution. It is interesting to notice that the surplus which originally served the general good by building reservoirs and levees was, in time, diverted to construct immense pyramids which served no practical need. The portents of the future are written on those monuments.

---

11   The Machines Move In

The first industrial revolution waited until about 5,000 years after the beginning of civilization. But then it hit society like a spade hits an anthill. We need to learn all we can from that experience, because we are already seeing the start of the next industrial revolution. If we are to turn this one to human advantage—or even survive it— we have a lot to learn.

Groundwork

The Roman Empire pressed to the brink of the industrial revolution, but it did not come at all near to going over. It took the Middle Ages to create the conditions for the first industrial revolution.

For one thing, the Middle Ages saw the end of significant slavery in Europe. The Romans used slave labor as the basic form of production, and labor saving devices therefore created little interest among them. The Middle Ages also saw technological improvements in agriculture which for the first time allowed efficient farming outside alluvial valleys.* Improved agriculture yielded a sufficient surplus for the revival of trade. Europe again had the wealth for trade and the power to open trade routes. And this trade in turn brought new influences back to Europe. Moreover, trade created the town and then the city in Western Europe, as well as the class of merchants who profited by trade. These merchants, the bourgeoisie, came to be a powerful group with very different objectives than the rural aristocracy.

Technological improvements enabled more people to stay alive than could be absorbed into the feudal social structure. Feudalism provided rather few sockets, and those who were unintegrated ultimately provided the labor pool for industrial production. In the earlier period, they became monks, soldiers, and bandits. English society was able to support Robin Hood and his merry band even though they neither sowed nor reaped.

The rise of the Protestant religion also created a climate favorable to industrialization. Protestantism, with its emphasis on hard work, and with its tendency to equate divine duty with earthly tasks, was as congenial to the mentality of the merchants, as it was alien to that of the rural aristocrats. It was the Protestant bourgeoisie who developed mercantilism, a new economy developed within feudalism but antithetical to it.

Critical Inventions

Inventions were not in and of themselves the cause of the industrial revolution. The steam engine was essential, but it had been invented before, by the ancient Greeks and possibly before them by the Egyptians. James Watt's reinvention of it when society was prepared to use it was nevertheless important, for the use of mechanical

---

* For example, the deep plow was developed. This plow was adapted to the Northern European soils and brought under cultivation large areas of rich land that could not be cultivated by Roman techniques. Similarly, the horse collar made it possible to harness horses efficiently in a way that was unknown in Roman times. The horse's faster metabolism provided a significant increase in motive power over the slower but more readily harnessed ox. Crop rotation was also brought into widescale practice as a means of preventing soil exhaustion. See Samuel Lilley, *Men, Machines, and History* (New York: International Publishers, 1966), pp. 18–19.

power was a basic characteristic of the new technology. Water power had long been used, but it had evident limitations.

A second critical invention came from America. Eli Whitney, usually associated with the cotton gin, probably made a far more significant contribution by pioneering interchangable parts. In 1798 Whitney proposed to make rifles in a radically new way. Always before, rifles had been made by skilled craftsmen who made one gun at a time by fitting each part individually. It was Whitney's genius to conceive of a system of making guns in which unskilled laborers used elaborate jigs to produce identical parts which could then be assembled randomly by other unskilled laborers.[1] He had difficulty selling his idea; he finally got a government contract, although it appears the military had little understanding of the importance of Whitney's proposal.* But once proven, Whitney's system spread rapidly.

A third critical development was the mass distribution of cheap goods. In the past, goods used by the masses had been made by the individuals using them or by village craftsmen; the centralized urban production had been of quality goods for the small luxury market. It came to be recognized that greater profits could be reaped by selling to the poor at a penny profit than by selling to the rich at a pound profit. The dollar watch was an early example of this approach.

The First Industrial Revolution

All this added up to a technological revolution. The system which emerged was characterized by the intercoupling of men and machinery; the machinery provided speed and power and performed the most repetitive operations, and the men remembered the program and performed the more complex manipulations.

The development of the power loom by Cartwright in 1785 could perhaps be taken as the beginning of this industrial revolution, and from then until 1945 the system expanded and developed. This was an era of linear change in which machines got better and better, operators became more and more skilled, and the organization of the system became more and more efficient. As time passed, the system was applied in more and more difficult areas. It was first used in

---

* The reason the military was interested in his system was that weapons with interchangable parts could be repaired more easily. After a battle new parts would not have to be fitted to each particular gun that had been damaged.

areas such as textiles where power-driven machinery was easily applied. It came very late to operations such as house building.

The result of the first industrial revolution was not only a new system of production, but also the radical transformation of society. For example, the military sector was fundamentally altered. Machinery had been used in warfare before—the cannon and the rifle were preindustrial forms of power-driven machinery. But the application of industrial technology meant that complex weapons could be produced in extremely large numbers and at low cost. Quite simply, that part of the world that was industrialized conquered the part of the world which was not. The Gatling gun was an early version of the machine gun, and some unknown British soldier observed in India:

> Whatever happens
> We have got
> The Gatling gun
> And they have not.

Moreover, the whole purpose of warfare changed. Wars had recently been struggles for political control in Europe, or for gold or land in the New World, but with industrialization they became a struggle for sources of raw materials and markets. In addition, the expense of war to both the victor and the loser entered a period of rapid increase.

For the first time, society found itself confronted with the urgent need to teach children things their parents did not know. In addition to literacy, the industrial revolution demanded a continuous upgrading of skills; this required a separate institutional sector through which new skills could be introduced. And so the whole enormous system of the public school was called into being.

As already noted, the family was severely buffeted by the revolution. In the very early factories the family worked as a family, but the demand for efficiency quickly led men, women, and children to be assigned different tasks. The family group thereby lost one of the few functions remaining to it.

The revolution touched off a period of vast scientific development, and for good reason. In the past, science had been mostly a rich man's hobby unrelated to work-a-day tasks. But physics, chemistry, and mathematics were crucial to the new technology and were encouraged accordingly.

Mass communications grew out of the new technology. At the beginning of the eighteenth century, the king of England had at his disposal essentially the same techniques of communication that the Roman emperors or Egyptian pharaohs had. But by the beginning of the twentieth century, radical new systems of communication were in use. When Mark Anthony spoke over the grave of Caesar, his eloquence was limited to those who could crowd within the sound of his voice. But when Hitler spoke to the German people, his voice was carried by modern technology to the farthest corners of the world.

Both government and the economy grew much more centralized during the nineteenth century, and a struggle ensued between them for leadership. To a considerable degree the Civil War resulted in transferring effective control of society to Northern industry at the expense of the Northern (and of course the Southern) government. It was not until the Depression of the 1930s that the governmental sector was able to reassert its power and reemerge as a leading sector.

During the industrial revolution population growth was tremendous, reflecting the greater efficiency of the new technology. The entire increase of humanity up to 1750 had resulted in a world population of one billion. That had doubled by 1940 to two billion, and by 1970 was approaching four billion. It is beside the point that most of these billions were hungry because most of the one billion people in 1750 were hungry. It is a demonstration of the degree of efficiency of the new technology that with only part of the world industrialized four times as many hungry people can be sustained.*

The society had not nearly begun to complete the secondary changes in response to the first industrial revolution when the next technological revolution began. It was not apparent at the time—such changes never are—but with hindsight we can see that it was in the late years of World War II that the second industrial revolution began.

---

* Hunger was part of the *means* of the revolution. Thus in England living standards went down among the masses during industrialization. By driving living standards down to the subsistence level and holding them there while production was continually increasing, surplus was accumulated and used to build new factories until finally there was enough to continue expanding production *and* to raise living standards. The same thing happened in the United States. The only mitigation here was the open land in the West to which the worker could escape if he had the initiative. The situation was also similar under communism. Russia sacrificed a generation by holding living standards down while they desperately built industry to catch up with the capitalist world. And significant rises in the living standard were allowed only when Russia too passed the point of industrial sufficiency.

More Groundwork

The second industrial revolution, like the first, had certain pre-conditions. Fundamentally, the first revolution was a prerequisite for the second. More specifically, the second revolution requires that the society have a tremendous accumulation of capital available for building complex productive systems. It must also have access to a high level of science and technology and to a pool of highly skilled workers and technologists—people who assimilated the techniques of the first revolution in childhood. Production must be highly centralized, for the new technology is effective only in huge units. Finally, at least in capitalist countries, high labor costs provide a strong incentive to replace men with machines.

The Critical Invention

Given these preconditions the indispensable invention was the electronic servo-mechanism. The vacuum tube, which was first used to amplify radio signals, took on greater significance when it made possible the first computers during the Second World War. Servo-mechanisms as devices to maintain steady states were hardly new; they had been used in Greek water clocks. But electronics made possible infinitely more complex servo-mechanisms than the simple mechanical ones heretofore utilized. HAL, in *2001*, was a servo-mechanism of extreme complexity, although he might seem much less complex in the actual year 2001.

The Second Industrial Revolution

The shape of the new technology is already evident in certain areas of production. Whereas the first industrial revolution created systems which intercoupled men and machinery, the second industrial revolution creates systems of pure machinery. The linear development within the first revolution led to a system which depended more and more upon the machine and less and less upon the human operator. With computers, this change became nonlinear, and the human operator disappeared entirely.[2]

The transition can be illustrated by what happened to anti-aircraft systems. At the beginning of World War II, anti-aircraft systems were characteristic of the first revolution. There were men intercoupled with machinery: a gun, a range-finder, proximity fuses, a slide rule-type calculating device—all interspersed with trained personnel. But as the planes became faster and faster, human reactions were simply too slow, and better and better machines were devised. The human observer was replaced by radar, the man with the hand calculator with a computer, and so on, until today the system is entirely automated. The human factor enters into the operation only at the on–off switch which keeps the anti-aircraft missile from shooting down the 7:35 flight from New York to San Francisco. And even that switch is becoming automated as computers are programmed to recognize scheduled flights.

Like the first revolution, the second began in areas where its particular technology was most easily applied. This time, however, it was not textiles, but petroleum refining which was most congenial to the new technology. For a decade we have had petroleum refineries covering acres in which no man labors. Gradually the techniques are being adapted to more and more difficult sectors of the productive system.

The second industrial revolution opens up the possibility of an indefinite expansion of production—as big factories automatically produce litters of little factories, and so on. But this possibility depends on the availability of enormous resources of power and raw materials, far beyond the demands of the first industrial revolution. The problem is complicated by the fact that the first revolution has already consumed a considerable fraction of the earth's fossil fuels and available minerals.

And yet the power and materials for the second revolution are probably at hand or nearly so. Nuclear energy will provide the necessary power, but not from the kind of power plants we have today; they are too expensive, too dangerous, and produce by-products so antithetical to life that it is almost impossible to dispose of them.* The new power source will be the hydrogen reaction of nuclear fusion (rather than the fission of heavy metals). But it may be tapped in one of two ways. The sun is an immense hydrogen reactor, and

---

* We already have tanks of radioactive wastes so hot that if they are not mechanically cooled they will boil and burst. The tanks will last only a few decades, but no living thing can approach them for centuries. The cooling equipment must be maintained by robot equipment which, once used, also becomes contaminated. See Gene Schrader, "Atomic Doubletalk," *The Center Magazine*, Vol. IV, No. 1, pp. 29–52.

with existing space technology it would be entirely possible to orbit as many square miles of reflectors as we chose in order to concentrate and beam to earth as much energy as we wanted. On the other hand, we are very close to developing working hydrogen reactors on earth, and it is estimated that the seas could provide enough heavy hydrogen to provide one thousand times our present power consumption for a billion years.[3] It seems probable that by 1985 one or both of these techniques will be advanced to the stage of today's uranium power stations.[4]

Certain specific raw materials may come into very short supply or even run out. But man's ability to synthesize or to develop substitutes is developing so rapidly that it seems unlikely that shortages will halt the productive explosion of the second revolution. To be sure, there is a price: to synthesize or to substitute usually requires more power than the original material did. Harrison Brown has contended that ultimately most of man's industrial needs could be synthesized from seawater, air, sunlight, common rock, limestone, and phosphate rock, but at an enormous cost in power.[5] Thus the solution to the problem of materials reduces itself to an aspect of the need for power.

Unless man perishes from war or pollution, the enormous productive potential of the second industrial revolution is almost certain to be realized. The first revolution produced goods on a scale unimaginable by previous standards; the second will produce goods on a scale unimaginable by the standards of the first revolution.

It can be safely assumed that the impact of the second revolution on the rest of society will be as pervasive as that of the first. If coupled with sensible population control (already practical, given modern contraceptives and communications), the new technology could mean that scarcity would cease to be a problem; that for the first time in human history it would be possible to produce all that everyone wanted and needed, including leisure.

Inevitably, all of the other sectors of society will go through a radical transformation just as they did in adapting to the first revolution. Actually, they are being compelled to begin this process of adaptation before they had fully adapted to the first revolution. It is very difficult to say precisely what will happen to the economy, the military, the government, the church, the school, or the family (although later chapters contain some guesses).

In the coming decades, great transformations will inevitably occur, and man could change his social structures to suit himself within the enormous limits circumscribed by the new technology. But the potential is also there for the development of autosystems so vast and remote that they pass entirely beyond human control.

---

12   The Ecological Gauges

The balance of nature included primitive man. But industrial man has built a system which sustains a vast population and vast consumption per individual. Having moved his productive system outside the old balance of nature, man must also provide his own systems to maintain his supply of materials and to absorb his pollutants. Thus he could establish a new balance of nature which included industrial man. Or he could wreck the planet.

The first industrial revolution enabled living standards to rise until the great mass of the population had sufficient quantities of the daily necessities. The second industrial revolution promises levels of production which could satisfy all man's material desires. But precisely because these technologies are capable of such enormous production, they impose proportionately great strains on the environment from which the society draws its raw materials and to which it must return its waste products. Pollution and declining resources have never before been serious problems, except on a local scale.

The Good Old Days

Local problems did arise. For example, in Dalmatia on the shores of the Mediterranean, there were originally rich forests interspersed with fertile glades. The Venetians cut down these forests to build ships. With the forest cover removed, erosion became a problem. Sheep and goats were introduced to graze on the remaining vegetation in such numbers that this too was destroyed. The erosion thus aggravated, the soil of Dalmatia washed down to the sea. Today, peasants eke out a living on the barren slopes by carrying the small quantities of remaining soil back up the hillsides in baskets and packing it carefully behind retaining walls which they build out of the abundant rocks. But the devastation of Dalmatia was a local phenomenon; elsewhere around the Mediterranean Basin the soil has continued to be fertile.

Similarly, pollution has been an urban problem ever since cities were developed. Until the twentieth century, the death rates in urban areas were so high that regardless of the birth rate, cities were able to maintain their population or grow only because of migration from the rural areas. The pollution in London in the sixteenth and seventeenth centuries was apparently something to stagger the imagination. Refuse of all types—waste, litter, excrement, dead animals—was not disposed of in any systematic manner. The only disposal system seems to have been a sort of trough which ran down the center of the streets toward which the refuse was thrown from the second floor windows of the houses. There it festered until rats ate it or the rain washed it down into the turbid Thames.[1] Small wonder that London's population was repeatedly reduced by plagues. But the pollution was a local phenomenon; far healthier conditions prevailed in the open countryside only a day's journey away.

Historically, conditions away from the cities have been similar to those which prevailed in a region of the Canadian bush where I spent my summers as a child. In this region, population density was extremely low, in part because the soil was not well suited to agriculture, and in part because there were no roads—the only access was by boat across 40 miles of lake. Under these conditions, pollution was hardly a problem. We used outhouses, but had we dropped our excrement in the open, flies could have carried the germs only to the family from which they came since habitations were so far apart. There were far more deer than people. We drank raw lake water, and also threw our fish heads in the lake; the lake was so large that the natural balance easily kept it pure. Even litter was no problem; finding trash in the woods or on the shores was such a rare event that it was exciting, not offensive. Nor was exhaustion of resources a problem. The available resources were quite adequate to sustain the sparse population by trapping, hunting, fishing, and gardening. Nature absorbed us easily.

Exhaustion of Resources

Here and now the situation is very different. The consumption of resources by modern technology simply overwhelms the mind. We had a mountain range of iron ore in the United States; it seemed unlimited. And yet today the Mesabi range is exhausted, for practical purposes, leaving in its place a man-made Grand Canyon. Fossil fuel deposits (coal, oil, and natural gas) have accumulated in the earth for a billion years to make the equivalent of perhaps four trillion metric tons of coal. This represents over one million pounds for each man who ever lived, including those now living. And it is only in the last 100 years or so that these resources have been heavily utilized—100 out of a million years of man's existence. It is doubtful that these fossil fuels will last as much as 400 years longer.[2]

As resources dwindle, the energy required to collect necessary raw materials increases. More and more quantities of lower grade materials must be refined, and deeper and more inaccessible deposits must be utilized. And as we saw in the last chapter, when substitute materials become necessary, they usually require more power to produce than the materials they replace; that is why they were not used until the original resource was exhausted.*

Pollution

Pollution becomes a problem only when the normal ecological balance is disturbed. The different life forms have evolved together in a complex relationship wherein one's wastes are another's resources. The number of each species is also adjusted to the available resources and to the capacity of the environment to absorb its wastes. Earth has always been a spaceship in which all products were necessarily recycled.† A stream can absorb the normal wastes of the organisms which dwell in it or beside it. In fact, these wastes are an essential part of the balance; the fish excrete substances which are utilized by other organisms in the overall food chain. But as man's numbers have multiplied and as his technology produces ever larger quantities

---

* Occasionally, to be sure, there is a serendipitous discovery of a substitute which requires less energy to produce than the original, or a new way of processing which uses less energy and lower grade materials. But these are the exceptions.

† Except of course energy, which has been largely imported from the sun.

of by-products per individual, the stream can no longer absorb them and becomes "polluted." It becomes overloaded with one particular set of by-products. The whole original balance of the stream then collapses, and man must develop artificial systems to break down human and industrial wastes into products which nature can absorb or man can utilize. Having built a technology which was not part of the balance, he must compensate for it by creating technological means of establishing a new balance. The problem of resources and the problem of pollution are two facets of the same difficulty. Man must cooperate with nature in turning his waste products into something that spaceship earth can absorb, recreating the balance which will again provide him with the materials he needs.

The key to the whole problem is energy. It takes energy to produce raw materials, and it takes energy to recycle waste products. Given the energy, man can solve the problem—providing he is willing to make intelligent efforts to solve it. In this light, the forthcoming breakthrough in the area of power from nuclear fusion assumes tremendous importance.

Crackpot Realism

As we struggle to face these problems, we encounter crackpot realism in several forms. For example the urgent need for conservation of resources and for the recycling of pollutants is met with the charge that it is simply unrealistic, that it is not practical in the competitive world of business. This might be true, but it only proves that the system must be changed in order to *make* conservation practical. But the voice of the autosystem demands continuation of the present system, and brands as unrealistic any solutions which lie outside that system. The words are spoken by servo-men who have been so programmed that they will accept the destruction of their world to defend the autosystem, believing that they are serving their own vested interests in so doing. But is the current value of a rich man's stock portfolio really more important to him than whether he can live on the air he breathes? Or is he the system's greatest dupe?

Another form of crackpot realism contends that worry is unimportant because over a billion years things have always worked out in the end. This is true, but many species have become extinct as things worked out during those billion years. *Something* will work out, obviously, if it is only a planet barren and sterile of life. But we had better think about *how* things are going to work out. For better or worse man can no longer fall back on the balance of nature; he has taken over that balance. I recall an engineer who took me to task at a cocktail party because of my concern over the exhaustion of petroleum resources. "Why, there's enough for another couple hundred years!" he told me, feeling he had absolutely devastated the basis of my concern.

A third form of crackpot realism contests the necessity of population control. The argument states that we will find a way to feed more people in the future, just as we have in the past. Up to a point this may be true. Harrison Brown estimates that the world could ultimately keep alive some 50 billion people. But before this conclusion is seized upon to justify unlimited population growth, it is well to note that the conditions under which these 50 billions would have to live render life hardly worth living.[3] And the problem of population growth would *still* have to be faced because the world would then have been pushed to the ultimate limit of its resources. Since a stand must be taken, why not take it now when a decent style of life may still be possible? But the autosystems are programmed to regard population growth as a factor which will facilitate their own growth and development.*

The crackpot realism of the autosystems hinders efforts to face the enormous problems created by the new technology, despite the evident fact that man's very survival is at stake. If we allow this crackpot realism to prevail, the new technologies will simply mean the failure of the human experiment. But then again, we could take a stand.

---

* The argument against population control is frequently wrapped in the guise of individual freedom—it is contended that it would be wrong to interfere with a person's right to have as many children as he chooses. But those who voice this argument are usually curiously indifferent to many other forms of coercion of the individual, such as the draft, the prohibition of abortion, or the withholding of contraceptive information.

13   Beyond Crackpot Realism

Because of technology, man alone of all the animals is able to cure his diseases and extend his average lifespan into old age. Because of technology man can escape drudgery and surround himself with things to please his senses and excite his mind. It is also because of technology that man is threatened with nuclear and ecological disasters. It is as unrealistic to rail against technology as it is to leave the technological autosystem uncontrolled. We must learn to accept or reject each new technological possibility in terms of human interests.

At present, the technological autosystem is programmed for unlimited growth and development. The mere discovery of a new resource is taken as reason enough for its exploitation if the system can use it to promote its cancerous growth. A case in point is the Alaskan oil deposits. As someone commented, these deposits had been taking care of themselves for millions of years and presumably would continue to do so until they were really needed; but such wisdom is mostly ignored. Similarly, the mere creation of a new artifact is taken to be reason enough for its production, provided only that men can be persuaded to desire it. The electric toothbrush is a case in point. We are confronted, quite literally, with technology for the sake of technology.

Yet man's interests do not necessarily coincide with the program of the technological autosystem. It has become apparent that not all technological developments should be encouraged or even allowed; but in terms of what criteria would evaluations be made? We must now begin to attempt to provide *human* criteria as an alternative to the criteria of the autosystem. The following list is hardly definitive, nor need it be. The point is to encourage recognition of the need to establish human criteria for the evaluation of technological proposals.

Environmental Considerations

First, a technological development is not humanly acceptable if it significantly lowers the quality of man's environment. More specifically:

1. It must not place excessive strain on available raw materials. For example, given the importance of preserving the remaining fossil fuels for petrochemical production, further development and refinement of the internal combustion engine is of doubtful acceptability (quite apart from the problem of atmospheric pollution). In contrast, development of other means of locomotion which do not exhaust precious resources would be desirable. For example, flywheel-driven vehicles seem promising. Far more power per pound can be stored in an ultra-high velocity flywheel than in even the most efficient batteries. With the present state of the art, flywheel-driven cars can probably be developed to have an adequate range for town use (in excess of 100 miles) and be capable of freeway speeds.[1] The ultimate source of power is electricity which, if generated by nuclear fusion, would be pollution free.*

2. A technological development must not produce toxic or offensive waste products. For example, the aluminum beer can seems a dubious advance over the steel beer can which would rust away naturally. Similarly, further development of chemical pesticides seems unacceptable because living organisms can be used to feed on agricultural pests.

3. A technological development must not involve excessive demands on energy. For example, since the power required to go faster tends to increase exponentially with each increment in speed, a point of diminishing returns is encountered. Supersonic flight is a clear case in point, quite apart from the problems of noise and pollution associated with it. In contrast, developments which increase passenger comfort during flight would involve little demand on energy and be quite acceptable.

In a similar way, technological developments might be acceptable if they replaced another approach which was less acceptable. Specifically:

4. A technological development may be acceptable if it replaces

---

* Fusion reactors generate heat as a byproduct; this heat may or may not pollute, depending on its use.

some similar device which imposed a greater strain on resources. For example, the development of electrical power generated by nuclear fusion will constitute a great improvement over generating electricity by combustion of fossil fuels.

5. A technological development may be acceptable if it produces less toxic and more disposable waste products than another similar device. An excellent example is the trend toward biodegradable household products.

6. A technological development may be acceptable if it requires less energy than the existing devices. For example, the transistor requires considerably less energy than the vacuum tube which it replaces.

Human Considerations

But the above criteria reflect only part of the picture. Even those technological developments which meet them should not automatically be implemented. Does the new technology benefit humans in some clear way that is demonstrably independent of the urgings and pleadings of the autosystem? So much of our presumed technological progress has simply served to make life more confusing, noisy, cluttered, ugly, busy, and aggravating. Technology is not its own justification; it must make a real contribution to the quality of human life. Specifically:

7. A technological development may make a contribution by extending the human lifetime in a meaningful way. The heart transplant operations of the 1960s seem to have failed in terms of this criteria; the pain, frustration, and ultimate tragedies seem to have outweighed the very small extensions of life which were achieved. But leukemia research, while not yet providing cures, has enabled afflicted individuals to extend their lives quite meaningfully.

8. A technological development may make a contribution by reducing illness. Such reduction must not be achieved by isolating the individual in a supersanitized environment. The ultimate implication of that approach would be to assign the individual at birth to a separate underground padded cell where he was safe from all dangers—until the ventilating system broke down. In contrast, developments like the Salk polio vaccine enable the individual to live in the world without risking certain diseases.

9. A technological development may be acceptable if it contributes to meaningful new experiences. While a supersonic flight is

new experience for most people, it seems insufficiently meaningful to justify its evident drawbacks. In contrast, the development of the motion picture created a whole new art form which has significantly broadened human experience and can potentially broaden it even more.

10. A technological development may be acceptable if it makes some form of experience fuller and more accessible. Meaningless gadgetry such as the CO_2-powered corkscrew could not qualify. In contrast, skindiving gear has vastly extended the capacity of man to experience his world.

11. A technological development may be acceptable if it makes a significant contribution to the growth of human knowledge. Spy satellites and electronic snooping devices are spurious examples. But radio telescopes, electron miscroscopes, and perhaps even space probes (if their enormous consumption of resources can be justified or reduced) do make valid contributions to man's understanding of himself and his world. And although some have not learned to cultivate it, understanding can be an extremely meaningful and exciting form of experience.

12. A technological development may be acceptable if it makes a significant contribution to the availability of human knowledge. There is an urgent need to provide an individual with easy access to available knowledge at *the moment of his curiosity*. A household device which gave instantaneous access to the data presently stored in libraries (which the average man has neither the motivation or skill to utilize) might go a long way toward reducing the intellectual stagnation and atrophy which afflicts so much of our population.

13. A technological development may be acceptable if it contributes to freedom from drudgery. The value of TV dinners may be doubtful, but it is hard to be critical of the vacuum cleaner—especially if one beat rugs hung over a clothesline as a child.

14. A technological development may be acceptable if it helps to free men from tyranny. This criterion would hardly justify a Department of Defense which threatens the annihilation of mankind under the pretense of safeguarding liberty. But it is intriguing to think of how one could use modern electronics in the defense of the individual. Instead of allowing the government to "bug" the phones, offices, and homes of citizens, we might seriously consider routine, mandatory "bugging" of the phones and offices of government officials. Such monitoring devices could be made to broadcast over special

radio frequencies so that any citizen could listen in on his government as it actually operated. The resulting loss of privacy on the part of the officials should certainly be one of the expected consequences of occupying a powerful political status.

15. Finally, a technological development may be acceptable if it creates an opportunity for human inefficiency. This is a rather subtle point, but it may be one of the most important. If an increase in technological efficiency frees people to behave inefficiently (from the viewpoint of the autosystem) and in ways that are more meaningful in human terms, it may be very valuable. It would be intriguing, for example, to try to devise economic and technological systems which would enable men to work at the hours and days of their own choosing without any fixed schedule. This would, of course, vastly reduce the efficiency of the systems; but if the systems were themselves efficient enough, they might be able to make up for the loss and still produce what was really needed. The human gain—by counterposing systemic efficiency and human inefficiency—might be enormous. Unfortunately, up to now the tendency has been to accept the autosystems' blind demand for maximum human efficiency regardless of how high the level of production becomes. Man has thus been further enslaved through the very developments which should have helped to free him.

Taking Control

The fifteen criteria listed above are not crucial. Doubtless some categories have been overlooked, and some of those listed could be combined. More important, many conflicts would occur in practice between different criteria which would have to be resolved on an individual basis. The essential point is that technological developments can no longer be blindly accepted but must be evaluated in terms of criteria which reflect human interests.*

The autosystem, of course, will vigorously protest any such re-

---

* Moreover, in view of the extremely large number of technological developments which have already been implemented, and remembering that technological change produces primary, secondary, and tertiary changes which cannot be entirely predicted, it would seem expedient to err on the side of caution. After all, a development which is shelved can always be implemented later if the need for it becomes obvious. Research and experimentation can continue in the meantime.

striction of its tendency for endless development and expansion. Through its servo-men it will argue that *any* given development does in fact meet *any* criteria which are established. This resistance and propaganda must be anticipated; in fact, it is not bad. Some technological developments are good, and programming the technological system to press continuously for development and expansion is one way to make sure that a large number of new developments are available from which to choose. But it is also necessary to prevent the autosystem from implementing the innovations unless men choose to allow this.

In practice, the evaluation of and selection among new technological developments would involve the creation of a new system in charge of such evaluations. Such a system would presumably show the usual tendency to become an autosystem in its own right. But again, this is not necessarily bad. The point is not to eliminate autosystems but to control them and to force them to serve rather than dominate humanity. It may be practical to divide and conquer. In Sweden there is one government bureau which is programmed to harass and challenge the other government bureaus in defense of individual interests. No doubt it has become just as bureaucratic as all the others. But out of its conflict with the other bureaus considerable human benefit may result. In the same way, men may find it advantageous to create a rival autosystem whose program directs it to challenge and resist the tendency toward overenthusiastic development which is properly built into the technological autosystem.

Part Four: The End of Economics

14   Economics as Rationing

Malthus had a point. Preindustrial societies rarely had enough food—except briefly after a plague or the introduction of a new technology. Industrial societies have enough food, but people still want lots of things they don't have. When there isn't enough to go around, there has to be some form of rationing, even if it's only the principle that the biggest club gets the biggest share. Economics is merely the rationing system of society.

Early Economies

As already noted, hunting societies have few possessions and have compelling reasons for sharing the available food. The chief might receive first choice, or even all he wanted, but for the rest a hunting economy is usually equalitarian and not very complex. It is with agriculture that the economic system begins to be elaborated. Private ownership of the means of production becomes possible. Over a period of time some individuals may be able to acquire more land and even a partial monopoly over the lands of the group. If they have more land than they can cultivate, they may arrange to have some landless individuals cultivate it for them, thereby dividing the society into classes: groups of people who share a particular economic situation, such as landowner, landless tiller, and so on. The landless tiller receives a part of the harvest and the balance goes to the landowner. Such an economic system based on classes requires enforcement since it cannot be assumed that the landless tillers are pleased with the arrangement. Government is therefore elaborated as a means of enforcing the economic system, and Marx's comment that the state is the means by which one class establishes its control over the society is quite appropriate.

In a class society, wealth comes to confer prestige: rich equals good. The next development is what Veblen called "conspicuous consumption"—the demonstration of wealth through ostentatious display.[1] To evoke prestige, a rich man may display upon his body the wealth which he has acquired. If the wealth is more than he can thus display, he may display it in his home, or on the wives and servants who depend on him for support. One of the effects of conspicuous consumption is that the demand for wealth becomes insatiable. There is a limit to the amount of wealth that one man can *use,* but there is no limit to the amount of wealth that he can *display.* The path is thus paved for more and more ruthless exploitation of those at the bottom in order to provide for the competitive displays of those at the top. The rule is Catch-22, which reads: "They have a right to do anything we can't stop them from doing." [2]

A Paradigm

To see how an economic system rations goods, let us use a simple paradigm. Imagine a little island on which there is a fantastic factory which will manufacture anything and a fantastic field which will grow anything. At the other end of the island is a little village. In between we will need some sort of conveyor belt by which the goods and foodstuffs are delivered to the village.

The paradigm suggests in simplified form three basic aspects of society: the field and factory are the technology wherein material things are produced, the conveyor is the distributive system which is the essence of the economy, and the village is the consuming system wherein material things are utilized.

If, as usual, there is not enough to go around, some form of rationing will have to be incorporated into the conveyor. It could be entirely equalitarian, some could be assigned more and some less, or there could simply be a daily snatch session to see who gets what.

It is convenient to have some uniform form of ration points. If the factory produces flutes and books, for example, it may be that some people are more interested in one than in the other. Equal quotas of each to everyone will not be satisfactory. A universal ration coupon which could be exchanged for either books or flutes could allow individuals to take more of their total share of production in one or the other according to preference. Such universal coupons, of course, are called money.

The way value is assigned to particular items is determined partly by the nature of the economic system.* Under an essentially communistic system, the number of ration points assigned to a book or a flute can be manipulated from time to time according to convenience. If enough flutes cannot be produced, the price can be raised so that the available ration points cannot buy as many. If there are flutes left over, the price can be lowered. Or wages (the number of ration points distributed) can be raised or lowered.

Thus in communist economic systems, currency is purely a system of rationing, and prices and wages can be altered without regard to profits, costs, or other such capitalistic considerations. All of the goods which can be produced by the fantastic field and factory can be delivered for consumption. (Of course some will be consumed in maintaining and enlarging the field and factory.) Production need not be limited for fear that people will lack coupons to buy them. Were it not necessary to ration goods because of scarcity, they could simply be given away; in fact, this has long been an ultimate objective of communism.†

Problems in Communist Economies

In actual communist economies there are certain typical problems. Unlike the island paradigm, the technology of a country such as the Soviet Union is enormously complex. Vast varieties of goods are produced in thousands of factories spread across a subcontinent, requiring the coordinated activities of tens of millions of individuals. The administration of this whole system has traditionally been done through a highly centralized bureaucracy in Moscow; all of the com-

---

* Although it reverses the usual procedure, let me use a discussion of communist economics as an introduction to a later discussion of capitalism.

† To be sure, wages have been used in communist economies as a means of forcing men to labor: those who didn't work, didn't eat. But this is simply another aspect of rationing; there would have been less production if all men had not been forced to work. Automated technology increasingly removes the necessity of human labor in the productive process, and thus the need to force men to work.

mittees which determined production priorities, quotas, prices, and wages were located there.

Such a vast system develops all the problems inherent in any bureaucracy. Some of these have been rather humorously described in books such as *Parkinson's Law* . . . ,[3] which points out that a bureaucracy tends to expand even though the work to be done remains the same or decreases. Similarly, *The Peter Principle*[4] states that a bureaucracy will tend to promote any individual until he reaches a job for which he is incompetent, leaving the system studded with ineffective components. Ossification, as described above, destroys the ability of the system to make realistic decisions. All of these problems have been very apparent in the Moscow bureaucracy.*

Another problem is that the centralized system leads to vast concentrations of power which are difficult to control. Statuses are set up and programmed to make extremely far-reaching and important decisions, but there is no real mechanism for checking the use of this power. Nominally the control of the autosystem lies with the people, but it seems doubtful that there is much effective control from that quarter.†

At various times the Russians have tried to reduce inefficiency by holding contests; quotas were established, and the manager who could push his production above quota was rewarded by money, promotion, or honors. But the manager who overfilled his quota oftentimes did so by disrupting production elsewhere and upsetting the overall integration of output.‡

Another problem is to locate and correct inefficiency. A factory may be operating at a low level of efficiency, but reports may be

---

* One of the reforms which began under Khrushchev and still continues is decentralization. By moving some decision making from Moscow to the outer regions of the Soviet Union, it has been hoped to make the system a little more efficient and a little less Parkinsonized, Peterized, and Putneyated. But as would be expected, the Moscow autosystem regards any attempt to dismember it as murder, and responds accordingly.

† In view of the fact that 99 percent of the population always votes for the existing party, only two conclusions can be reached: the party is 99 percent perfect or the population is not exercising effective control. See Djilas, *The New Class* (New York: Praeger, 1957).

‡ For example, after World War II steel was in short supply. There was a desperate need to replace agricultural equipment which had been destroyed or worn out during the war. A certain amount of the available steel was allotted to tractor factories, and a certain amount to combine factories. But if the combine factory manager had better political connections than the tractor factory manager, he could divert steel from the tractor factory to his own. He could then overfulfill his quota by 200 percent, but at the cost of no tractors produced to pull the combines.

falsified and the political connections of the manager may have more to do with his fate than the efficiency of his operation. There is no bankruptcy for Russian factories.

Despite these problems, the system obviously works. Russia is the second industrial power in the world, and it is second to the United States primarily because it began industrializing later and lost much of its industry in World War II. The point is simply that the system has certain characteristic problems, mostly deriving from the bureaucratic inefficiencies inherent in very large-scale administration, planning, and coordination.

One solution to many of these problems would be to institute some form of automatic penalty for inefficiency—a penalty which was not dependent on the accuracy of reports, and which was immune to political influence. For example, a point value could be assigned the materials and energy used by a plant, and to the labor which it utilized. The total could then be divided by the number of units produced to attain a cost per unit which could be compared with similar plants. This type of procedure is inevitably followed in capitalist economies, and, since Khrushchev, Russia has experimented along these lines. Those who wish to believe that communism cannot work have been delighted by what seems to them to be the introduction of capitalism into Russia. But it is not capitalism; the fundamental characteristics of the system are unchanged. They have superimposed a sort of "monopoly game" on top of their communist economy as a means of attempting to devise automatic means of evaluating efficiency.

To date neither the attempts at decentralization nor the introduction of accounting systems has proved a complete solution to the problem. Capitalism avoids some of the problems inherent in communism. But, as we shall see, it does so at a price and has inherent problems of its own.

---

15   Capitalism

Capitalism is neither god nor devil, but merely a particular system of rationing goods when there aren't enough to go around. Just as with communism, problems arise in practice to undermine some of its theoretical virtues. But for all that, like communism, it has been a workable system. Capitalism has difficulty, however, in distributing all the goods that the technology can produce, and that is going to turn out to be the crux of the problem.

What Is Capitalism?

Were it not for our familiarity with the custom, it might seem very strange that anything as essential to the entire group as the means of production should become the private property of individuals. Yet this is the essence of capitalism. Not only are the instruments of production privately owned, but they are operated with the expectation of selling the goods for more than it cost to produce them. The surplus remains in the hands of the owner as profit.

A second characteristic of capitalism is the rationing of goods by money, which in turn is acquired by labor in the instruments of production. In this regard it resembles current communism (although the communists contend that this practice is for them a transitory phase). In capitalism, however, money may also be obtained from profits derived from the ownership of the means of production.

A third characteristic of capitalism is the expectation that those who cannot labor (children, the aged, and the infirm) and those whose activities do not yield wages (wives) will be supported privately by those who are employed.*

A final major characteristic of capitalism is an ideological program which stresses values such as: work is good, wealth is good, competition is good, human happiness is a result of wealth and power, and those who succeed in occupying powerful statuses should be rewarded with a larger share of the society's production.

---

* Although this expectation lingers on, it is increasingly contradicted in practice, especially with regard to the aged and the infirm. Private support fundamentally means support through families, and the family is hardly strong enough to discharge such obligations any more. Thus, support of the nonworking passes to other systems, notably the state, but with misgivings and uneasiness all around.

Advantages of Capitalism

A number of advantages are claimed for capitalism. For example, it is contended that capitalism turns private greed into public benefit.* Fundamentally, the argument is quite simple. Under capitalism, pri-vate greed leads the entrepreneur to try to make as much money as he can by besting his competition. To do so, he must make a better product, or sell it at a cheaper price—or both. He will then get business away from his competitors and become wealthy, thereby fulfilling his greed. But along the way, capitalism will have forced him to benefit the public by creating a better or a less expensive product.

A second major advantage claimed for capitalism is that automatic control mechanisms are established which render unnecessary the bureaucratic controls needed to coordinate a communist system of distribution. For example, capitalism is supposed to coordinate the various forms of production through supply and demand. To return to the example of the tractors and combines, if they are sold on an open market it is contended that they will automatically be forced to adjust to each other. No government bureau is needed to decide how many of each should be produced; each factory will sell what it can, and what it can sell will be determined by the demand.

In a similar way, it is contended that under capitalism, inefficient units are automatically warned, and finally removed. In contrast to communism, the inefficient unit will simply be unable to compete and will be forced to reform or go bankrupt.

Finally, capitalism is said to provide automatic pressures to keep men working without the necessity of external coercion. Slaves must be driven to work, but the free laborer—knowing that he must work to eat—will not have to be driven.

Problems of Capitalism

Despite its theoretical virtues, capitalism has a number of problems in practice. For one thing, when the means of production are

---

* Bernard Mandeville was one of the first to express this idea in 1714 in a little book called *The Fable of the Bees* (Oxford: The Clarendon Press, 1924).

privately owned, the rest of the society—although dependent on these means of production—is not able to control their use or development. The American railroads are as important to the American people as the Russian railroads are to the Russian people. Yet what control do the American people have over privately owned railroads? In practice this particular problem has led to the development of government bureaus to regulate the railroads in the public interest. This solution, however, may involve the worst of both worlds since it entails both government bureaus and private ownership.

Moreover, when the instruments of production are operated for private profit it cannot be assumed that this operation will necessarily be in the best interests of the public. As noted in connection with ecological problems, the greatest profit may involve policies which result in pollution and in the destruction of resources.

Another problem arises from the fact that the logical outcome of free competition is its opposite—monopoly. If the bigger dogs continue to eat the smaller dogs, in the end only the very biggest dog will be left. Thus oil companies competed freely in the nineteenth century until Standard Oil had destroyed or absorbed so many other companies that competition ended. The resulting monopoly led to the creation of government bureaus whose job was to enforce free competition through regulation—an ironic result, since free competition was supposed to remove the necessity for government bureaus. Similarly, in practice, price fixing has prevented the operation of competition, and led to the creation of yet other bureaus to try to enforce the "automatic" laws of supply and demand.

Finally, advertising goes a long way toward preventing private greed from resulting in public good. Improving the product or lowering its price has little to do with sales in the modern economy. In fact, the assumption today is that the product should not be too good (so it can wear out or become obsolete), not too cheap (lest it get a poor image). One is supposed to use the large profits derived from producing a poor product and selling it at a high price for advertising—to make people want to buy the product. Competition thus comes to be between different means of advertising and exerts no pressure for improving products or lowering prices.

Thus capitalism in practice does not possess all the virtues that can be claimed for it in theory. The "automatic" mechanisms do not avoid the need for government bureaus; such bureaus are necessary to keep the mechanisms working. The situation is parallel to the theory versus the practice of communism.* Both systems work, and both have difficulty manifesting their presumed virtues. In fact, the most striking thing about the two systems may be the degree of their similarities despite the very different ideological bases which supposedly underlie them.

The Basic Problem

There is, however, an additional difficulty in the capitalist distributive system which has already caused serious problems and which will be greatly aggravated by the second industrial revolution. In fact, because of this problem, it is doubtful that capitalism can survive this revolution.

Return to the paradigm of the island, with the fantastic field and factory, the conveyor belt, and the village. Under a capitalist system the factory and the field will be privately owned and their products will be sold at a profit. The bulk of the villagers will work in the field and factory, and receive wages with which they purchase their ration of the daily output. Now a strange and little understood aspect of capitalism would appear. At the end of the day some goods would remain on the conveyor belt after everyone had run out of money. The wages and the dividends would have all been spent, but products would be left over. These could not be used since they could not be paid for. Under communism they could simply be given away, but under capitalism to give them away would entail a loss for the owners and interfere with future sales.

Let me describe the problem in slightly more traditional terminology. Gross National Product (GNP) is the sum total of all the goods and services which are produced and placed on the market. In the paradigm of the island, it is the total output of the field and fac-

---

* For example, because Russian industry is not operated for private greed, one might hope that it would have less tendency than American industry to waste resources and pollute the environment. In fact, however, Russian industry has until recently been as bad as American industry in its indifference to the environmental consequences of its operations.

tory. Purchasing Power (PP) is the total of monies and credits available to purchase back the products which have been produced and placed on the market.

In the illustration, the gross national product and the purchasing power are equal in (a). This would mean that all of the goods could be purchased, and that all of the purchasing power would be used up in buying the goods.

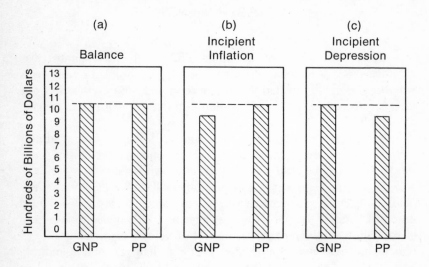

In (b), the purchasing power somewhat exceeds the gross national product. This is not a normal situation, but when it occurs it is a powerful cause of inflation. A small excess of purchasing power has a strong tendency to bid up the prices of the available goods.

The natural tendency under capitalism, however, is shown in (c). Here, as we predicted in the island paradigm, gross national product exceeds purchasing power with the result that a small amount of the production cannot be utilized because there is no purchasing power to buy it.

Although this imbalance seems to be the natural tendency in capitalist economies, it is not clearly understood just why this is so.* In fact, it is not even generally acknowledged that it *is* the natural condition, despite the fact that two of the most persistent characteristics of capitalism, expansion of public debt and inflation, are primarily results of this imbalance. Moreover, as we will see in the next chapter, economic policy is primarily directed toward evading this imbalance. Yet traditional economists tend to ignore it, to treat it as a frequent (but somehow unusual) occurrence, or to sidestep the issue by contending that analyses such as mine are oversimplified— but without offering any counterinterpretation of the phenomenon involved.

The consequences of having less purchasing power than gross national product are profound. The obvious way to close the gap is to reduce production to the level of the available purchasing power. This procedure, however, has the unfortunate consequence of laying off workers, reducing corporate profits, and therefore further reducing purchasing power. This further reduction, of course, must be met by further reductions in production, which leads to further reductions in purchasing power. The resulting downward spiral eventually results in the collapse of the distributive system. This is the path that led to the Great Depression of 1932. And every American administration since has desperately struggled to prevent such a depression from recurring.

The full absurdity of depressions (and their smaller cousins, recessions) tends to be obscured by familiarity. Let us think again of 1932. In this country, people were suffering great privation because the distributive system had collapsed. There was nothing wrong with the technology—the factories, farms, workers, power, and raw materials were still there. But they could not be used to fulfill human needs because they could not be manipulated to yield a profit. So the tractor factory was closed, the tractor worker was unemployed and

---

* Some of the reasons for such a gap may be suggested, however. Certain types of saving result in the removal of some purchasing power from the system. Flow of capital overseas may have the same effect. Under some conditions, reserves and inventories may also reduce available purchasing power. But the essential point is that the gap exists.

hungry, the farmer who would have liked a tractor could not buy one or even sell the food he produced. The whole country slowed down and suffered because the distributive system had failed.

And the fundamental reason the distributive system had failed was that the gap between purchasing power and production had finally caught up with the system. The tendency toward this gap is peculiar to capitalism—Russia suffered no such depression in the 1930s nor at any other time.* Within capitalism the gap may be temporarily closed, or its consequences may for a time be avoided; but the problem remains.

It seems very unlikely that the American people would have accepted the privations of the 1930s had there been a general recognition that nothing was wrong with the country except the failure of our specific system of distribution. But at that time the American people still thought of disasters primarily in rural terms. A rural disaster is usually a natural phenomenon: a drought, a plague of grasshoppers, a flood; little can be done about it except tighten the belt and wait for better times. The same fatalism was inappropriately extended to the collapse of the man-made distributive system. Of course the autosystem encouraged people to blame "hard times" or themselves for unemployment, and discouraged them from asking dangerous questions about the root cause of the problem. It is characteristic of autosystems to regard the suffering of millions as an acceptable price for the protection of its own basic structure.

But it is doubtful that such rural attitudes dominate the American population today. Another collapse would be likely to bring an overwhelming demand for change in the distributive system. It is the recognition of this fact that leads the government to agonize continually over the economic indices. The tendency toward a gap between production and purchasing power is still there, and there is continuous danger of a downward spiral as great as or greater than that in the 1930s. There are various ways of attempting to prevent such a spiral without going so far as to abandon the system; we will look at these in the next chapter.

---

* Russia's problems in the thirties were nearly the opposite type; she was technologically unable to produce all the goods that she needed.

---

16   The Deepening Crisis

The thing about capitalism is that it doesn't produce quite enough purchasing power to buy everything that gets put on the market. To avoid a recession, you have to give it a jolt of borrowed money. So we keep increasing the national debt. This could probably continue for a long time, except that automation is going to create more goods and fewer jobs. How much strain can the weak link take?

It has been increasingly recognized since the Depression that the capitalist system of distribution is not automatically stable. Economists and politicians try to manipulate the economy to prevent it from lapsing into a recession. They avoid discussing the fact that there is an inherent gap between purchasing power and production, but they try hard to close that gap.

Fundamentally, all of the remedies attempt to close the gap by increasing purchasing power. The alternative—reducing production— is utilized only to the extent of regarding a certain level of unemployment and idle productive capacity as normal and acceptable. But to attempt to close the gap completely by reducing production would guarantee a major depression.

There are a variety of ways in which purchasing power may be increased.

Favorable Balance of Trade

One of these is to sell more to other economies than is purchased from them; that is, to have a favorable balance of trade. Such a balance, in effect, imports purchasing power from other economies. The United States did this for decades, until by World War II it had gathered some 95 percent of the capitalist world's gold supply.

Unfortunately, the effects on the other economies are so disastrous that the favorable balance of trade has become obsolete.*

Inflation

Another means of closing the gap between purchasing power and gross national product is inflation. By expanding the currency and credits available—simply by issuing more ration points—purchasing power is increased. Of course, the expanded purchasing power makes price increases possible and inevitable as industries seek to maintain their actual profit levels in spite of the inflation. Higher prices in turn bring demands for higher wages which it is politically inexpedient to ignore. The end result, of course, is for the price and wage increases to offset the effects of the inflation. The reason inflation tends to close the gap at all is that there is a time lag between the expansion of the currencies and credits and the increases in wages and prices. During this time lag, purchasing power is somewhat increased.

Unfortunately, as economic medicine, inflation is extremely dangerous. Once begun, it is difficult to control. As people become aware of inflation, they press harder and harder for continual increases in wages and prices in order to hold their own in spite of the inflation. The expectation of inflation becomes profoundly inflationary. The danger is a runaway inflation which, once started, cannot be stopped until it wrecks the economy.†

In the United States the government attempts to maintain the annual rate of inflation at between three and five percent—this being the maximum rate which it is believed the economy can endure with-

---

* In recent years the U.S. has had an unfavorable balance of trade. It still tends to sell more abroad than it buys, but its massive military operations throughout the world create a net deficit.

† I happened to visit Shanghai in the very last days of Chiang Kai-Shek and saw the runaway inflation there. In a ten-day period, the Chinese Nationalist dollar went from eight million per U.S. dollar to 11½ million. Banks handled money in bales. Someone would enter to make a deposit accompanied by his coolie carrying the bale of money. On the bale was a note asserting that there were so many billion dollars in the bale. The bank could not possibly count the money and made no effort to do so. They merely kept the bale intact with the note still on it, and when someone came in (with his coolie) to make a withdrawal, they would push the bale to him and say "So and so said there was this much money in this bale—do you want to count it?" The answer was invariably no, and the little note became in effect the denomination of the bale.

out letting inflation get out of control. Such inflation closes part, but not all, of the gap between gross national product and the available purchasing power. Inflation is thus a partial—but only a partial—solution.

Private Debt

Since the entire gap cannot be closed by inflation, other means must be found. One of these is the expansion of private debt. To return to the paradigm of the island, if goods are left over on the conveyor belt, a deal could be made with a villager to take a flute or a book home tonight and pay for it with tomorrow's wages. This is installment debt. Private debt expansion tends to close the gap; it distributes the goods left over by increasing purchasing power. But that purchasing power was obtained by taking it out of the future. This produces a kind of economic hangover because the following day brings its own problems. Once again there are more goods than funds, and part of that day's purchasing power has already been used!

To put the matter a little differently, private debt must be repaid, and in the long run, it wipes out the gains that it created. In addition, there is a limit to how much debt the consumer can assume. But the expansion of private debt can help temporarily. President Eisenhower, who was not noted as an economist, nonetheless grasped this point when he suggested during a recession that if all patriotic Americans would buy something on the installment plan the economy would recover.

Public Debt

There is yet another source of purchasing power to close the gap, and that is public debt. Superficially, public debt seems to resemble private debt. Obligations are created on which interest is paid until the principal falls due. However, private debt and public debt are totally different because public debt is *not* repaid.

Fundamentally, the mechanism is this: the government incurs an indebtedness by issuing bonds. These bonds borrow purchasing power from a hypothetical future in which they would be repaid. (If they were repaid, of course, that future would find itself gravely short of purchasing power.) The government can spend the money it receives from sale of the bonds, and those who buy the bonds can use them as security for borrowing money, thereby expanding credit. The government can therefore spend more money than it receives through taxes, introducing new purchasing power into the system and closing that part of the gap which inflation could not close. It is essential for the federal budget to be unbalanced; it is relatively unimportant which expenditures made the budget unbalanced.

The entire system runs on faith, on the traditional assumption that government bonds are the most secure of investments. Should this assumption ever come to be generally doubted, the bonds would become worthless, and the system would collapse at once. To maintain faith the government must always pay interest on the bonds. The bonds themselves can be paid by issuing new bonds when the old ones fall due, as long as faith endures.

The added interest on each increase in the federal debt becomes a permanent item in the federal budget; increasingly larger sums must be set aside for interest payments. This is one of the prices we must pay for an economic system which cannot fully purchase the goods it produces.

The purchasing power which the government creates by debt expansion can be introduced into the economy in many different ways. It can, for example, be given to the rich. The oil depletion allowance has enabled those in very high income tax brackets to avoid much of their federal taxes by investing in oil leases. To the extent that the resulting loss of revenue to the government was made up by an increase in the federal debt, purchasing power was increased and funneled into the economy.

It is equally possible to give the money to the poor. Any form of welfare, social security, or medical care will have the proper effect, insofar as the programs are supported by debt increase rather than current taxes. That part of any program paid out of current taxes does not add to the total purchasing power since the taxes remove as much purchasing power as the expenditures add.

Or we could use the additional purchasing power to subsidize industry. For example, the aerospace industry has received massive federal support for many years. The amount of this support which resulted from an increase in the federal debt added purchasing power to the system.

People can be hired to do things which do not result in a salable product. The Works Progress Administration, Public Works Administration and the Civilian Conservation Corps of the 1930s, and the Job Corps and VISTA of today are examples. To the degree that the wages of individuals in these programs led to debt increase, purchasing power was increased. The Soil Bank Program and other agricultural subsidies which pay farmers for not producing food-stuffs are another means of pouring money derived from debt expansion into the economy.

In short, from an economic viewpoint it does not matter how the funds enter the economy as long as the federal government operates in the red.* There is, however, a psychological problem. The average citizen is not an economist, and in fact has a distaste for economic theory. Under these conditions his appraisal of economic issues is quite unsophisticated. The average citizen looks at the federal government in the same way he looks at his own household, and he applies the knowledge he has acquired in the management of his household to the activities of the government. He knows that if he consistently spends more than he earns, he is going to get into trouble. When he applies the same logic to the government, it leads him to demand that the government balance *its* budget.

But to balance the federal budget (except perhaps for a single year) is almost to guarantee economic disaster. The entire gap between purchasing power and production would then have to be closed by runaway inflation, or production would have to be severely curtailed, thereby initiating the downward spiral of a depression. Eisenhower apparently was sincere in his efforts to balance the budget and bewildered in his inability to do so.† More sophisticated administrations such as the Kennedy administration gave lip service to the balanced budget but never seriously intended to achieve one. The Nixon administration quit even speaking of a balanced budget in its middle years and began speaking of planned deficits.

But the private citizen demands justification for deficit budgets, and they cannot be justified to him on economic terms. To do so

---

* It may, of course, matter a great deal in human terms how the money is used: for example whether it subsidizes the rich or the poor, or whether it results in the pollution or the restoration of the environment.

† The economics of the Eisenhower administration have always reminded me of a story about a farmer who became obsessed with how much money he could save if he did not have to feed his horses. He tried to train them not to eat by feeding them a little less each day until finally he was not feeding them at all. But he had bad luck, and everytime he got one fully trained it died. Eisenhower had much the same luck; every time he got the budget balanced the economy started to go into a tailspin and he had to take the government back into the red to straighten things out.

would involve admitting a grave defect in the very nature of the system. What is needed is some way to justify deficit budgets to the voters which is easily understood, readily accepted, and does not encourage lines of thought critical of the autosystem.

Armaments

The same citizen who wants a balanced federal budget will agree that the protection of the country has an even higher priority than balancing the budget. It can be explained to him that although the government certainly intends to balance the budget and will do so very shortly, the danger of an invasion from the Eskimos is so great that it will be necessary to rearm, which will entail a temporary deficit budget. Unless, of course, the voter would prefer a large tax increase. . . . And to show good faith, the government promises to save the taxpayer some money by cutting in half all aid to the Indian reservations. Since the voter dislikes taxes even more than unbalanced budgets, he doesn't call the government's bluff.*

It is not true, as is sometimes said, that the only reason the U.S. has diverted such a monumental segment of its production into armaments is economics. That is one of the reasons;† we have also produced these arms for use—as is abundantly evident in Korea and Vietnam.

The Unresolved Crisis

In 1932 the economy ceased to function without the help of inflation and unending debt expansion. That crisis has never been resolved; it has only been sidestepped.‡ The question arises; what happens next?

---

* If he did call its bluff and arms production were fully financed out of current taxes, the armaments would no longer contribute to closing the gap between purchasing power and production.

† By 1971 there were signs of a change. The voters were showing less enthusiasm for arms production, and a greater tendency to accept deficit federal budgets as an economic necessity to maintain prosperity. Such a shift in attitudes would still leave the underlying problem unsolved, but might make the world a little safer place.

‡ Roosevelt began using an unbalanced budget in an effort to get the economy going again. Although they seemed huge at the time, his deficits were not on a big enough scale to be highly successful, and by 1939 recovery was only partial. In 1939, the war in Europe created a final opportunity for a favorable balance of trade—the European countries wanted arms so badly they did not worry about sacrificing the rest of their gold reserves. The arms sales

There are two theories. One states that the economy has a terminal illness, and the other that it has a chronic illness. A chronic illness is one that the patient will not get over, but which can be kept from killing him by suitable medication. An example would be malaria, which traditionally has been incurable but controllable with quinine. A terminal illness is one which eventually kills the patient even though medication may delay death. Both theories accept the necessity of medicating the economy continuously through a combination of mild inflation and steady debt expansion. The argument is whether the illness is terminal or chronic.

Most economists seem to believe that it is chronic. It might be suspected that this merely reflects their stake in the status quo, but there is some evidence to support this view.* But with the technology moving into a period of nonlinear change, generalizations based on past experience are of limited utility. The second industrial revolution will vastly increase production and will greatly reduce the need for human labor. In human terms, it is hard to see this as tragic. If we can produce what we need without having to work for it, why not?

But the second industrial revolution will be disastrous for the economic system because it will throw an intolerable strain on precisely the weakest link in the capitalist chain. It will almost certainly

---

fully closed the gap and got the American economy going. In 1941 America went into the war itself. During the war years of 1941–1945 arms production was on such a vast scale that debt expansion went far beyond what was necessary to close the gap. In fact, debt was expanded so rapidly, and civilian goods were in such short supply, that people had more money than goods. A serious inflation threatened, and the government responded with the great war bond drives. War bonds were used as a sort of sponge to soak up the surplus purchasing power. In 1945, at the end of the war, there was a large backlog of surplus debt expansion stored in those bonds, and it was rather startling how rapidly it was used up. By 1948 the gap was reappearing, and by 1950 the economy was showing serious signs of a downward trend. In 1950 the economy was rescued by the beginning of the Korean War, and the U.S. went back on a massive arms economy, part of which was financed out of debt expansion. In the decades since, armaments have continually been used to justify unbalanced budgets. Obviously, the fundamental problem has not been touched.

* The percent of the gross national product that is used to pay the interest on the federal debt is a critical figure. As the economy expands and inflates, it can presumably afford to make bigger interest payments on a bigger debt. But if the interest on the debt began expanding more rapidly than the economy, the end would be in sight, since the government eventually would have to default on the payment of interest on the government bonds, and the whole system would collapse. But it appears that over the last decades the percent of the gross national product that has been going for interest on the national debt has stayed roughly constant. This lends support to the view that up to now, at least, the treatment has been able to control the illness.

make it impossible to distribute goods by selling them at a profit to wage earners.

There will be one last-ditch effort to salvage the system, and it is already taking form. We are moving rapidly toward a guaranteed annual wage. Essentially this will be an attempt to keep the system going by utilizing an idea from the Monopoly game, giving everyone a certain amount of money for passing "Go." They could then buy goods even though they were unemployed. The money to pay them, of course, would have to be raised in taxes placed on profits and the wages of those who were still employed.

Philosophically, the guaranteed annual wage is interesting. In order to salvage capitalism and continue distributing goods for profit, it proposes to give people the money to buy the goods. It is remotely possible that this bit of sleight of hand might succeed, but it is very difficult to see how the system could be financed within a capitalistic framework.

---

17   The Next Step

It would seem that the next step may be a long one. With automatic machinery to produce the goods, and with people largely retired, it is hard to imagine that mankind will continue playing Monopoly. If there is really enough to go around, then neither wages, profits, nor conspicuous consumption is going to mean very much. The transition to the next type of economy may come easily, or it may come hard; but it is almost certainly coming.

The Decline in Conspicuous Consumption

As the enormous productive forces of the second industrial revolution make goods more plentiful, that part of the demand for them which was based on their use as prestige symbols tends to disappear. This has already happened in particular areas. In America we have long ago passed the point where being fat conveyed prestige

—simply because the food supply is so great that nearly everyone could be fat. Yet through history, being fat has usually conferred great prestige. The automobile has even declined as a prestige symbol.

This trend is especially obvious in the youth culture. For quite a long time, the young have increasingly regarded their vehicles as mere means of transportation, and if they become psychologically involved with them, it has been to personalize them in ways unrelated to conspicuous consumption. They have painted them, built living quarters into them, and devised ingenious means of keeping them running, but fewer and fewer are in the market for the newer, larger, and more powerful models. The same is true of the approach of the young to housing.

Unemployment and Unemployability

It is often argued that automation creates jobs; while it may eliminate the job of a file clerk, it creates the job of a computer programmer. But the number of computer programmers hired is far smaller than the number of file clerks displaced; indeed, that was the whole point of replacing them. Moreover, the individual who loses a job as a junior assistant file clerk, may not be intellectually or emotionally qualified to be trained as a computer programmer. A larger and larger group are finding themselves without a status in the economy to provide their wages.

This trend even reaches into the professions. One of the effects of the first industrial revolution was to enable the most gifted entertainers to use mass communications to extend their activities to a much larger audience, at the expense of the opportunities of the less gifted. The entertainment industry thus became much more competitive, and the neighborhood fiddler was eliminated. This process is now reaching professions such as teaching, where use of video tapes enables the extremely effective teacher to reach a much larger number of students. In so doing, he eliminates or greatly downgrades the role of other teachers.

For the unusually bright, the highly educated, and the talented there may always be jobs, but by definition the bulk of humanity is average. The average individual finds his opportunities increasingly restricted.

Unemployability has not been too obvious until recently because it first struck the most vulnerable groups: the minorities and the young. It is interesting to note that when overall unemployment was only five percent, black unemployment in some neighborhoods ran to 80 percent and to 60 percent among unemployed youth in many areas. But unemployability does not mean simple unemployment; it means the lack of any realistic prospect of a job. It is unemployability that is now rapidly spreading into other segments of the population. It can no longer increase much among the minorities or the young.

Nearing the End

The effect of all this, of course, is to overstrain the capitalist system of distribution. More and more products are thrown on the market in a period when there may be a decline in demand and when the number of people who can secure wages may be diminishing. It seems clear that things are building to a crisis.

In some ways the coming crisis resembles the one predicted by Marx. He predicted that capitalism would be torn apart by the development of forces which in themselves were a natural outgrowth of the system but which could not be contained within the system. The new technology is outgrowing the economic system in which it was born and is creating forces that strain the capitalist economy.

Marx, however, seems to have believed that class conflict would be the means by which capitalism would be destroyed. He seems to have thought much more about political upheavals motivated by economic inequality than about economic changes as a result of technological revolutions. Could it happen this way—could capitalism be destroyed through class conflict? Let's try to imagine a scenario.

Scenario One

Let us assume that present trends continue—production rising, automation spreading, employment falling, and unemployment reaching further and further into the middle classes. They will respond with incomprehension and fear. Let us assume further that an aggressive, conservative government attempts to cater to this fear. Such a government would restrict welfare even though unemployment was rising, and would pretend to seek a balanced budget while continuing arms expenditures. Considerable suffering and even hunger would result among the minorities, lower classes, and among those of the young who could not get support from middle-class parents. Over time, many engineers, teachers, and retailers would find themselves joining the ranks of the unemployable as the economy constricted. Some of these would become radical and would begin looking for new solutions to economic problems. They would make intellectual leadership available for the larger masses.

At this point the government could be expected to crack down harshly on youths, dissenters, blacks, and other potentially revolutionary groups. The National Security Act might be revived to detain large numbers of politically unreliable individuals.

Rigid production quotas might be established in an effort to limit production without allowing a downward spiral. Each factory could be required to produce just so much, and their customers could be required to purchase just so much. Despite these efforts, the economy would necessarily slip downward. It would be reasonable to expect some sort of general's coup in an attempt to cure what they would term the softness of the civilian government in dealing with the crisis.

Under these conditions a class conflict along classic Marxist lines could very well develop. The economy would progressively deteriorate and finally collapse. More and more individuals would become hostile to the government until finally a general strike was organized. The civilian National Guard would go over to the insurgents, and attack the professional army. Washington would fall, and the victory of the revolution would be proclaimed.

How likely is this scenario? It is possible, but it does not seem probable. Quite apart from the difficulty of imagining a violent revolution in America, the history of twentieth century capitalism shows much more flexibility than this scenario allows. The capitalist autosystem is willing to make substantial compromises to avoid disaster, as welfare legislation and antitrust laws show.

Scenario Two

Let's try another scenario allowing more flexibility to the system. We begin with the same premises—production climbing and unemployability rising. As the crisis deepens and goods are being produced which cannot be bought, the government acts to introduce a guaranteed annual wage. Perhaps in its earliest form this takes the shape of a Negative Income Tax where families are all guaranteed a minimal level of support. Soon it is expanded into a general guaranteed annual wage. In the early phases there would be great opposition and national debate. Dire prophecies would be made that with a wage guaranteed, nobody would work. In spite of this opposition, the program is pressed forward.

In order to pay the guaranteed annual wage as the percentage of employable people shrinks more and more, heavy taxes are levied on remaining salaries and corporate profits. These tremendous taxes produce discontent and grumbling; however, the increase in the productive forces comes so rapidly that the burden can be borne. In time, the distinction between those whose money comes from jobs and those whose money comes from the guaranteed annual wage becomes unimportant, since both are able to obtain substantially everything they need. A job comes to be valued more for itself than for its wages —those who have something constructive to do are envied by those who are condemned to a lifetime of leisure.

Under these conditions, the private ownership of the means of production would become substantially meaningless. What is the advantage of owning a factory if everyone can have all he wants of everything? A national corporation might be established to include all of the productive apparatus. Stock in this corporation could be issued to each citizen at birth with a sufficient dividend attached to enable him to buy his full share of the national production. At this point capitalism would have ended—not with a bang, but by being forgotten. The autosystem would have gracefully allowed itself to be transformed into something very different.

This scenario is possible, but how likely is it? Perhaps more likely than the class conflict scenario, but it seems to entail more flexibility than the economic system is likely to show. Moreover, it is by no means certain that maximum taxation and debt expansion could finance a guaranteed annual wage throughout the transition away from capitalism.

Can we imagine an intermediate version? Let's try again.

Scenario Three

The same situation is occurring—production is expanding very rapidly, jobs are declining, and economic crisis threatens. As in the second scenario, a progressive government establishes a guaranteed annual wage, beginning with a negative income tax. However, the expense of this program is so great that as more and more individuals lose their jobs it simply cannot be sustained by any possible level of taxation. Therefore the guaranteed annual wage has to be restricted to nothing more than a food stamp program with rent stamps added.

Meanwhile unemployability continues to rise and production to increase. At this point the government attempts to institute various economic measures that have proved effective in ending recessions in the past.*

Despite this, a massive downward spiral occurs as factories close to reduce losses. The Dow Jones Stock average drops to 350; more factories close, and most of the remaining jobs evaporate. The situation is similar to that of the 1930s, but more severe. Whereas in the 1930s the entire Keynesian bag of tricks was new and unused, now every known trick has already been used.

The autosystem tells the people to tighten their belts, that prosperity is just around the corner and that they have nothing to fear but fear itself. There is a great deal of confusion in the public mind; the average citizen suddenly discovers that he has an interest in economic theory. Debate occurs, various radical spokesmen come forward—and suddenly find an apt audience.

Then some charismatic leader propounds what he terms the "wheelbarrow theory," and it catches on. Like most popular economic theories, the wheelbarrow theory is a simple one: it suggests that in a society where the productive forces have grown able to produce enough to go around, it is needless to mess with sales, advertising, or wages. Instead, issue everyone a wheelbarrow and let him walk home from the warehouse with whatever he wants. The theory has the advantage of timeliness and simplicity—and is even roughly practical, given the enormous productive force unleashed by the second industrial revolution.

The supporters of the wheelbarrow theory organize themselves into a political party which wins at the polls. A military coup attempts to take the victory away from them, but the groundswell is too strong and the autosystem too weak. The new economic system is proclaimed from the steps of the White House, and the wheelbarrows begin

---

* For example, interest rates are lowered to encourage increases in consumer debt—but too few consumers have jobs to establish significant installment debt. Very large federal deficits are incurred in an attempt to stimulate purchasing power, but most of the funds end up in the hands of industry to offset losses rather than in the hands of consumers. Wage and price controls are rigidly established to offset the inflationary pressure but end by inducing general panic.

squeaking as the productive forces are let loose and their output is carted off. At first there is chaos and hoarding, but as the automatic factories saturate the demand, private property becomes too plentiful to be particularly meaningful, conspicuous consumption dies, and advertisers, wholesalers, and retailers join the railroad firemen and the mule breakers.

Is this scenario possible? Yes. And I believe it is the most probable of the three.

Where Does It End?

Where will it all end? If we survive pollution and neglect to blow ourselves up with nuclear weapons, we are heading toward an economic system that will be basically different from what we now know. The productive forces of the second industrial revolution make possible Marx's utopian dream of a society which asks from each according to his ability, and gives to each according to his need.

Throughout most of human history individuals have defined their fundamental role in life in terms of their status within the productive system. Ending this preoccupation might create a real utopia in which men were freed from the drudgery of labor and developed their full potentialities. Or it might lead to a hell of escapism and boredom in which men found no meaning or purpose in life and drowned themselves in safe and legalized narcotics to endure endless bland entertainment until they could stand it no longer and took the final walk to the sanitary and painless State Suicide Parlor. The only safe prediction seems to be that nonlinear change will occur. The society of the future may be unclear, but capitalism seems unlikely to survive the second industrial revolution.

Part Five: A Hard Look at the State

18   Cooking Fish

The citizen keeps getting asked to swear allegiance to the state; but the state never has to swear allegiance to the citizen. A lot of the things the state does and a lot of the rules it makes up seem more designed to contribute to the state of the state's steady state than to the honest-to-goodness good of its goodly citizens.

On a dark night several years ago I was walking across a paved mall on campus. Suddenly I heard a car start up far down at the end of the mall. Without any lights it came charging toward me. It just missed me and raced to the other end of the mall. And then I saw what it was all about. It was a police car, and at the other end of the mall a girl was riding a bicycle. There were rules against riding bicycles on campus—presumably to protect me. So I walked over to where the officer had captured the girl and said: "You very nearly ran over me!" He answered: "Well, yes. You didn't get out of the way." "But this mall is closed to all traffic," I objected "Yeah. But this girl was riding her bicycle across the mall and I had to get her." Now given the choice of being run over by a bicycle or a police car I will always choose the bicycle.

Somewhere along the line the state has gotten out of control; it enforces its rules against bicycle riding no matter how many people it has to run over. Thousands of years ago the Chinese sage Lao-tse suggested: "The state should be governed as we cook small fish, without much business." [1] But try to tell that to the servo-men of the autosystem.

What Is the State For?

In the early civilizations, the state made no pretense of serving the general welfare. It existed as the means by which the will of the ruling group was enforced on the rest of society. The man in the hut knew where things stood and what to expect. It was only with the rise of modern nationalism in Europe that it was conceived that the state should serve the general welfare. Not that it did, of course. But it helped if the French soldier believed that he was some-how involved in the glory that would shine forth when France conquered Russia. It helped to give meaning to frostbite, hunger, and death.

Today every gradeschool student has learned that the state exists in order to promote the common good. And to some extent, this may be true. The state has ceased to serve the interests of any single class exclusively and has become instead the basic regulatory agent of the society.

Thus the state is the agency that most intentionally manipu-lates the other institutional sectors. Presumably this is done to pro-mote the welfare of all. And sometimes this seems to be the case; for example, the regulation of the economic sector by the Pure Food and Drug Administration. In other cases it is difficult to see any public benefit from the regulation—for example, the regulation of the family through the marriage laws.

The state also undertakes the organization of large-scale proj-ects. For example, it undertakes to provide a safe and adequate water supply to cities. But it also organizes such large-scale under-takings as the Vietnam war.*

Then, too, the state regulates individual behavior. Such restric-tions as those against driving the wrong way on the freeway seem clearly in the public interest; but others, such as the regulation of sexual activities between consenting adults seem to serve no evident human purpose.

The fundamental problem is that although the state may have largely ceased to be the means of enforcing the will of a particular class, it remains an enormously powerful system which is difficult to control.

The Psychotic Leader

For one thing, the state attracts to it a particular type of indi-vidual: one who enjoys giving orders, and who is untroubled by

---

* The other day I was listening to a commercial for one of the health funds and I thought how different it would be if the health programs were funded out of state funds, but war funds had to be solicited through private contributions: "Send your dimes and dollars to blow up Laos!"

doubts over his right and ability to make decisions for others. Things might work out better if there were some way of coercing men of exactly opposite tendencies into assuming political leadership.* But the modern state is hardly led by its wisest, most moral members. In fact, the history of the modern state is studded with psychotic leaders who have driven misguided populations toward disaster. Their names live in the history books, and thousands have died in the battles they precipitated; but what human benefit has resulted? In *The True Believer*,[2] Eric Hoffer has detailed much of this sorry history.

When the state has not been preempted by a psychotic leader, it is likely to be serving its own interests as an autosystem. This can take a variety of forms.

The Abuse of Bureaucracy

The modern state must develop a complex bureaucracy to function at all. Bureaucracy is not altogether bad; it is merely a means of routinizing the decision-making process when very large numbers of decisions have to be made. It is the essence of bureaucracy to define categories of situations and carefully establish a standard decision for each category. The bureaucratic form of decision making has the advantage of objectivity; the decisions are made in terms of clear and public criteria. The student who applies to the bureaucracy of the college for admission does not have to worry about whether it has a prejudice against brunettes or Catholics. Bureaucratic procedures thus not only speed up the process of administration, they also protect against many types of personal abuses.

Unfortunately, bureaucracies also tend to become autosystems. As such, they lose sight of the individual and attempt to force all cases into their standardized categories. But there are always a minority of cases which do not properly fit any category and must be decided on a personal and nonbureaucratic basis.

For example, several years ago a young man applied for admission to college. He was required to submit various documents

---

* The Hopi Indians' example might help us. Their culture taught them to avoid leadership; they found it necessary to assemble in the kiva and allow no one to leave until someone had been forced to assume the role of leader. Ruth Benedict, *Patterns of Culture* (New York: The New American Library, 1953), p. 91.

including a high school diploma. Unfortunately, he had attended high school in Europe and his diploma was written in Danish. Obviously his file was one of those which did not fit the standard categories of the bureaucracy; the fact that there were documents which the clerk could not read demonstrated that. But his case was forced into the nearest standard category—applications lacking a high school diploma—and he was refused admission.* The problem here is not bureaucracy but its abuse. At its best, by making standard decisions in recognizable types of cases, bureaucracy can free the senior staff to deal with nontypical cases on an individual basis. But as an autosystem, bureaucracy tends to abandon this flexibility.

Canonizing the Rules

As bureaucracy evolves toward autosystem, rules cease to be guidelines and become sacred principles. Thus the legal profession speaks about the Rule of Law as if the mere existence of a law gave it sanctity. But a law deserves respect only if it serves a respectable function for people. From the viewpoint of the autosystem, however, the law matters for its own sake.

I once had the tiniest of automobiles, and it seemed an enormous waste to park it in a parking space intended for large American cars. In the crowded parking lot by my office I found a tiny stall, a leftover space that even a normal compact car could not fit into. So I would park my mini-car there in order to leave the regular spaces for the regular cars. But the police objected that my action violated the parking laws and gave me repeated parking tickets. To no avail I explained that the reason this space was not officially designated was because it was too small for any other car and that I was performing a public service by parking my mini-car there. The servo-man looked out from behind the badge of the autosystem and told me that the law could make no exceptions.

The state comes to be primarily concerned with the maintenance of its own steady state, or, in Dick Tracy's most revealing slogan: "Law and Order First." From a human viewpoint it is human welfare first; law and order matter only if they promote human welfare.

---

* By the time he succeeded in clarifying the situation through a considerable exchange of letters, he was informed that although his application was now recognized to be complete, he could not be considered because registration was now closed.

But the autosystem glorifies itself and people really come to believe that the system is more important than they are. President Kennedy found a willing audience for his demand: "Ask not what your country can do for you, ask what you can do for your country!"[3] For some reason I was not properly shocked by this slogan until I heard a student correct it to say: "Ask not what you can do for your country, but what your country is doing for you." What *is* the country? Merely an arrangement of statuses, roles, and institutional sectors at varying degrees of centralization. What really matters? Only the people.

Democracy to the Rescue?

The problems I have been discussing are found in all modern states; they are in no way peculiar to the United States, the Soviet Union, or Japan. To a considerable degree they merely reflect the by now familiar tendency for any complex social structure to become an autosystem preoccupied with its own steady state, and trying to program its human components to acquiesce in its ascendancy.

The founding fathers of this country greatly feared the state, and the system which they established deliberately weakened it. Thus, they divided state power among three separate systems—legislative, executive, and judicial—and further divided the legislative system into two houses. They had reason to fear the state; they had seen the behavior of the European monarchies. Yet the state which they feared was far smaller, far less complex, and far less powerful than the states we have today.

In order to establish a controlled state which would serve the interests of the people and avoid the excesses of other states, they proposed to establish a democracy. This choice was guided by certain fundamental assumptions which it may be important to recall.

19   Behind the Picket Fence

Democracy wasn't always a cliché. It was conceived as a means of keeping the state in line. The idea was that men knew what was good for them, and would vote accordingly. The whole idea has a certain innocence about it. And well it should; it is the product of a more innocent age.

The Essence of Democracy

All too often, sentimentalities pass as definitions of democracy; clichés are strung together by commas and semicolons. Democracy becomes the smell of mom's apple pie cooling on the windowsill, and of autumn leaves burning behind the picket fence as a barefoot boy and his mongrel dog trudge past the white wooden church toward the fishing hole. . . .*

But democracy is not apple pie or motherhood or the steeple on the white wooden church. It is merely a system of getting people into and out of certain central statuses in the political sector of society. When defined in this way, it abruptly becomes something less glamorous and sentimental—and considerably more real.

Democracy is often confused with capitalism. Yet it is a political system which has no necessary connection with any economic system; capitalism may be combined with dictatorship as readily as with democracy, and socialism in no way precludes democratic rule. It is also easy to think of democracy as majority rule. But although it usually involves rule by the majority, it may involve rule by the largest minority. Hitler at one time had a majority of the German

---

* William H. Whyte, Jr., once constructed a similar satire on meaningless, emotional definitions of free enterprise. He had hoped to contribute to meaningful thinking by a *reductio ad absurdum*. He was upset to find that a firm wanted 1,000 reprints of it to send to their customers, since it was such "a magnificent expression of real Americanism." See William H. Whyte, *Is Anybody Listening?* (N.Y., Simon and Schuster, 1952), pp. 30–31.

people behind him, but that majority rule did not make Germany a democracy.

It is also common to think of democracy as elections. The device of elections is commonly used in democratic governments. However, it is not essential. Other means of determining the public will could (and perhaps should) be devised. Moreover, the more presence of elections does not guarantee democracy, even if those elections are free from fraud. In the Soviet Union, for example, elections are held which observers agree are honest and secret. Yet the Soviet Union can not be termed a democracy in view of the very limited opportunities for public debate and discussion.

The essence of democracy is found in the freedom of the minorities to agitate for their views, and if one of them succeeds in becoming a majority (or perhaps the largest minority) to take power in some prescribed manner. Only if these conditions exist is there a democracy; if they exist, the other details of the system are inessential.

Democracy was proposed in the hope that the state would thereby be rendered less oppressive, inflexible, and autonomous.

Once Again: The Age of Reason

The philosophy of democracy as we know it is a product of the eighteenth century, the Age of Reason. This brief and exciting era, as we saw in the Prologue, was a time when men were tremendously impressed with reason and with the idea that men as reasoning animals were going somewhere important.

There is a very close parallel between the assumptions underlying classical economics and those underlying democratic theory. Classical economics involved the idea that private greed would result in public good as entrepreneurs competed in the market, and as rational consumers forced them to produce the best product at the lowest price. The theory of democracy assumed that there was a comparable marketplace of ideas, in which competition for the allegiance of rational voters would result in the victory of the best ideas and the disappearance of the rest.

Man as Rational

Underlying the idea of democracy is a view of man which is profoundly characteristic of the eighteenth century.[1] For example, it is implicitly assumed that the individual wants to assume responsibility for his own destiny, and can therefore be counted on to involve himself in the burdens of the political process. Eighteenth century intellectuals viewed man as inherently eager to joust with life. The theory also assumes that the individual can understand the issues which confront him and that he will perceive his own best interests within these issues.* Then, as each voter sought his own best interests, the majority would automatically steer the government toward the policies most beneficial to the greatest number.

At the very core of democratic theory is the assumption that the voter arrives at his decisions exclusively through a rational process. This entails quite a number of conditions. Obviously the voter must first be free from external coercion; he must be free from fear that he will be punished for his decisions. But it is not only *overt* coercion which matters. If the voter's decision is to be meaningful, he must also be free of *covert* coercion—subtle manipulations which shape his decisions perhaps even without his awareness. The consumer of ideas, like the consumer of goods, must be free to make his own decisions.

The assumption that the voter is free from *internal* coercion is even more basic to democratic theory. He must not be impelled toward some particular judgment because of his complexes, his background, or his secret urges. He must be sufficiently free from inner biases to enable him to respond to the external situation on its own terms and on its own merits.

Finally, democratic theory assumed that after the voter has arrived at his reasoned appraisal of the situation, he will be able to see and understand the results of his decision. Then, if an error is made, its consequences will be noted by the voters, and the whole affair can be set right at the next election.

All these assumptions add up to the image of a man who wants to assume control over his own fate, who sits down uncoerced and free from compulsion to evaluate the various political positions, who chooses among them in terms of an enlightened self-interest, and who then watches the effects of his decisions and prepares himself for the next round. Granted this image, it is easy to understand

---

* At times democrat theorists have argued among each other over whether some particular segment of humanity—women, the young—could understand the issues. But they all assumed that those whom they were willing to enfranchise would be able to understand the issues.

why it was hoped that democracy would alleviate many of the problems which the state poses for mankind. With such voters, the state could not become the means by which a dominant class enforced its own interests, but instead would serve the best interests of the greatest number. Moreover, the state could not become the vehicle for psychotic leaders to fulfill their warped ambitions, nor would it be allowed to become an aloof and self-determining autosystem.

Or so it seemed in the eighteenth century.

---

20   Democracy versus the Twentieth Century

It is easy to see why democracy was advocated in the eighteenth century; it is more difficult to see why it is still advocated in the twentieth. The simple fact is that the twentieth century has abandoned every one of the assumptions which underlie the theory of democracy.

Irrational Man

Democracy's fraternal twin, classical economics, is dead. Modern economics no longer assumes that the marketplace is guided by the force of reason. In fact, the whole theory of modern advertising is based on the opposite premise—that the purchaser is fundamentally motivated by irrational forces. The advertiser seeks to understand these forces, and to use them to manipulate the consumer. A sense of power and virility is sold, not an automobile; a sizzling suburban sociability is sold, not a barbecue; social acceptance is sold, not a deodorant.

If the modern view of how economic decisions are made is right, it bodes ill for democracy; democracy would be expected to result in the greatest good for the most wily manipulator, not for the greatest number. The theory of democracy depends on the very assumptions which the advertiser has abandoned.

The assumption that the individual wants to assume responsibility for himself has also been abandoned. Existentialist philosophies have become the pervasive viewpoint of the twentieth century, and their common and fundamental element is the insistence that man finds responsibility for himself painful, and will go a long way to attempt to evade it. Democracy thus seems to confront man with precisely that which he seeks to escape.

Whereas the theory of democracy necessarily assumed that the voter can understand the issues, the experience of the twentieth century suggests that he cannot. The issues have become so enormously complex that even the specialist who devotes his life to their study finds them difficult to appraise. What chance, then, has the part-time citizen who has also the responsibilities of a job and family and has an understandable interest in recreation? The voter is called upon to appraise the response of his government to complex crises in countries he could not even locate on a map and to evaluate programs to deal with problems whose causes are completely unknown to him. Modern political candidates recognize these facts and avoid any direct discussion of fundamental issues. It is simply assumed that the voter neither understands them nor cares to think about them. Instead he is offered contrived oversimplifications—preferably expressible in terms of slogans such as "domino theory," "missile gap," or "law and order." And perhaps even the slogans are unimportant; some believe that the sex appeal or charisma of a candidate is more crucial than his platform.

Voters who are unable or unwilling to grasp the issues can hardly be expected to understand their own interests within the issues. Therefore the state undertakes to steer the voter by persuading him to identify with an issue; the voter does not steer the state by his perceived interest in the issue. An interesting example occurred during the war bond crusades of World War II. It was assumed that the voter could not perceive that his interest lay in preventing a serious inflation by absorbing surplus purchasing power into war bonds. Instead, the government attempted to persuade the voter to buy war bonds on the falsified claim that the dollars were essential to buy weapons and munitions for his loved ones who were fighting. Apparently presenting the economic reality to the voters was never seriously considered; nor did they perceive and raise the real issue on their own.

Democratic theory also assumed that the voter was free from overt external pressures. Yet this is hardly the case in modern society where dossiers are kept on millions of citizens, where police agents infiltrate all unorthodox organizations, and where faces at rallies and demonstrations are systematically photographed and filed. The citizen is quite aware that people are punished for expressing certain viewpoints, and the free competition of ideas is correspondingly inhibited.

Moreover, *covert* coercion—coercion without the awareness of the one coerced—has reached the level of a sophisticated art in the modern world. And covert coercion is even more of a problem to democracy than overt coercion. When voters are menaced by rifles at a demonstration, all are at least aware of it. But when the opinions of the voters are controlled through subtle manipulation, the problem may not even be noticed, let alone solved.

Most of the issues on which the voter is expected to make a decision involve things beyond his immediate experience. He is therefore necessarily dependent on outside sources of information, and the whole effect of modern means of communication is to centralize the sources of such information. A great deal of power results from the ability to influence these centralized sources. Such power may be used for political purposes in obvious ways. It may also be used for commercial purposes; the newsmagazine and television station try to keep their audiences by giving them the type of news they want to hear to the exclusion of a great deal of less exciting information which would be more useful to the citizen in the decisions he is required to make.

Covert coercion takes other forms. A special type of entrepreneur has developed whose profession is conducting political campaigns. It is interesting to note their assumptions about success in political contests. One famous firm will accept the account of a candidate only if he gives them complete control of everything he says during the campaign. They justify this policy on the grounds that a candidate who opens his mouth independently invariably makes a mistake, is likely to lose the election, and thus hurt the agency's winning reputation. Once the candidate has agreed to their terms and paid their high fees, they conduct the campaign in terms of simple slogans carefully contrived to manipulate the voters. Typically, the slogans have nothing at all to do with the issues at hand, and they may say nothing at all. Such tactics make a mockery of democracy.

Overt and covert coercion aside, democratic theory also assumed that the voter was free from *internal* coercion. He was to decide his position by applying reason to the facts, according to eighteenth century theorists. But in the nineteenth century, Freud founded the study of the unconscious and produced partial maps of this *terra incognita.* He pointed out, for example, that individuals have a strong tendency in their adult relations to the state to reenact their infantile experiences with their parents. And it is quite plausible that they should do so, since the state stands in somewhat the same relation to the adult as does the parent to the child. But if the voter's decisions are determined by what happened decades ago, what are the implications for democracy? *

The twentieth century sees the individual as being largely controlled by inner and outer forces which he does not understand and probably does not wish to understand. It is presumed that his reason is used primarily to find justifications for the conclusions that these forces have preordained. Man is seen as rationalizing, not as rational.

Finally, the rate of change in the modern world may be so rapid that the results of any given political decision cannot be isolated and evaluated. In the mosaic of events, even the specialist may have trouble determining the results of a past policy—let alone whether it was wise or misguided. The situation is hardly helped by the autosystems' use of the mass media to obscure past mistakes. The probability of the voters correcting past mistakes is correspondingly reduced. Some decisions, moreover, have implications which could never be corrected in a subsequent election, however obvious their effects. The decision to initiate a nuclear war is a clear-cut example, but the effects of certain decisions regarding resources and pollutants may be equally irreversible.

A Matter of Faith

In brief, the twentieth century has totally abandoned the view of man and political process which led to the formulation of the

---

* After Freud, one could no longer say (as one could in the age of Jefferson) "I have studied the situation, and arrived at a conclusion." One had to say: "I have studied the issues, and keeping in mind my generalized tendency to rebel against authority, and compensating for it, I have tentatively concluded. . . ." Marx further complicated the picture by showing how profoundly the individual's position in society influenced his perceptions of that society. One could no longer merely consult with one's analyst to compensate for internal bias; it was also necessary to allow that one had been socialized, say, as a petit bourgeois in the capitalist economy of the Northwestern United States in the 1940s.

theory of democracy in the eighteenth century. The system, such as it is, lingers on; but we no longer hold the beliefs which could lead us to expect it to work. Instead we expect it to work because the glories of our democratic system have become an article of religious faith among us. We have never been encouraged to examine democracy dispassionately. But it is high time we quit worshipping our presumed democracy and began trying to find out if there is a way of making it work.

---

21   The Taming of the State

It is not enough to point out the faults of our democracy, for as Winston Churchill said, "Democracy is the worst of all systems, except for all the others." Instead of either praising or damning it, it might be interesting to look for things that might give democracy a better chance of working.

The state is not being effectively controlled by our present version of democracy; it is largely running itself and the people in it. There is perhaps no more urgent task than to try to create the means by which the modern state could be brought to heel.

Discourage Existential Cop-outs

For starters, it might be helpful in building a democracy if we abandon the myth that men yearn after freedom, and accept the harsh reality that they often fear and despise their own freedom. The myth gives an easy, false security in the struggle to build a free society. A great deal of thought is needed on how to discourage people from retreating into existential cop-outs by accepting servo-man status.

Changes in the socialization process are quite evidently necessary; children need to be encouraged to be self-accepting and self-affirming. They need to understand the temptation to evade their responsibility for themselves; they must attach a positive value to assuming this responsibility. Existential courage must replace the courage of the gunslinger as a basic value and model.

Restrain "Putney's Law"

In 1835, de Tocqueville wrote about the "tyranny of the majority" in America.[1] He feared that the holding of minority viewpoints was becoming more and more difficult in our democracy as the pressures to conform increased. Such intolerance of political debate is the antithesis of the open forum envisioned in democratic theory; it leads to efforts to restrict the very freedoms which are essential to the meaningful operation of democracy.

This is a principle which I modestly call *Putney's Law: If the people of a democracy are allowed to do so, they will vote away the freedoms which are essential to that democracy.* The idea that all viewpoints should be heard is a very abstract and difficult doctrine; it is easy to accept as a slogan, but hard to maintain in practice.*

In a democracy, everyone seeks to restrict those ideas which he regards as dangerous and irresponsible, and in the end the tyranny of the majority will allow nothing but the prevailing viewpoint to be expressed. In any society not on the verge of collapse, most of the people either support the status quo or are indifferent to it. This majority will not be interested in expressing unconventional ideas. Therefore the majority will have an illusion of freedom whether or not such freedom in fact exists. But the critical test of democracy

---

* Test it in terms of one of your own favorite convictions. If you are devout, do you really think atheists should be allowed to teach children? If you are atheist, do you really want to have Christian teachers in the grade school?

Of course you believe in the freedom of everyone to express his views, especially those sensible enough to agree with you. You also believe that other *responsible* viewpoints should be heard (that is, viewpoints which are similar to yours except for unimportant details). You will even agree that people whom you regard as cranks and crackpots should be heard; they are no threat, anyway. And so you conclude that you really believe in the freedom of speech.

But if you are pressed you will almost always find that there is a fourth group: people with ideas which have a certain powerful attraction, especially to the unsophisticated, even though *you* know them to be false. These are dangerous ideas, and despite your allegiance to the principle of freedom, the expression of these ideas must be restricted.

Such ideas, of course, are the ideas that you find threatening, and they are threatening because they offer answers which derive from premises significantly different from your own.

is whether the minority is encouraged to attempt to become the majority (not merely to become like the majority), whether "dangerous" viewpoints are allowed to compete freely with the prevailing ones.*

Putney's Law simply reflects the tendency of the majority to want to forbid the expression of viewpoints which it finds threatening. In the United States, the operation of Putney's Law is somewhat restrained by the Bill of Rights and the difficulty in amending the Constitution. The people resent this restraint, and there is much talk about modifying the Supreme Court so that the Bill of Rights will no longer prevent the American people from voting away their freedoms as rapidly as they would like. The Supreme Court has, in fact, sometimes allowed the restriction of freedom and has sometimes resisted it, although there has been a steady but slow progression away from freedom.†

If democracy is to be seriously attempted, we must restrain the operation of Putney's Law. The Supreme Court and the first ten amendments must be scrupulously protected merely to keep things from getting worse. Education can help. A self-fulfilling prophecy is one which makes itself come true; there can also be self-defeating prophecies. Popularization of Putney's Law could help to make it self-defeating. An understanding of the nature of the temptation and the reasons for it can provide the individual with a better opportunity to resist it.

---

* I once heard a Southern judge criticize the American Civil Liberties Union for being a communist-front organization. Now the ACLU is one of the few organizations which really attempts to preserve the freedom of speech. It takes the difficult view that all ideas should be heard; they have simultaneously defended in court the Ku Klux Klan and the NAACP, the American Nazis and the Communist Party. The judge cited statistics to show that 90 percent of the cases which the ACLU had taken during the 1950s concerned communists, and he took this to prove that the ACLU had communist affiliations. But of course he missed the essential point: it was precisely the right of the communist viewpoint to be heard that was the test of freedom in the 1950s.

† Perhaps the best way to test the degree of freedom in a society is to stand on a streetcorner and express those ideas which are currently and locally regarded as the most dangerous. The time interval before you are arrested is directly proportional to the degree of freedom. In some countries you will need a stopwatch; in others, a calendar. The time interval will be shorter in the United States today than in England, and shorter in the Soviet Union than in the United States. In Spain it will be shorter than in the Soviet Union.

Discredit the "Hidden Persuaders"

It may be useful to recall how Vance Packard popularized the phrase "hidden persuaders." [2] He described how modern means of communication combined with depth psychology made possible the deliberate manipulation of people without their knowledge. We must recognize and honestly admit that democracy is meaningless if the public is trained and conditioned to hold certain attitudes. To build an effective democracy, some form of restriction must be placed on the types of campaigning that are used.

I am far from believing that these restrictions should be established through laws; it would be much more appropriate to utilize education. Means of mass manipulation should be publicly explained in such a way that even the average voter has some idea of how he can be manipulated and therefore acquires some capacity to resist manipulation. It might also be useful to satirize the techniques of the hidden persuaders while dignifying a rational approach to decisions. At present, the reverse situation prevails. Through advertising, be it political or commercial, the average American is subjected to several hundred appeals a day which are intended to encourage him to respond to manipulation rather than to reason.

The Presumption for Anarchy

During his studies in Siberia, Prince Kropotkin became impressed with the degree to which cooperation within a species could be a trait favoring survival. He contrasted this view to the popular interpretation of Darwinism wherein all creatures were seen as struggling against each other for survival.[3] Generalizing his ideas into the political realm, Kropotkin came to feel that mankind might fare much better left alone in small cooperative groups than under an arbitrary and distant state apparatus. That is to say, he became an anarchist. Among Americans it has somehow become an unquestioned article of faith that anarchy is impractical, that if attempted, it would result only in mass rape, robbery, and slaughter.

Yet the simple truth is that mankind has usually lived without the state, in "anarchy." Most of man's million years have been spent in small families or villages which had little if any formal social structure.* Historically, the state emerged as a means of extracting labor and tribute from the villages, not because the villages somehow required the state. It is not anarchy that is impractical; the ability of men to live without the state has been abundantly demonstrated. What may turn out to be impractical is to group mankind into such large and technologically complex units that the state becomes essential to the coordination and control of the system.

We need to reexamine the assumption that the answer to all problems is to enlarge the state by making new rules and establishing new agencies of control. It might be far more productive to reverse the presumption and first ask whether a problem can be resolved by repealing legislation or dismantling some part of the state apparatus. The struggle to deal with the "problem" of abortion by laws and the battle to enforce these laws is a convenient example. Only after vast misery and injustice was it accepted that the solution was simply to repeal restrictive legislation.

As an autosystem, the state propagandizes for its essentiality and can be expected to make the most dire prophecies for any reduction in its role. But that is precisely what an autosystem would be expected to do; we need not take its warnings too seriously.

To make the presumption for anarchy requires merely that we check first whether a problem cannot be better dealt with by means other than the state, or if a cure via the state may not be worse than the problem.† If careful checking indicates the need to retain a law or agency or to establish a new law or agency—well and good. But when for many the police have become more of a menace than the muggers and when the state insists on defining as crimes numerous acts which have no victims, it is time to abandon the presumption in favor of the state.

---

* I have visited isolated villages in Mexico where this is still the case. The people are not really aware that they live "in Mexico," have no contact with the federal government, and live without any statuses or institutions beyond the family. They have an informal social structure based on prestige, but no laws, no officials—in short, no state. Although they have no police, somehow they very rarely rape, rob, or slaughter one another.

† In many cases advice may be much more effective than regulation. Advice, which the individual knows he can ignore, invites him to assume responsibility for his own decision. And in making his decision, he may well consider the advice. Regulation invites rebellion. Small craft warnings at sea are purely advisory, but most sailors take them very seriously. Drunk driving is dangerous *and* illegal, but many people don't avoid driving when intoxicated.

Stress Local Decisions

President Tito of Yugoslavia is one of the few communist leaders who has tried to build a meaningful democracy. Tito has contended that the masses are most able to deal with those issues which are relatively local and closely related to their daily experience. On abstract matters of national policy he feels the democratic process is much less effective and much less essential. The thrust of the Yugoslavian government has therefore been to try to create meaningful democratic forms at local levels. It has not fully succeeded, but the ideal seems an interesting and important one.[4]

In contrast, in the United States local elections usually bring out relatively few voters. Such elections are not given the glamour and spectacle of the national elections. And yet the people are more able to judge whether the streets are being maintained in their neighborhood than whether American economic aid is effective in Latin America. People are much more able to appraise the wisdom and integrity of their mayor than of their president.

It might be very useful to emphasize local elections, and to move as many issues as possible from the national to the local level.

Keep Home the Vote

B. F. Skinner, in his proposal for Walden Two,[5] dignified those who chose not to involve themselves in the political process. He attempted to define a society in which those who were politically uninformed and indifferent were encouraged to express their indifference and lack of information by abstaining from the political process. This would seem to have evident merit in that it leaves the political arena for those who have more information and motivation. What are the real implications of our present practice of pressuring voters to go to the polls who do not wish to, who have not informed themselves, and whose vote can only dilute the votes of the more thoughtful? It is all very well to encourage the citizen to interest himself in politics, but if he remains uninterested, it seems foolish to urge him to vote nevertheless.

Voting "No"

Americans have taken pride in the fact that they make a choice between candidates, whereas the Russian merely votes yes or no on a single slate of candidates. The American system has the advantage of giving the voter more than one distinct possibility to choose from. But if none of the alternatives are appealing, the American voter is in a dilemma. He is reluctant to vote for someone he doesn't favor merely because the other candidate seems the greater evil, but he is equally reluctant to throw his vote away by voting for some minor party which has no chance of winning. And he is reluctant to abstain, because he does have opinions. Under these conditions it would seem desirable to have a "No" on the ballot. If neither candidate were acceptable, the voters could force a new election with new nominations by a majority "No" vote. There would be a reasonable possibility of such a majority, whereas under present conditions the protest vote is split among all the minor parties, the "lesser evil candidate," and the abstentious. A combination American–Russian ballot—with several candidates and "No"—would seem likely to increase the effectiveness of democracy.

Similarly, on issues of national policy, it might be well always to separate issues and personalities. Let the voter vote on the issue without complicating it by having him voting for a candidate at the same time. Let him vote for peace directly, not just for a peace candidate.

Select from among the Better

There are many factors which currently enter into who becomes a political leader in America. Traditionally, most leaders come from law or business. They also come from the wealthier classes, not only because campaigning is expensive, but also because the wealthier classes have the background and orientation to seek office. They almost all lead—or appear to lead—conventional lives; divorcees, intellectuals, and men of exotic interests and backgrounds are conspicuously rare. Increasingly, those who rise to the highest offices must be effective on television. Obviously, political leaders are more personally ambitious than the average citizen. Yet none of these qualities are relevant to making the man a good leader for humanity. Qualities like humility, morality, ability to understand complex social processes, ability to understand divergent viewpoints, and so forth are simply not part of today's selection process.

Plato, in his disgust with Greek democracy, proposed that society develop a special leadership caste. The finest specimens were to be selected from each generation and trained from infancy to be leaders morally worthy of leadership. It may be neither practical nor desirable to go that far in selecting leaders, but it might be practical to devise means of eliminating some of the least desirable candidates and perhaps improving the rest.

For example, it does not seem unreasonable to require men who seek the highest offices to undergo some psychotherapy to increase their awareness of their own inner mechanisms and hidden motivations, just as psychiatrists have long been required to do. Some training in humanities and liberal arts seems a reasonable prerequisite to great political power—minimally, perhaps basic courses in anthropology, history, and social structure. Certain civil service-type exams could be devised to insure minimal knowledge of world and national affairs. A fascinating problem is to devise means of discovering individuals who would make desirable leaders, but who lack the personal ambition to volunteer for leadership.

Fundamentally, I am suggesting that certain minimal standards be defined for those who assume positions of great power. The democratic process could then select among them. If such a procedure seems undemocratic, it is no more so than any check on popular sovereignty, including the Bill of Rights.

Elaborate Repeal and Recall

As our democracy has developed, the whole emphasis of the apparatus is on determining who gets into office and on what laws will be enacted. Our means of removing a man from office once he is in, or of removing legislation from the books, are more of a rudimentary afterthought. We ask the people to exercise their judgment under conditions when apathy is most likely to be a serious problem and when ignorance is likely to be the greatest. It is before the man is elected that the least is known about him, it is before the law is enacted that it is most difficult to visualize its consequences.

It would seem that the voters are best able to recognize a bad leader after he is in office, or a bad law after it goes into effect. Democracy must therefore have highly developed procedures to get rid of bad leaders and bad laws quickly.

For example, several people have suggested that a little switch placed in the homes of all Americans could be made to give an instantaneous total of the number of people opposed to the current conduct of the government. Whenever a voter felt that he was opposed to continued power of a particular leader, he could turn his switch to "no." A constitutional amendment could provide that any government official was automatically and instantly removed from power when the proportion of the citizens who had turned on their "no" switches exceeded 50 percent. Everything would then have to stop until a new official could be installed. Such a device might do much to prevent disasters such as the interminable extensions of the Indo-China war; and it would certainly end the present practice of assuming that the voters will forget unpopular actions by the next election.

Admit the Need To Change

The specific proposals I have attempted are less important than the general point that we must abandon the idea that we *have* a workable democracy. A workable democracy has never existed—at least in a large and complex society. If we wish to continue to experiment with democracy (and I hope we will), we will have to give a great deal of thought to it, be prepared to work very hard at it, and expect to meet formidable obstacles. At the moment, the state is out of control.

22   Why There Is War

We've all heard the argument, "I admire your idealism in wanting to end war, and I wish it were possible. Unfortunately war is just part of human nature. There have always been wars, and there will always be wars, and we might as well accept the fact." Now, this argument is crackpot realism. It has a ring of hard, rational thinking to it, as opposed to sloppy sentimental thinking. But in point of fact, the argument is completely fallacious.

Crackpot Realism Again

To argue the universality and inevitability of war is to generalize from a particular period in human history to all of human history, and from particular civilizations to all mankind. *Violence* is universal (although some cultures are much more prone to violence than others); it may always have been with us, and may always be with us. But there is a great deal of difference between violence and war. The violence that is universal consists of personal acts for personal motives; war is a group action for objectives defined by the leadership of the group. In fact, violence for personal reasons is usually frowned upon or forbidden in war.

Many societies, such as the Eskimos, have never participated in wars, and are entirely unable to understand the practice. It is only because war is such a basic element in our own culture that we project it as a universal to other cultures. A *truly* realistic statement about war, however, would go something like this: War is a cultural trait whose origins were fundamentally associated with the beginnings of agriculture some ten to fifteen thousand years ago, and which will end with the second industrial revolution in the twentieth century—either because wars end mankind or, we hope, mankind ends wars.

All men were hunters for about a million years, and there are various reasons why hunters do not make war. Fundamentally among hunters there is really nothing important to be gained by it.

The hunter knows that his neighbor's possessions are essentially the same as his own and that to take them would merely increase his burden as he migrates. Similarly, he knows that it would be harder to seize the day's hunt from his neighbor than to hunt for himself. The hunter, in other words, knows that his neighbor has only the possessions he carries with him, and no food reserves at all.

Moreover, hunting groups avoid contact with each other for the same reason that they avoid any large groupings; it is necessary for them to remain in small, isolated groups to avoid exhausting the game or driving it before them faster than they can migrate in pursuit. Sporadic territorial clashes are about the only conflict that can occur between hunters. But each band has its own migratory routes, and further territory would not necessarily be an advantage. Moreover, they cannot take time from hunting to patrol their boundaries. There are strong motivations on all sides to work out a system of accommodation with neighboring groups; for the most part, territories are recognized and respected. Warfare plays no role in their culture until they come in contact with peoples who have made the transition to agriculture.

Nomads and Villagers

Agriculture provides the first real motivation for warfare. Agricultural groups settle, and unlike hunting groups, can be attacked at a fixed location. More important, the harvest of an agricultural group represents a six- to twelve-month food supply acquired all at once and is well worth stealing. Similarly, the animals of a herding people provide a large bonanza to the one who seizes them. War thus begins as the nomadic groups who are still hunters attack their neighbors who have made the transition to agriculture or herding.

Imagine a scenario. A group of men are practicing neolithic agriculture in a small valley. They have cleared an area and planted crops with digging sticks. They have a few half-domesticated animals that feed on the stubble of their fields. On the hill overlooking this valley, a group of nomadic hunters pause as they follow the game. Their leader looks down, and an idea forms in his mind: Why hunt when we can go down there, massacre them, take their harvest, slaughter their animals, and enjoy all we can eat for a month or so? The nomads confer briefly and charge down on the village.

At this point in history, warfare has been invented. Thus it is in the sites of the early agricultural villages that specialized man-killing tools are first found. The scenario can be continued to the next stage. After awhile, the nomadic leader has a second inspiration. After destroying a number of villages it occurs to him: why kill all of them? He begins to see that if he leaves some of the villagers alive and takes only part of what they have, he can come back again to raid them again. Why kill the goose which lays eggs? At this stage, the raider comes down from the hills, kills a few villagers to impress the rest, takes part of the harvest and part of the animals, and leaves them just enough to survive and start over, rather like a beekeeper taking honey from a hive. In time, the raider becomes an expected part of the villagers' lives and a system of tribute is established whereby the villagers share their produce in exchange for being allowed to live.

A third phase of the scenario begins the day the raider arrives to collect his tribute, but finds the village burned, the crops taken, and the animals gone. He realizes that someone has encroached on his territory, and he becomes aware of his symbiotic relationship with the village. He discovers that he has a vested interest in protecting the village against other raiders. The raider then settles down and provides protection for "his" villages in exchange for being supported luxuriously off the small surplus that the villages can produce.*

The essential point about this bit of imaginary history is that war becomes a fundamental part of the raiders' culture *because it pays*. It would be absurd to suggest to the raider that he should renounce warfare; with him it is a successful way of life.

Shifting Functions of War

When the urban revolution occurred in the alluvial valleys, warfare increased in complexity. The simple arts of the nomadic raider were elaborated into the complex arts of modern war, involving armies, battles, and chains of command.

Through history, the precise functions of war change. What re-

---

* Such are the origins of many aristocracies. It is common to find in early agricultural societies that the aristocracy is of a different ethnic origin than the peasantry. On closer inspection it is discovered that the peasantry are descended from the neolithic agricultural villages, whereas the aristocracy are descended from nomadic hunters.

mains constant is that wars are undertaken in the expectation that they will pay. The great innovations made by the Romans in the art of war were motivated by the need to provide foodstuffs for Rome. Caesar was not in Egypt to woo the fair Cleopatra but to seize Egyptian grain.*

With the discovery of the New World the function of war changed again.

The Spaniards were interested primarily in gold and estates. They moved into the civilized areas of the New World seizing the wealth and massacring the local aristocracy in order to replace them.

With the first industrial revolution, the function of war changed again to become a quest to control sources of raw materials and markets for manufactured goods. The industrialized fraction of the world attacked and conquered the rest of the world. Throughout the history of warfare, war has been undertaken in the quest for some kind of profit. War is not a perverse quirk of an evil human nature; it is a means by which societies have sought certain objectives.

From Profit to Loss

The industrial revolution, however, had some unanticipated effects upon warfare. The vastly improved weapons which enabled the industrial nations to conquer the world also escalated the expense and destructiveness of war—so greatly, in fact, that it became impossible for the industrial nations to profit from warring against each other.

World War I was the first major conflict in which this change became evident.† In the peace negotiations following the fall of Germany, the Allies seem to have been bewildered by the fact that there was no way of extracting from Germany the cost of the war

---

* But the Roman population outgrew this food source too, and the armies pushed farther and farther into less fertile territories, ultimately even to England. It was no accident that the three notable areas of Roman achievement were *armies* to conquer territory, *roads* to transport foods and goods back to Rome, and *law* to control the conquered territories.

† The United States under Wilson seems to have been rather precocious. In America, for the first time in history, a war was waged under the slogan "The war to end all wars." This slogan may depend on very doubtful logic, but the fact remains that it does not reflect an expectation of profit.

plus a reasonable profit. The Treaty of Versailles, to be sure, attempted to do just that; but although impossible reparations were demanded of Germany, they still fell short of making the war profitable to the victors.

This was a decisive event in human history, just as the day when the nomads first swept down on a village was a decisive event. The nomads discovered a new and profitable undertaking, and the signatories at Versailles discovered that this undertaking was no longer profitable.

That discovery, of course, did not end war. There is a great deal of inertia in societies. World War II came along, and the recognition that war was no longer profitable was more general. Neither England, France, the United States, nor the Soviet Union seems to have expected to benefit from World War II. Rather, they fought in an attempt to maintain a status quo against what seemed to them to be worse alternatives. Germany and Japan, however, still viewed the war as a potential source of gain. In the aftermath of their defeat, and with the new horror of nuclear weapons, the recognition finally spread throughout the industrial nations that wars could no longer be profitable between them.

From the time of the invention of agriculture to the time of the industrial revolution, war was a practical undertaking. It would have been absurd to attempt to preach pacifism to Cortez as he burned his ships on the shores of Mexico. But today war has become an impractical undertaking. There is simply no way the industrial powers can fight each other without annihilating themselves. Minor powers might make minor gains through minor wars, but only if the industrial powers do not intervene—which they are more and more likely to do.*

Military Gauges in the Red

When industrial powers realized wars are unprofitable and even self-destructive, the gauges of the military autosystem went into the red. The functions of the military was to fight wars, and wars had

---

* Thus the Vietnam war—between a great power and a very minor power —kept the world in anxiety lest another of the major powers should come to the defense of Vietnam. And the Egyptian–Israeli conflict has been repeatedly restrained for fear that the major powers would become involved in it and thereby precipitate World War III and the end of mankind.

become impossible. The situation is rather analogous to the crisis in the March of Dimes after the successful implementation of the Salk vaccine. How can the system save itself from dissolution when its function becomes obsolete?

When normal innovation can no longer keep the gauges of a system out of the red, there are only two alternatives. The system can disintegrate, or it can .transform itself so that it can function under conditions which previously would have destroyed it. Unable to move the needle out of the red, the system must rearrange its internal structure so that the red zone moves away from the needle.

This is exactly what the military sector did in response to the realization that war had become impractical. A number of years ago I was introduced to a colonel at a cocktail party. Having a bit of the devil, and a bit of the grape, in me I said as I shook his hand, "I am a pacifist." To my utter amazement he responded as he shook my hand, "I'm glad to meet you; I'm a pacifist too, which is why I wear this uniform." I retired to a corner with a fresh glass of punch to contemplate this mystery. After a while I could see what underlay his comment. The autosystem, whose servo-man he was, had accepted the fact that war could no longer be fought, and had even accepted the necessity for preventing war. But the autosystem had managed to redefine its function and justify its continued existence by claiming that it now existed to prevent war. The slogan which reflected this redefinition was "If these weapons are ever used, they will have failed in their function."

Thus, for the first time in history, mankind is confronted with a military apparatus whose function purportedly is not to fight wars, but to prevent wars. Caesar or Napoleon would be amazed. In past eras one side may have armed defensively because it perceived that its opponent might see some advantage in attacking. But now all sides arm defensively (for the Soviet military autosystem has made the same adaptation as the American). Yet each knows that the other can have no rational incentive to launch an attack.

Brinksmanship

The contention that military preparations are the best way to end wars creates anomalies. For example, bluff replaces bout. John Foster Dulles elaborated this into the strategy of "brinksmanship." This is the art of attempting to win concessions by convincing your opponent that you are insane enough to initiate a nuclear war even though you would perish in it along with him. Having convinced him of your insanity, you attempt to wrest concessions from him to placate you. It becomes a contest of who can profess the greatest insanity. Unfortunately, it is difficult to give credibility to your insanity without doing insane things, and there is always the danger that your simulation of insanity may get out of control or may drive your opponent so insane as to initiate the war before you can.

Another anomaly is that the preparation for war comes to be justified for its own sake. In the past, preparation for war was undertaken with the expectation of conducting a war. The nomad on the hill sharpened his weapons because he intended to use them, and Caesar drilled his legions in order to attack his neighbors.

But today preparation for war is defined as a means to coerce an opponent, in spite of the fact that war is impossible, and also as a means to prevent war. There is no historic justification for this view of war preparation; historically, preparations for war have not produced peace. But the obvious means of achieving peace—the abandonment of war preparations and the preparation for peace—would threaten the survival of the military autosystem.

The military has undergone an elaborate adaptation to the new situation. This adaptation has gone through several definite stages which are important enough to consider in more detail in the next chapter.

---

23   Systematic Insecurity

The adaptation of the military autosystem to a world in which it can no longer wage wars has been ingenious. It has adapted to successive stages of technological proficiency, much to the detriment of mankind. Madness has been systematized and then compounded until even the military has recoiled and sought to retreat toward safety. Unfortunately, there is nowhere to retreat within the perimeters of the military frame of reference.

Immediately after World War II, the United States had a monopoly on nuclear weapons; it was assumed that no other nation was likely to develop them for some time. Moreover, the American military was at its peak strength, and the American industrial apparatus had survived the war undamaged. All the other major powers had suffered considerable damage to their industry and military systems. In the glow remaining from the idealism professed during the war, it seemed that the United States would use its unparalleled military advantages to insure the peace.*

Minimum Deterrence

The strategy which the military evolved during this first period was ostensibly designed to fulfill its new function—keeping the peace. This strategy was given no special name at the time, since it seemed to be the only possible strategy. Later on, when other strategies evolved, it came to be known as "minimum deterrence."[1]

In essence, the strategy was this: nuclear weapons were so devastating that only a few of them could destroy any country in the world. For example, it would be very difficult to find more than 500 areas in the Soviet Union worthy of an atomic bomb. Allowing two bombs for each such area, and doubling the number to make a huge allowance for failures, interceptions, and so forth, some 2,000 bombs and perhaps 1,000 bombers were all that would ever be needed. Given these bombs and planes, no country would attack the United States (or any country it pledged to protect) because we would at once destroy all the cities of such an aggressor. Nuclear weapons were thus seen as a deterrent, as a means of preventing war. And only a few of them were necessary to accomplish this objective.

In 1948, however, the Soviet Union developed its own nuclear weapons. This produced a vast turmoil in the United States. Americans had for so long underestimated the industrial potential of communism, that the initial reaction was that the Russians must have

---

* In those days nuclear weapons seemed so terrifying that another war was unthinkable. Although those weapons were puny by modern standards, nevertheless the cities of a nation could be destroyed from one day to the next. It seemed impossible that men could live under continual threat of annihilation. We forgot that one way of adapting to such a situation was to refuse to think about it.

"stolen the secret" of the bomb. Culprits and scapegoats were sought, and the witchhunt ended in the tragic execution of the Rosenbergs.[2] It was only when the Soviets beat the United States to a workable hydrogen bomb some two years later that America faced the fact that Soviet science and technology were the equal of their own.

But the end of the American monopoly on nuclear weapons rendered the strategy of minimum deterrence obsolete. For if the airfields and bomb storage areas could be subjected to a surprise nuclear attack, the deterrent itself could be neutralized.

Second Strike Capacity

Once again the military had to rethink its situation. Naively, one might have thought that the spread of nuclear weapons, and the prospect of a war fought by two nuclear powers, would have led to the abandonment of the whole idea of security through weapons. But such a thought was unthinkable to the military. Instead, it devised a new adaptation which not only provided a crackpot-realistic justification for armaments, but even rationalized a great expansion of them.

The new strategy was second strike capacity, which was the policy of the United States from 1948 into the middle 1950s. The essence of the strategy was to provide guarantees that there would be enough nuclear weapons and delivery devices to absorb an unexpected attack and still be able to destroy the opponent's cities and industry. Presumably, therefore, no such attack would ever be made.

There are fundamentally three ways of trying to guarantee second strike capacity. The first is concealment. A variety of methods have been proposed.* Ultimately the most effective form of concealment was to hide nuclear submarines on the ocean bottom or even under the polar ice cap. Thus they could fire their missiles even though the United States were utterly devastated.

---

* One was to mount the American nuclear weapons on railroad cars which would continuously tour the country in a random pattern (never, of course, becoming involved in train wrecks). Another means, used for several years, was to keep a certain proportion of our bombers in the air at all times so that they could attack the Soviet Union on a moment's notice, and even though their airfields were destroyed.

The second means of trying to guarantee second strike capacity is "hardening." This simply means bombproofing the weapons. The most effective means of hardening has been the silos in which the Minutemen solid-fuel missiles are deployed. These silos, dispersed in the desert, are incredible containers of steel and concrete which are designed to withstand anything but an absolute direct hit by a nuclear weapon. It is reasoned that it would be impossible to score direct hits on all the silos and that a second strike capacity would thus survive any attack.

An unfortunate by-product of such hardened missile sights is the guarantee that in any nuclear exchange a large number of weapons would be "ground burst" in the effort to destroy as many of these silos as possible. The implications of this seem not to be generally understood.* But the fallout generated by such an exchange would practically guarantee the annihilation of both countries and perhaps of the world through fallout, even though no bombs were directed toward cities.

The third way to try to guarantee second strike capacity is proliferation, building enormous quantities of weapons and delivery systems in the hope that no matter how many of them were destroyed, there would still be enough left to wipe out the attacking country.

Minimum deterrence and second strike capacity were both defensive strategies. However dubious the assumptions on which they rested may have been, they did assume that a nuclear war could not be won, and that the role of military preparations was merely to prevent such a war. Unfortunately for mankind, the enormous proliferation of weapons which was undertaken in the United States to guarantee second strike capacity—and to justify expansion of the federal debt—suggested another and infinitely more aggressive strategy. This strategy, which emerged in the middle 1950s, was never the acknowledged policy of the United

---

* If a nuclear device is detonated at a considerable altitude, its primary effects are thermal; it causes everything flammable to burst into flame simultaneously in an area perhaps sixty miles across. Such air bursts produce total devastation in particular areas, but relatively little radioactive fallout. If, on the other hand, a nuclear device is detonated on the ground, the thermal effects are not so great (heat waves, like TV signals, travel in straight lines), but the fallout is enormously increased as the debris from the blast is rendered radioactive and carried to high altitudes from which it can travel around the world. In order to knock out hardened missile sites, several devices must be ground burst near it in the hope of achieving one direct hit.

States. It was only in 1962, when we officially *renounced* this policy, that we tacitly admitted that it had guided us for years. Such an admission was hardly necessary, however; the effects were obvious for all to see.

Counterforce

The strategy which grew out of the proliferation of American weapons is called counterforce. It is an aggressive strategy which seeks not to prevent war, but to win concessions. It holds out the dream of winning a military victory without fighting, purely through the preparation for war. It is one of the most insane pieces of logic ever evolved, and it was responsible for inflicting upon the world the most horrendous arms race conceivable. The final result could well be the end of humanity. Today even the American military acknowledges the madness of such a strategy, but much of the damage has been done.

Counterforce is the mad fantasy of a military planner surrounded by nuclear plenitude; and it can only be explained by a fantasy. Imagine, if you can, the following scenario.

One day the President of the United States gets on the hot line and calls the Premier of the Soviet Union. After the usual preliminaries about the weather and their respective families, he gets down to business. "Old buddy," he says, "you think you've got second strike capacity."

"Yep, sure do," responds the Russian Premier.

"Well, you're wrong. Are you recording this conversation?"

"Of course.'"

"Good. Then check these data with your intelligence. You have the following missile sites: I will give you the latitude and longitude of each of them." A long list of *all* the locations of Russian missile sites follows. "We have deployed against each of these sites three missiles with multiple warheads which are ready to fire from the following locations." The latitudes and longitudes of the United States missile sites are given. "Check these data with your espionage. You have the following nuclear equipped submarines; they are at present at these locations." More latitudes and longitudes. "Each of them is being trailed by three American killer submarines. I have told our commanders to move within sonar range, but to withhold attack at present. Verify their presence with your submarine commanders. You have in the air the following flights of bombers. . . . They are being followed by our interceptor groups which will now move within radar range but will not at present attack. Verify this with your aircraft commanders. You have, moreover, the following miscellaneous installations. . . ." And again a list of weapons and of the counterforce available against them. The American president demonstrates that every weapon the Soviet Union possesses can be at once destroyed. Although the Soviet Union thought they had second strike capacity, in fact they do not.

"Well," says the Soviet Premier in this fantasy, "I don't know. Obviously I'll have to check the whole thing out. Tell you what, I'll call you back in an hour."

"Fine."

The Soviet Premier checks with his generals, his intelligence, his submarine commanders, and his air force, and discovers that it is all true. So he calls back, "You old goat, you! You really did it! Well, I guess that's the way it goes. We surrender. When can you get the army of occupation over here? By the way, I hope you and the missus will have dinner with me at my dacha when you come to take over the Kremlin."

This insane dream led us to undertake the most incredible proliferation of weapons. It is insane because it is impossible. We now acknowledge that there is no way in which all of their, or our, weapons can be successfully located and reliably destroyed. There will always be enough left to annihilate the aggressor.

Overkill Ratios

The proliferation undertaken while the American military pursued the chimera of counterforce has led to amazing overkill ratios. An overkill ratio is the number of times you could destroy your opponent if it were possible to destroy him more than once. The American overkill ratio was pushed up and up until it has been variously estimated that we could destroy from 100 to 1,000 Soviet Unions.[3] Meanwhile the Soviet Union did not seek nuclear parity with the United States, but they nevertheless increased their weapons in an effort to guarantee second strike capacity.* The Soviets have an overkill ratio of about half that of the United States.

---

* The Soviets never believed that counterforce was practical, and never attempted to develop it. They did, however, recognize the strategy that the

It is impossible to grasp the meaning of the magnitude of the destructive weapons which were assembled during this arms race. Let me try to summarize them in two ways. First, the American arsenal is so vast that for some years now even the Pentagon has been unable to find any justification for the further production of nuclear weapons. Second, if the megatonnage of the weapons in the arsenals of the United States and the Soviet Union existed in their TNT equivalents, and if TNT were edible, and if the entire population of the world ate nothing but that TNT for a lifetime, there would still be some left. Even a pound of TNT is very dangerous, but the equivalent of tons of it is available for every man, woman, and child in the world.

Disarmament

The proliferation of weapons and the ultimate abandonment of counterforce led, in different ways, to the idea of arms control. This strategy is an effort to counteract the insanity of the arms race by lowering the overkill ratios to the minimum which is conceived "necessary" for national security. Each side retains the capacity to annihilate the other, but limits itself to that capacity. There is no real logic in arms control, except perhaps that it might permit parts of the Southern hemisphere to survive a nuclear war in the Northern hemisphere.

Some steps toward arms control agreements have been reached; for example the ban on nuclear weapons in outer space and on the ocean floor. But the main reason for advocating arms control is the hope that mechanisms can be worked out (within the presumed security of retaining the capacity to destroy your opponent) that could later be extended into real disarmament. Such real disarmament, obviously, holds out the only security for mankind.

Real disarmament, unfortunately, runs into the problem that both the American and the Soviet military autosystems are paranoid. A paranoid is one who reasons that he is in some particular kind of danger (perhaps being trampled to death by an elephant on the sidewalk). He becomes fixated on this particular threat, and will ignore other risks of all sorts to avoid it (he may walk down

---

United States was pursuing, and became extremely paranoid that we might attempt to win a counterforce victory.

the middle of a busy street to avoid any elephants which might appear on the sidewalk). Not only are both autosystems paranoid (together with the servo-men which they have programmed), but their fantasies are mutually aggravating.

Thus when the U.S. negotiator sits down to discuss disarmament with the Soviet negotiator, he has the obsessive fear that the Soviet Union is going to *cheat*. It is possible that they might; this is one of the many dangers with which he must deal. But he becomes so preoccupied with this *particular* danger that he is willing to run almost any risk of other dangers (such as an accidental nuclear war) in the effort to reduce the possibility of Soviet cheating to absolute zero. As the U.S. negotiator sits at the table he is always thinking of a scenario in which the United States disarms in good faith, only to have the hot line ring and the Soviet Premier announce that they have cheated and still have 25 missiles hidden under the Ural Mountains. In response to this fear, the American negotiator demands inspections. And lots of inspectors. He will run any risk of the negotiations breaking down in the effort to assure himself that he has left the Soviets no possibility of cheating. His fear is not ungrounded; it is his assessment of the relative dangers of different courses of action that is insane. And so he demands 100 inspectors permanently posted on Soviet soil; on second thought he makes it 1,000 inspectors, and on third thought, 10,000.

Meanwhile the Soviet negotiator is equally paranoid, but he imagines a slightly different scenario. Recalling the long American flirtation with counterforce, he is obsessed with the fear that the United States does not want to disarm at all, but only wants to ferret out the remaining secret Soviet installations. He imagines that as soon as disarmament is supposedly ready to begin and the American "inspectors" are all at work, the hot line will ring and the American President will announce that the inspectors are spies, and that all the Soviet secrets have now been discovered. Immediate surrender is therefore demanded. The Soviet negotiator consequently decides that he can allow only 10 inspectors to visit for a month, and on further reflection he decides that it had better be only one inspector for a week.

At this the American negotiator faints from fear, because he *knows* that the reason the Soviets don't want inspectors is because they intend to cheat. When he recovers, therefore, he demands 100,000 inspectors. Thereupon the Soviet negotiator faints, because he *knows* what all those inspectors are really going to be doing, and when he recovers he insists that there is no need for any inspection at all.

Under these conditions, disarmament negotiations are extremely difficult, since both autosystems demand total guarantees against their particular obsessive fears, and since such guarantees are mutually contradictory. And thus the most advanced nations of the world remain armed and dangerous, and hope that somehow they will be able to avoid destroying each other and themselves.

Meanwhile, in other regions of the world, the situation is very different. . . .

---

24   Country X

There is another part of the world which is not afflicted with affluence or alienation, and where the overkill ratio is zero. Call it underdeveloped, emerging, colonial, or third world; it is the part of the world least influenced by the industrial revolutions, and most alien to the suburban-born American. Even the presumed experts of the USA and the USSR often misunderstand its real nature. It is the world of the man in the hut.

The affluent nations have long exploited the preindustrial regions. But even when they try to be benevolent, they project their own problems and aspirations onto the preindustrial peoples. At best, such projections lead to "assistance" which is not related to the realities of these regions; at worst, these projections lead to disastrously misguided interference in the affairs of these regions.

Let me attempt to describe the unfamiliar reality of the preindustrial world by means of a hypothetical example, Country X. This imaginary country illustrates the common elements of such regions, be they in Latin America, Africa, the Middle East, the Far East, or the Caribbean. Details vary, of course, but the basic elements are surprisingly similar.

The Villages and the River

Country X is largely a natural region which is drained by a large and complex river system. Along the banks of the tributaries of this river are fertile lands. Rising in the background are mountain ranges which partially ring the drainage basin of the river. The population is concentrated in the fertile area along the river; the mountain ranges are relatively uninhabited.

The history of Country X begins in the obscurity of antiquity. Thousands of years ago agriculture began to be practiced along the river. Agricultural villages appeared along the river banks, each one substantially independent of the others. The villagers had a strong identity with their own village, and no sense of identity beyond it. After a while, the villagers were born on land that their ancestors had tilled for longer than the folk memory could recall. They lived all their lives on this land in ways not greatly changed from those of their ancestors, and they looked ahead to a future in which their descendants would practice the same life in the same villages after their deaths. There is a remarkable stability, insularity, and timelessness in these villages.

There really is no Country X—that is the key to everything. It is only the villages that are real.

Conquerors

The villages first came to the notice of the outside world when one of the ancient agricultural empires "discovered" the river many centuries before Christ. The representatives of this empire established a base at the river mouth, and proceeded up the river informing the villagers that they were now members of an empire and would be privileged to contribute some of their harvest to the emperor every year. But beyond the collection of this tribute, the empire had little effect on the life of the villagers which went on as it always had. A few new ideas and artifacts were assimilated through the centuries without producing fundamental changes. Time rolled on. The empire declined, its boundaries receded, the tribute collectors came irregularly, and then not at all. The mountain tribesmen became bold and made occasional raids into the valleys. After a few centuries, new conquerors came up the river to demand tribute in the name of a new emperor. The centuries passed, and that empire too receded, and the cycle repeated yet again. The most obvious result of all the conquerors was the gradual development of a port at the river mouth. This port was in every respect alien to the region. Built and inhabited by the conquerors, it was the base from which they controlled the river and transshipped the tribute.

Time passed, and in the seventeenth century the first Europeans arrived. They were strange in many ways, but some of their behavior was quite familiar: they viewed the villages as a resource to be exploited. Toward the end of the eighteenth century the Europeans came to stay. For a period, control of the port passed from one European country to another; then it stabilized, and the Europeans settled down. It was they who defined the nation and its boundaries.

The Europeans differed in one important way from the ancient conquerors. They did not merely demand tribute. They were interested in extracting raw materials and in growing cash crops. They therefore grouped the villages into European-controlled plantations. They took the best lands and forced the villagers to grow crops on them for the European market. The villagers retained the less desirable lands on which they eked out their living. The European conquest fundamentally disrupted village life; the ancient conquerors had taken a percentage of the harvest; the modern conqueror took away the land.

Other changes were introduced by the Europeans. European products and customs entered the villages. Alcohol or opium became available and sometimes were forced upon them. Firearms were introduced. New diseases swept through populations lacking natural immunity. The life of the villagers suffered a disastrous decline.

Xopolis

At the mouth of the river there was a sense of progress and development among the conquerors. The port now developed into the city of Xopolis. And Xopolis became a characteristic European city. Indeed the reality of the villages came to be hidden behind the façade of Xopolis.*

---

* If you had visited Country X on a Cook's Tour, you might have been impressed by the quaintness of Xopolis; but it would seem quaint only because all cities all over the world are much the same and minor differences are thus

In order to administer their country, the Europeans established a bureaucracy which used "Xoners" in the lower statuses and Europeans in the highest. Thousands of natives worked in this bureaucracy, and became Europeanized. They were either born in Xopolis or had left their villages when young. Of necessity, they spoke the European language. They came to admire and to imitate European ways (even though they might secretly hate Europeans). The native bureaucrats became imitation Europeans totally alienated from the reality of the region.

The Europeans established the University of Xopolis, an institution which granted degrees primarily in medicine, law, and letters. Its graduates, while not numerous, greatly exceeded the demand for their services; degrees were sought for prestige, not for their economic utility. Xopolis had far more native physicians than could practice medicine. The Europeans went to European doctors, and the natives were mostly too poor to afford any kind of medical care. And none of the doctors ever went to the rural areas where the villagers lived and died as they always had with only their own traditional remedies.*

The Europeans also created an army to defend their colony against other European powers and to guard against native revolt. This army was a mercenary force trained and commanded by Europeans. In its ranks were natives whose ties to the villages were severed and who would fight the white man's battles for a price. Prominent in the army were crack troops recruited from the mountain tribesmen who had a traditional contempt for the villagers. The army governed the country insofar as the interests of the Europeans were involved, and left things as they were insofar as the interests of the Europeans were not involved. Life in the villages went on in whatever imitation of the past was possible within the plantation system.

---

emphasized. But the broad streets, the tall buildings, the shops and the stores, are all fundamentally European in nature. If you felt adventurous on your tour you might have visited the "native quarter" and thought that you were seeing the reality of the country there. But, in fact, the "native quarter" is as alien to the villages as is the European sector of the city. The native quarter is where those who have become detached from the village life live their lives in poverty under semi-European conditions. They, too, are aliens. And no Cook's Tour travels to the villages.

* The situation was similar among the lawyers; there were more lawyers in Xopolis than could ever practice law. And the graduates in letters competed desperately for the few teaching positions at the University.

In Xopolis a superficial industrial development took place through foreign capital which built factories in order to exploit the cheap labor of the urbanized natives. This industrial development was proudly shown to all visitors, but actually had little meaning in terms of the economy of the region. That economy remained centered in the villages.

Village Uprisings

Throughout the nineteenth century there were sporadic uprisings of the villagers. These were essentially suicidal outbreaks with no thought of sustained revolution or of permanent accomplishment. In some particular plantation, perhaps, the overseer was unusually oppressive, or bad harvests threatened starvation. But for whatever reason, an uprising would begin among the young men of a village. The other villagers would at first discourage them (knowing well the consequences), but once the youths acted, all knew that all were doomed, and all joined in. They would take such agricultural tools as could be used for weapons and fall upon their tormentors—the overseers and local administrators. (The landlord was likely to be an absentee.) They would then seize the available foodstuffs and alcohol, burn the plantation house, and settle down to enjoy themselves until the inevitable gunboat came up the river. And then they died as they had known they would. Perhaps the adjacent villages died too, as the troops drove home the lesson. Then things would be quiet in that region, but after a year or a decade the pattern would repeat somewhere else. As the tempo of such suicidal uprisings gradually increased, the ruthlessness of the army similarly increased.

Nationalism

The twentieth century came without substantial change, and the First World War was barely noticed. By the time of the Second World War, however, certain winds of change were stirring. For one thing, the European concept of nationalism caught on among the native bureaucrats, the native army officers, the small merchants, the graduates of Xopolis, and especially among the occasional native graduates of European universities. Nationalism is an idea totally alien to the villagers; their loyalty and identity is with the village. They feel no loyalty to the nation which was organized to exploit them. But to the Europeanized native in Xopolis, the idea of Country X as a nation among nations seemed to be the antidote to the domination and arrogance of the Europeans.

Then, too, the European hold on Country X was subtly weakening. By World War II, colonies were ceasing to be profitable. The cost of keeping the colony subdued was escalating at the same time that the profits from the colony were declining. Moreover, humanitarian sentiments at home were forcing certain expensive changes in the operation of the colony. The war further weakened European political control by distracting the attention of the Europeans during the critical war years.

In the aftermath of the Second World War came independence. After a few years of maneuvering and sporadic violence, the higher levels of the bureaucracy were vacated by the Europeans and occupied by native nationalist politicians. For the first time in history, Country X was a separate political entity. In the eyes of the world Country X was now launched on its path into the modern world. Its representatives sat in the United Nations.

But independence was another of Xopolis's illusions. The villager found no independence. The landlord still controlled the plantation. At most, the European landlord might have been replaced by a native landlord from Xopolis, who was likely to be even more ruthless in his exploitation than the European had been. Xopolis was now the conqueror of the villages.[1]

The native government became even more corrupt on its own than it had been under the Europeans. Bribes had always been a way of life because salaries were so low that the lesser bureaucrats needed them simply to live. But in the absence of the restraining influence of the business-minded Europeans, the government became absolutely corrupt at all levels.

The government spoke about its plans for the development of Country X, by which it meant the development of Xopolis into an industrial economy. The government welcomed foreign capital within certain restrictions, and the villages were exploited even harder to support the industrial façade. Suicidal village uprisings increased in frequency, and the army of Xopolis—now led by Xoner officers— held the villagers in absolute contempt and met unrest with increasing terror and persecution. Gradually the gauges of Xopolis began moving into the yellow. In the national palace, the dictator sat surrounded by his relatives and his entourage of yes-men. His eyes were not on the gauges.

---

25   Revolution in Country X

The revolution in Country X was fundamentally the revolt of the villagers against the alien city. The man in the hut was finally learning to strike back. Neither the Xoners nor the Americans nor the Russians understood the revolution; but it was a simple and natural phenomenon. Or it would have been had not American interference turned it into an immensely destructive catastrophe. All in the name of freedom.

Losing Friends

The rulers of Xopolis had never had the support of the villagers, and they gradually began to lose what support they had in the city. For different reasons, group after group found themselves coming into opposition to the government. For example, the callous indifference of the government to living conditions in the city alienated the lower class Xoners who were its chief victims.

The rulers saw their positions first and foremost as an opportunity to create personal fortunes—which they safely hid in numbered Swiss bank accounts. The businessmen often found their interests in collision with those of a government official. A particular businessman may have seen an opportunity to make a fortune by building a modern cement plant; cement was imported except for one inefficient local factory. He soon discovered, however, that that local plant was owned by the cousin of the brother-in-law of the chief of the army, and that no competition would be allowed. As he sat and thought of the money he could have made with his modern plant, he found himself coming more and more into opposition to the government.

The students were the first group to rebel openly. In the University they were filled with nationalist ideals which contrasted sharply to the corrupt and stagnant reality of the present government. In their enthusiasm to see Country X become a European-type country, the students studied European revolutionary theory, and conspired in the cafés. Whenever the government met a student demonstration with machine guns, the number of student militants was increased. Periodically the government cracked down and closed the University to disperse the students. After things cooled a bit, the University was reopened, the students were a bit more cautious for awhile, and then the situation moved toward the next confrontation. A tradition of hostility between students and government developed. Many students retained their radical views after graduation, especially if they were unable to find the jobs for which they felt their training had prepared them.

To a considerable degree, the government alienated even the army which it used to keep the other dissident elements under control. When the Europeans left, the higher ranks in the army were filled by young Xoner officers, European trained and indoctrinated. These young officers were strongly imbued with nationalism and with Western dreams of progress. They wanted to see Country X manufacture its own automobiles, they wanted honesty in government. Their careers depended on staying in the favor of the government, but secretly they found themselves thinking more and more of a coup d'état.

About the only friends that the government of Xopolis now had left were its employees and the landlords. The employees depended on the government for their livelihood, but they also were alert for signs of weakness which might suggest that they should begin ingratiating themselves with its successor. And the landlords were a dispersed group—some of them on the land, some in Xopolis, and more than a few in other countries. They hardly formed a cohesive basis of support for the government.

The government was unlikely to make any moves toward land reform—the one action which might have given it a base of support outside of Xopolis. It was not just that it was corrupt and dependent on the landlords for their support. Even if a group of idealistic young officers had carried out their coup d'état, driven off the dictator, and seized Xopolis, land reform would have been one of the last things on their mind. They would first of all have tried to deal with the corruption in the bureaucracy, and then focused their attention on expanding industrial production. These were the interests which derived from their nationalistic ideals. And expanding industrial production would necessarily have meant trying to extract just as much production from the villages as possible, to feed the city and to sell in foreign markets to buy machinery. But the peasants wanted the plantations to be divided up into small and inefficient parcels. Whether corrupt or reformed, the Xopolian government had a vested interest in opposing land reform.

An Impasse

At this point the gauges were clearly in the yellow. The government had no possibility of support outside the city, and was rapidly losing ground within it. The tourist who passed through the shops might see a calm surface, but the visitor who entered into the life of the city would find himself caught up in political ferment.

There were all sorts of political parties, both open and underground. The largest single party was the Communist Party, which controlled the unions. Varying coalitions formed and dissolved. Every night new handbills were printed, and every vertical surface, be it wall or post, was plastered with manifestos, announcements of congresses, pronouncements, and so on.

The jails became centers of political activity. The serious agitators were kept there permanently, but remained active through a host of political small fry who flowed in and out as the level of repression rose and fell. It became a sort of open secret that nearly everyone was to some extent a revolutionary.

Against the backdrop of all this political activity it is difficult to realize that it is all an illusion and that nothing is really happening.* But it is all only the ferment of Xopolis, and Xopolis really has nothing to do with Country X. Xopolis remained what it always

---

* I know. Once I spent several months in one of the Xopolises of the world and was caught up in the illusion that something was going on. Congresses would be called and issue pronouncements; parties would split and coalesce; students would riot and be shot; people would be thrown into jail. Only very slowly did I realize that it all meant nothing, which of course, was one of the reasons that it was allowed to happen.

had been, an alien structure. Within Xopolis, the conquerors of the villages were quarreling among themselves.

Out in the countryside, the peasants were willing to pay almost any price for change. Each village wanted its land back. But their consciousness did not transcend their local problems, and at the local level the problems could not be solved. As Fanon has pointed out, the villager does not need to be taught the necessity of revolution but to conceive the possibility of it.[1] And the villager who barely grasps the existence of Country X can hardly grasp the idea of a revolutionary change in its government.

The urban intellectuals had the understanding which the peasants lacked, but they lacked understanding of the peasants. The revolution which the intellectuals wanted was not at all the revolution the peasants would have wanted, if they had understood what a revolution was.

And so, for a time, the situation achieved a stability of sorts. Where were the Communists? The Chinese were far away. The local Party was Russian oriented, and this fact rendered it ineffectual as a revolutionary pivot. On the one hand, the Communist Party was primarily concerned with the welfare of the Soviet Union, and the Soviet Union in its efforts to avoid a nuclear confrontation with the United States tended to regard local revolutions as a bit dangerous. On the other hand, the Communist Party shared the Russian view that valid revolutions were necessarily led by industrial workers.* This orientation explains why the Communist Party in Xopolis had worked so hard to achieve control over the small industrial unions; it also explains why the Communist Party could not begin to establish a meaningful relationship with the peasants. Anyway, like other Xoners, the Communists took a dim view of the peasant's yearning for his own plot of land. In order to build an industrial country they wanted to maximize agricultural production through collectivization. The peasant did not want to be collectivized and work on a state plantation any more than he wanted to work on any other plantation.

Things therefore waited. The corrupt, incompetent government lurched along its inept route, becoming more and more ossified and

---

* Orthodox Marxism, particularly as interpreted by the Russians, has seen the industrial workers as being especially chosen by history to lead the next wave of revolutions. Peasants might participate in these revolutions, but only under the leadership and control of the industrial workers.

less and less able to govern. The peasants were subdued by sheer terror, but more by their inability to grasp the larger potential of their discontent. In Xopolis all sorts of groups plotted the revolution, but they could not agree with each other, and in any case, their revolutions would not have resolved any problems outside of Xopolis.

A meaningful linkage between the revolutionary intellectuals and the peasants would have quickly ended the era. But there were many factors preventing such a linkage. The revolutionary had probably neither known a peasant nor cared to know one. He was proud of his Xopolian heritage, of his education, and of the fact that he had risen above his peasant forefathers. If he made the enormous step of going to the country, it was only to harrangue the peasants in the hope that they would follow him back to the city and overthrow the government for him. And if the peasant listened to his speech he felt no community of interests; the revolutionary was simply another alien from the enemy city.

The Breaking Point

Yet the link was forged between a few intellectuals and some of the peasants. It came when a group of the most venturesome intellectuals fled Xopolis and attempted to organize the peasants into a guerrilla movement.* At first the intellectuals regarded themselves as destined to guide and teach the peasants, and the peasants feigned stupidity and refused to hear even those things to which they could well have listened. Villagers died as the intellectuals provoked needless massacres by government troops; intellectuals died as villagers betrayed them. But finally a few of the intellectuals began to realize that through the peasants they were seeing their country for the first time.† Because these intellectuals began to

---

* This could have happened during World War II if Country X had been occupied by Germany (as was Yugoslavia) or by Japan (as was Vietnam). Some of the intellectuals would then have found themselves fighting in rural areas, living with the peasants, eating their food, and in spite of their preconceptions, gradually grasping the realities of the peasants' situation. Such intellectuals who were still alive at the end of the war would have been transformed.

† Had the *Thought of Chairman Mao* been available, they might have learned a little faster. But then again, Maoism can also become a blinding dogma, as DeBray has pointed out—while propounding his own revolutionary dogma. See Regis DeBray, *Revolution in the Revolution?* (New York: Grove Press, 1967).

learn, the peasants began to trust them and to listen to them. And the peasants thus learning the one thing they needed to know: the potentiality for social change.

At this point, the gauges clicked into the red, and the revolution became a foregone conclusion. The idea of peasant revolt spread among the villages, and the government's lack of support became obvious. Groups of officers mutinied, not because they understood the peasant revolt, but because they saw their chance to dethrone the government. The dictator and his cohorts flew off toward their Swiss bank accounts, and Xopolis fell.

Those intellectuals who led the peasant cadres then took over, somewhat to the discomfort of the rebellious army officers and the Communist Party. Two possible outcomes could have ensued. If the intellectuals reverted at this point to their previous orientation, joined forces with the young officers and the Communist Party, future of the peasants was grim. Their basic desire for land reform would be denied as the intellectuals forced collectivization to build Xopolian industry. The peasant revolution would have had to be started again from scratch or abandoned. If, however, the intellectuals had been truly transformed, they would hold off the officers and the Communist Party and initiate immediate return of the land to the villages. Gradually, and much later, the government could try to persuade the villagers to join Country X and the twentieth century. Meanwhile, Xopolis, the foreign city, would have withered at least temporarily.*

America to the Rescue

However, these two outcomes are replaced by a third in view of the complexities of the world situation. The United States, especially, must be expected to intervene, and in a way which will fundamentally alter the situation. Long before the peasants and the intellectuals established their critical linkage, the United States would have been supplying dollars and military equipment to the corrupt and decaying government of Xopolis.

---

* A revolution which went to the heart of Country X's problems would necessarily deprive Xopolis of most of its functions—for its functions have been largely to serve the conquerors in their exploitation of the villages. This is why travelers report that Havana seems like a ghost town, while the countryside is developing.

To the credit of the United States, such aid is typically linked to demands for reform. When the American ambassador is approached for tanks and jets, he is likely to respond: "There is no way your government can continue much longer unless you undertake fundamental reforms." * He is given assurances that reforms will be forthcoming tomorrow. However, the government of Xopolis insists that the military aid be forthcoming today—unless, of course, the United States wants a communist takeover.

And so the aid pours in, and the stakes escalate. When the peasant begins his fight he is now confronted with an American-trained and paid army, using all the ingenious and expensive weapons that American industry can provide. And as the revolution grows, the American autosystem doubles and redoubles its aid and its commitment to the old government. The needles stay where they are— the government hardly becomes more popular or less corrupt. But the red zone is moved. The level of violence necessary to remove the government is continually increased. What could have been a relatively easy transition becomes an extremely destructive civil war. Thousands, perhaps millions, will die; the country will be literally blown apart. Caught between a government which can neither continue as it is, nor change into something which could continue, with the enormous power of the American autosystem committed to maintain the status quo, the future of Country X becomes problematic.

It may end, as in Vietnam, with the total destruction of the villages by bomb and bulldozer so that the surviving villagers can be driven into relocation centers where they become refugees dependent on the government for each day's food. With luck, as in Cuba or Yugoslavia, the revolution may be able to play one great power off against another, and win a respite. In many countries, such as Brazil or Greece, the story is yet to be written, but the process of trying to move the red zone away from the needles is well under way.

---

* Of course, being in Xopolis the American ambassador is likely to assign a higher priority to the reduction of urban corruption than to land reform. But at least he recognizes the need for *some* reforms.

26   Balancing the Blame

Great powers have always behaved badly: Rome eradicated Carthage, Spain raped Mexico, and Russia stomped Hungary. And the United States—the good guy of the 1940s—became the bad guy of the 1960s. Some see this misbehavior as the result of evil conspiracies on Wall Street or in the White House. But the real source of the tragedy is the relentless stupidity of our ossified autosystems.

C. Wright Mills introduced the phrase "balance of blame" in his little book *The Causes of World War Three*.[1] I have always liked the expression because it encourages a realistic approach to the question of blame. There is the human tendency to try to justify your own position completely, or, if that seems impossible, to reverse the field and assume that you are completely wrong. Many marital quarrels involve this type of oscillation. The concept of a *balance* of blame discourages such a black-and-white approach. But there is also a tendency, especially among liberals, to make the comfortable assumption that when there is blame on both sides, no real assessment of fault can or need be made. The concept of a balance of *blame* encourages recognition that although both sides may be grey, some greys are much darker than others.

It is useful to apply the concept of the balance of blame to the history of the cold war. When we do so, some interesting and disturbing conclusions emerge.

Misbehavior

In the period from 1945 to 1970 there was considerable misbehavior on both sides of the Iron Curtain; neither the United States nor the Soviet Union were always admirable neighbors to the rest of the world. For example, in the period right after the Second World War, the Soviet Union unbolted and shipped home the industry of every country it occupied; this was their means of trying to replace their war-devastated technology. Moreover, their trade relations were designed much more to benefit Russia than to contribute to the welfare of the countries with which they traded. The United States has been equally exploitative, in a somewhat different way. Our quest for low-priced raw materials has not only looted the resources of other countries, but has led us to support governments, however oppressive, which would maintain cheap labor and the low price of these raw materials. Neither the United States nor the Soviet Union has hesitated to effect direct military intervention in callous disregard of international law and international treaties when they felt it in their interest to do so: Hungary, Guatemala, Czechoslovakia, and Vietnam—the list is long and bloody.

In most specific situations, there seems to have been a distinct tipping of the balance of blame toward one side or the other. The Russian suppression of the Hungarian Revolution was undertaken in the name of protecting the "free and popular" government of Hungary against "fascist conspirators." Had the government of Hungary been free and popular, it is hard to understand why Soviet tanks would have been necessary to crush a handful of conspirators. The United States had a certain culpability for encouraging the Hungarian Revolution and then leaving it to perish, but the balance of blame in the Hungarian tragedy seems to have lain clearly with the Soviet Union.

On our side of the ledger, there is the Vietnam story. In the early days of the war there were no North Vietnamese troops in the south. The southern guerillas may have received moral support and organizational assistance from the north, but if the Saigon government had been the choice of its own people it could have easily dealt with a few troublemakers. Yet even with the most massive help from the United States, this government could not control its own territory. Throughout the whole Vietnamese tragedy, the balance of blame has lain heavily on the United States.

Trends in Blame

Admitting that in different situations the balance of blame has lain on different sides, the next question is whether there are any overall trends. I believe there are. In the period from 1945 to

1950—the first phase of the cold war—the balance of blame seems most often to have lain with the Soviets.

For example, the Soviets established satellite governments subservient to Moscow in every country where the presence of the Red Army enabled them to do so. This expansion was no doubt partly motivated by a fear of Western aggression, but that fear was hardly shared by the millions who lost their independence to provide a buffer zone for Russia. Meanwhile, the United States seemed to retain some of the idealism of the Second World War; it sincerely promoted recovery in Western Europe, supported the United Nations, and even proposed international control over its nuclear weapons under the Baruch Plan.*

In 1950 the Korean War began, and once again the balance of blame seemed to lie with the Soviets. There had been continual border incidents in divided Korea, but the communist claim that the South attacked the North seemed unlikely in view of the rapid collapse of the Southern army. A more plausible explanation was that the Russians, knowing well the unpopularity of the Syngman Rhee government, and assuming that the United States would not defend it, encouraged the North to attempt a reunification of the country.

In the first era of the cold war, it seems possible to say that the balance of blame lay more often with the Soviet Union than with the United States. The second era began in 1950, and extended until 1962. During this era the American government elaborated the "containment" doctrine which came to mean in practice that there would be no leftward change anywhere in the world if the United States could prevent it. The "policeman of the world" became America's self-image; it destroyed the popular government of Arbenz in Guatemala, invaded Cuba at the Bay of Pigs, and gave the CIA a free hand to undermine the Geneva Accord in Vietnam. Moreover, the adoption of the counterforce strategy precipitated, as we have seen, a vast and senseless arms race. No doubt the American actions were partially a response to Russian expansionism during the first phase of the cold war, but Stalin died in 1953, and by 1956 Khrushchev had launched the policy of "destalinization"; Russia was changing. But the proportion of situations in which the balance of

---

* The Baruch Plan was vetoed by the Soviet Union.

blame lay with America seemed to increase throughout the era.

The end of this second era came in 1962 with the Cuban missile crisis. Practicing brinksmanship, the United States went to the edge of nuclear war—from which only the sanity of Khrushchev rescued the world.* In the aftermath of that horror, a new era began.† Although the United States proclaimed that no deal had been made to secure the withdrawal of the Russian missiles, it reminded the world that the United States would not invade Cuba since American policy forbade the invasion of any country. Moreover, it was announced that purely as an economy measure, a number of military bases would be closed, and the size of the armed forces reduced. The Soviets retaliated by announcing a reduction in the size of *their* army, and the peace race suddenly seemed almost real.‡ This era, from 1962–1964, was the most hopeful of the cold war, and one in which the blame on both sides seemed to be declining. I remember giving a lecture in late 1964 which expressed the mood of that era. The main point was that for two years we had not made any major mistakes, nor gotten into any new messes. Two problems remained from the past, but they had not gotten worse, and if they could be solved, the cold war just might be ended. The two problems were Berlin and Vietnam.

Early in 1965 the next era began—with a massive escalation of the war in Vietnam. The good feelings of 1964 suddenly seemed

---

* The only justification for this American gamble, except perhaps to deprive the Republicans of a campaign issue, was that the missiles in Cuba increased the Soviet overkill ratio slightly. Given the size of the overkill ratios of both nations, and their inherent absurdity, it seems an incredible issue over which to risk the entire future of the human race.

† There were many indications. For example, *Playboy* magazine did a pictorial study of the women of Russia; *Holiday* magazine did an illustrated story on touring Russia; *Life* magazine did a sympathetic story of the Russian leaders including a picture of Khrushchev wrapped in furs and looking like a cuddly bear.

‡ America's dismantling of her Turkish missile bases during this era was particularly important. The significance of these bases was well understood by the Russians, although largely unrecognized by the American people. The bases were installations of liquid-fuel rockets placed in Turkey during the quest for counterforce. Unlike the modern solid-fuel rockets, liquid-fuel rockets cannot be protected by hardening. They are too complex, and have too long a countdown. They can never be used for defense in the modern world, since an attacker would certainly destroy any such highly vulnerable installations in the first salvo. Thus the only use that the Americans could make of these rockets would be in an American attack on Russia, or in the threat of such an attack. The removal of these rockets from Russia's borders was a good faith indication that America was abandoning the counterforce strategy.

a lie. From 1965 to 1970, although there were communist outrages such as the invasion of Czechoslovakia, the overriding horror of the Vietnam war left no doubt anywhere in the world (except perhaps in the United States) that the balance of blame in the cold war now lay with the United States.

By 1972 even the American people were strongly opposed to the recent American role in world affairs. The government alternated between ignoring this opposition, and making temporary concessions to it. For example, Nixon repeatedly announced that he was getting out of Vietnam, but somehow getting out always seemed to involve a continuation of the war. But by then the damage was largely done. Vietnam was a shambles, and—in a different way—so was America.

Reasons for the Blame

To me as an American, the fact that the balance of blame sometimes lay with us is unacceptable, to say nothing of the fact that our share of the blame has become increasingly larger. I want America to resemble the country I learned about in grade school civics—not the image I saw reflected from Vietnam. Why did America do these things? There seem to be two possibilities: evilness or stupidity.

Those who argue that evilness is the primary reason usually point to capitalism as the basic root of evil American behavior. They claim, for example, that oil deposits off Vietnam in the China Sea had a great influence on American policy in Vietnam. No doubt capitalism can sometimes lead to evilness, but it is hardly the whole story. In the case of the offshore oil deposits, as late as 1971 their existence had not even been verified by test drilling, and they had hardly been considered in 1965 when the massive escalation began. It was the *French* who originally had economic interests in Vietnam, not the Americans. An invasion of Chile to protect Anaconda and Kennecott Copper would have made more capitalistic sense than an invasion of Vietnam to protect French rubber plantations. And anyway, capitalism can hardly be the cause of the frequent misbehavior of the Soviet Union.

Evilness is not primarily a product of capitalism (nor of communism) but of uncontrolled autosystems. As we have repeatedly seen, autosystems will ruthlessly pursue their objectives in terms of their own assumptions, regardless of the impact on humanity. But evilness is not even the crux of the matter. To do evil is to make gains immorally. Much of what the American autosystems have done has not brought gains. Much of the behavior has been simply stupid; the American military and political autosystems are growing ossified.

For example, one of the characteristics of an ossified system is an inability to adapt its basic assumptions to fit changes in the environment. Now, a great deal of American foreign policy has derived from the assumption that the communist expansion from 1945 to 1947 is the prototype for all radical change. In 1945–1947, communism expanded because Russia was forcing the establishment of sympathetic governments in the countries it was occupying after the war. Since then, however, communism has expanded very differently. Local revolutions have been led by popular leaders who turned out to be much more nationalistic than pro-Russian. Thus communism came to Yugoslavia by a popular and local revolution, and by 1948 Tito had begun his break with Russia and with communist orthodoxy. Similar events occurred in China, in Vietnam, and in Cuba. Such communist victories are fundamentally different from Russian invasions, and cannot be dealt with in the same way. Yet the United States persisted for years in demanding that Moscow stop every revolution in the world as if it were in control of them. But it is doubtful that Castro would turn Cuba back to Batista even if the Russians told him to do so.

An ossified system also projects—it assumes that the conditions which exist within it also exist outside. This was very apparent in the Vietnam war as the American military attempted to cut the Vietnamese supply lines. The American military depends on roads and landing fields to move its heavy equipment. But supply lines have little importance to an army which fights with simple equipment, is largely supported locally, and whose major means of transportation are bicycles. The alleged Ho Chi Minh Trail, which the United States struggled so hard to destroy, could not be destroyed because it was not at all similar to Highway 17 in California. But throughout the war, the Pentagon persisted in acting as if it were. Then too, the American government persists in projecting American desires on the peoples of other countries. For years it has been firmly convinced that what the villagers in Country X really want is an opportunity to cast their votes in an honest election for the next president of Xopolis.

Another symptom of ossification is degeneration of the information inputs. One of President Johnson's close advisors finally pointed out what many outside government had long understood: the President is likely to be one of the most tragically misinformed people in America.[2] There are many reasons why American information has been inadequate. One has been the preoccupation with security. In a paranoid fear that a subversive individual might enter the information system, American ended by excluding nearly anyone with an independent or analytic mind. For example, by eliminating those who had been doubtful that Chiang Kai-Shek was the democratic hope of the East, the State Department for years excluded everyone who was informed about that region.*

The ossification of the America autosystems has been furthered by the fact that the theoretical constructs in terms of which our decisions are conceptualized are neither sophisticated nor accurate. In fact, the American systems have tended to be antitheoretical. The effect of being antitheoretical is not to avoid theory, but merely to avoid confrontation with the theory that is used. The antitheoretical tend to use uncritically whatever theory seems most obvious in terms of crackpot realism. Thus the domino theory hurt the American autosystem much more than it helped it.

In the era since 1965, stupidity seems a more prominent factor than evilness. American policies have had disastrous effects on the underdeveloped world, American prestige, the loyalty of American youth, and even American capitalism. The uncontrolled autosystems may be evil, but they are becoming unable to serve even their own interests effectively.

---

* This fault is also apparent in the FBI and the CIA—especially in the FBI because it is more public. The kind of screening that the FBI agent passes through weeds out those who tend to think independently, or entertain unusual ideas. It retains the most conventional minds with the smallest tendency toward any mental innovation. Yet intelligence gathered by such minds influences national policy. The Russians seem to fare a little better in this regard. The Russian agents we have discovered seem to be men of independent minds. The Russians have made use of their creativity, but kept them under continual surveillance by their own unimaginative FBI types.

---

27   Seeking a Defense

For all its opulent and apocalyptic armaments, the United States is a weak giant lacking both the means and the will to make a real defense of itself. The means could be developed, and the will invigorated. But it is not a Russian invasion which is our greatest danger. The American people and the Russian people must find the means to defend men against autosystems—their own as well as each other's. That is the real problem of defense!

From the human viewpoint, arguments for a radical restructuring of our military system are overwhelming. Our means of "defense" have become the most expensive aspect of our society, and one of the greatest threats to its survival. And somehow, in the name of defense, we find ourselves doing unpleasant and immoral things throughout the world. Controlling our military autosystem is not only a national problem; it is also a world problem.

Part of the problem is that we really have not thought through what we mean by defense, what we are trying to defend, and from whom. We have established a defense system which has come to generate its own answers to these questions, and we let it think for us. We can't afford to do that any longer.

The Weakness of the Giant

The Department of Defense defines its task somewhat as follows: it exists to establish effective means of using force to protect the American social system from being coerced or destroyed by some other social system. This definition is simply gritty with unexamined assumptions: for example that the welfare of the American people is identical with the welfare of the American social system, and hence that their annihilation may be risked to protect the social structure; or that force is the most effective means of defense, and hence that the primary path to safety is to develop systems of weapons.

Proceeding along the path defined by these assumptions, an awesome military apparatus has been developed. In spite of this, our defense position is actually rather weak. Although we could easily blow up the world, we would blow ourselves up with it, and most of our military equipment is of a type useful only in an attack. If we accept the premises that we will not be the aggressor and do not want to be annihilated in our own defense, America is relatively undefended.

Switzerland may actually be more secure than America. Recognizing its inability to fight aggressive wars, Switzerland has for some time concentrated on military preparations which *are* defensive in nature. They have focused, for example, on means of rendering an invasion of their country very difficult. Every major bridge, pass, and tunnel is mined, and can be instantly detonated. Moreover, their troops are trained for years on terrain immediately around their homes so that an invading army would be met by men fighting for their homes on mountains they had known and trained on all their lives.

Then too, the Department of Defense overlooks the essential element of the will to fight. For all our computerized weapons systems, our youth is alienated to the extent of being generally unwilling to participate in the defense system. In 1969 over 50,000 Americans deserted from the Armed Forces, and 150,000 went AWOL for shorter periods.[1] Those willing to accept the draft rather than jail showed little interest in fighting in Vietnam, and for the first time in American history a small but significant number actually defected and fought with the Viet Cong despite the tremendous handicaps of language, diet, and reluctance to fight their former comrades.[2]

But it is not only youth who may lack the will to fight. The flag-waving middle classes might not be eager to join a guerrilla movement to throw back an invader. As long as the water flowed from the kitchen tap and their television sets worked, I have a hunch they would acquiesce to any actual army of occupation. It could be observed in Europe during the Second World War that the businessman who avoided getting in trouble with City Hall when his own politicians occupied it, also tended to avoid getting in trouble with City Hall when it was occupied by Nazis. By the reports of travelers and the response at the Bay of Pigs, Cuba may well be stronger in this regard than the United States. With little of our complex equipment, the Cuban people would probably make a spirited defense against any aggressor.

Unquestionably America can destroy the world, but it is by no means certain that it could defend itself.

A Stronger America

Could America be made stronger, and if so, how? The Pentagon's response to any fear of weakness is some exotic new scheme for destruction, such as training the friendly porpoise to carry a nuclear weapon in a harness on his back. But if the goal is defense, it might be best to pause and ask just what kinds of equipment are useful in defense.

If our military apparatus is not to be used for aggression, then it seems only sensible to destroy unilaterally and at once all of those weapons systems which are peculiarly offensive in nature. Not only are these weapons useless, they give a false sense of security. Why not simply abandon our long-range missiles, long-range bombers, long-range submarines, and all of our large nuclear weapons? Immediate benefits would include enormous savings and a greatly reduced possibility of accidental nuclear war. A more subtle benefit would be to force us to think about means of *defense:* how would we deal with an invading army?

Given the resources and the territory of the United States, the possibilities of a defensive system à la Switzerland are enormous. Fidel Castro is reported to have admired the Rocky Mountains as an area for guerrilla warfare. Moreover, it would be possible to preorganize a resistance. Heretofore, resistance movements have been organized after an invasion under obvious difficulties. A preorganized resistance movement, with the full finances and resources of the government behind it, could have far more deterrent effect on a potential invader than intercontinental ballistic missiles that could never be used without annihilation. A country with the will to resist is extremely difficult to occupy, as the United States learned in Vietnam. Imagine the problems of attempting to subdue the American subcontinent with its 200 million people trained and organized for resistance. It would not be difficult to raise the stakes so high that any invasion would be unprofitable, if not impossible.

It is probably a mistake to become preoccupied with violent means of resistance; there may be more effective ways. I may sound whimsical if I suggest air-drops of vodka and dancing girls to meet an invading army, but I quite sincerely believe this is a more practical means of *defense* than Polaris submarines. The means of tempting, cajoling, and diverting an occupying force so as to render it ineffectual should be easy to develop in a country with the American capacity for corruption. *Chaos, carnival, and confusion may turn out to be more effective defensive weapons than guns, grenades, and garroting cords.*

Moreover, one of the most important means of building an effective defense would be to do everything possible to increase youth's sense that America is worth defending. The same youths who marched in Washington under Viet Cong flags might march with even greater enthusiasm under the American flag—if they felt the ideas for which that flag has allegedly stood were being practiced.

Specifically, ending racism in this country would do more to improve our defense than a fleet of supersonic bombers. Reordering national priorities away from destruction and toward ending poverty and saving the environment would do more to make America secure than the most enormous anti-ballistic missile system.

To turn our military system into a purely defensive one and to rekindle our American ideals would destroy the image of indifferent, imperialist America overseas. As we proceeded with the destruction of our offensive weapons, it would be wise to encourage inspection of the most thorough nature by anyone who was interested. Since we would not be cheating, there would be nothing to hide. America might once again emerge as the good guy of the world. And it never hurts to have friends when trying to defend oneself.

I am completely convinced that means such as I have suggested would guarantee the United States against the threat of foreign invasion. It is more difficult to devise means of protecting weaker friends against attack by a major power. Several points should be noted, however. Popular governments are rarely attacked by their neighbors. If we would cease supporting corrupt and unpopular governments we might find that our friends were in less need of assistance. Moreover, the results of our explanation of new means of defense could be exported. In any case, we are not really able to protect our friends now; we can blow up the world, or blow up the country we are trying to defend; but we cannot guarantee their safety.

Nuclear blackmail is another problem to be considered. Even though the United States were invasion proof, we could be blackmailed by some other nuclear power, told that unless we delivered them ten percent of our industrial output, they would begin blowing up our cities one by one. Of course that could happen now, and our only answer would be to threaten to destroy the world. The best means of dealing with such blackmail would seem to be to evacuate the threatened city, tell them to blow it up if they dared, and call for a worldwide protest and boycott of the aggressor. If the United States had returned to good guy status in the world, the tactic would have a good chance of success. No military means would seem to have any chance of success.

What Are We Defending from Whom?

Thus far I have limited the concept of defense to the conventional one: how to protect the American social system from another social system which sought to destroy, coerce, or replace it. But this concept ignores the fact that *the American social system is itself the most immediate aggressor against which the American people require defense.* The changes which would result if the Russian autosystem took over the American autosystem are greatly exaggerated —by the American autosystem. The real problem is not how to defend *America,* but how to defend *Americans.* Only in the propaganda of the autosystem are these two identical.

The critical question is how we can defend ourselves against all autosystems, domestic or foreign, against being turned into servomen, against being exploited or annihilated. Such defense requires, first, that people generally come to understand the differences between their interests and those of the autosystems. Moreover, they must develop a sense of human self-worth based on an affirmation of life and an understanding of their real needs. They must become autonomous.*

There is an enormous need to define the specific techniques

---

* In *The Adjusted American* (New York: Harper & Row, Publishers, 1966), Gail J. Putney and I attempted to describe the means by which an individual can achieve such autonomy.

by which such autonomous men can defend themselves against—and ultimately control—the autosystems. No doubt the techniques will have to be shaped by the specific problem, but let me suggest some ideas which may illustrate possible lines of approach.

One approach is to persist in dealing with the autosystem as if it were in fact operating to fulfill the human function for which it was established. I remember vividly a student who contended that the true function of a college was education, but that the system had obscured this function in a plethora of requirements, exams, degrees, and other such systemic paraphernalia. He decided to by-pass all that, and embarked on a career of auditing courses—some 15 to 18 units per semester. He worked hard, took the classes that interested him, did the assignments that were meaningful, devised extra work on his own, and generally treated the college as if it were an educational system. The system fussed and creaked a little, but found it impossible to spit him out. He got his education. (Later on he played the game a while and got his degree.) Fundamentally, I have been suggesting that we use this tactic on the Department of Defense—treat it as if it existed to defend us, and demand that it actually do so.

Another technique is to take up the excesses of the system and cooperate them to death. This may be far more effective than resistance. What Jew dared not wear his armband under Hitler? But when the popular King of Denmark began wearing the Jewish armband and invited all of his subjects to do so, the Nazis were forced to abandon armbands in Denmark. Similarly, given a government which makes extensive use of spies and informers, the traditional tactic is to counterinfiltrate, identify the informers, and eliminate them. But this creates a counter system which may become equally antihuman. It would be far more effective for everybody to inform continually in such a way as to generate a mass of data which could neither be evaluated nor utilized and leave the government completely in the dark as to what was really going on. Many variants of the technique are possible.

But the most effective and important technique I can suggest is to refuse to take seriously the propaganda of the autosystem and its servo-men. Imagine a mass of autonomous people assembled in a park, listening as a servo-man gives a war-mongering speech. Imagine them really enjoying the speech, for it is a truly fine war-mongering speech. The politician comes to the great climax and marches off to lead the people to war. But as he looks behind he sees people applauding like mad, but still sitting in the park. They can appreciate a good war-mongering speech, but they never considered taking it seriously. They sit there on the grass, drinking wine or making love, and talking about what a great speech it was. And the servo-man, alone, flaps his arms in frustration, shrugs, hesitates, and wanders back to join them—and perhaps ceases to be a servo-man.

To become a servo-man one must first become convinced that the autosystem is right. If we do not take the autosystem seriously, it cannot control or exploit us. We are its essential components, and in the end it can do nothing without us. Laughter rescues us from misplaced reverence, and joy affirms the validity of the individual human experience. Together, laughter and joy are the most powerful weapons against tyranny. A tyrant thrives on fear and survives on hatred; he cannot cope with the laughter of a joyous people. Neither can an autosystem.* The development of autonomous, joyous laughter as the fundamental technique for defending humanity against all autosystems may be our most important task today.

---

* When Jerry Rubin and his cohorts showed the country just how ridiculous the House Committee on Un-American Activities really was, by openly reducing its proceedings to the tragic-comic inquisition it had always actually been it lost its power like a witch in church. Yet this committee had terrorized a whole generation and wrecked many lives.

28   Triumphant and Irrelevant

The churches are doing just fine; they have become an integral part of America. Of course America is fundamentally unreligious, so the churches had to make a few changes in order to adapt. But it worked out well, and the few people who are really interested in religion can still do their thing outside the system.

The Church Triumphant

Some have predicted that the churches will save America and some that the churches in America will disappear. And in fact, the religious sector of American society presents a paradoxical appearance.

On the one hand, the churches are phenomenally successful. They are virtually unopposed. There are enormous quantities of proreligious literature, but virtually no antireligious literature. To make antireligious statements is considered at best inconsiderate or uncouth and at worst salacious or subversive. Yet large and unselected multitudes are asked to bow their heads for prayer without a thought that the irreligious might be placed in an uncomfortable position. Religion is respectable, and irreligion is not.

This was not always so true. Although we think of past generations as blue-nosed bigots, a Republican national convention once chose a notorious agnostic to deliver the keynote address.* Such a choice would be inconceivable today.

Statistics also support the triumph of the church. In 1950, it was a sociological truism that church membership in America had never reached 50 percent of the population. In 1965, American churches claimed a combined membership of 125 million which represented some 70 percent of the United States population over the age of 5.[1]

---

* Robert Ingersoll, noted anti-Christian writer and lecturer, gave the keynote address at the Republican Convention in 1876.

Opinion polls consistently show that around 95 percent of the American people say they believe in a God, and over 75 percent say they believe in personal immortality.*

Yet another indication of success is the economic prosperity of the churches. This was brought home to me when I sat with the investment committee of a mortgage company. I was surprised to find that applications for church mortgages were being routinely approved. The committee explained that church loans were excellent risks; the churches had plenty of money and paid regularly.†

One can certainly make a strong case that the churches are doing very well in America. But there is another side to the story.

The Church Irrelevant

There is quite a bit of evidence that the churches are irrelevant to the lives of Americans. For example, research usually fails to detect significant differences between the religious and the non-religious apart from their religious convictions. In some studies of my own, for example, I failed to detect important differences in behavior between the religious and the nonreligious, although the religious tended to feel a little more guilty about a few of their actions.[2]

The immense secularity of American society also suggests the irrelevance of religion. To talk about strong religious convictions (except in church) is to be regarded as a nut. Let anyone who doubts this stand on a street corner and hand out religious tracts or attempt to discuss religion at a cocktail party. It is true we use the slogan "Pray for Peace" to cancel stamps, but it is clear that most Americans have more faith in the Strategic Air Command than in prayer.

---

* Thus, the *Gallup Opinion Index* (Princeton: Gallup International, 1969), pp. 15–17, records that 98 percent of the subjects interviewed claimed they believed in God, 85 percent believed in Heaven, and 65 percent believed in Hell.

† I had anticipated that church loans might be controversial since it would be poor public relations to foreclose a church, and besides, what could one do with a church building if one did foreclose? But the committee told me that there was never any need to foreclose; the problem, they said, was to make the prepayment penalty strong enough so that the churches did not pay off the mortgage prematurely.

One tale can summarize the point. A new minister came to a prosperous Protestant church. He was a real live wire: pleasant personality, athletic appearance, good education, liberal views, lovely wife. He took this already successful church and made it really go; he launched new projects and a massive membership drive.

There was a particular woman in town who was the queen bee of a clique of young business and professional people who were going to be the business leaders and city fathers in a few years. Several members of this clique had already joined his congregation, and if he could get the queen bee, the balance would probably follow. So he did his homework, and went to her house. He rang the bell, smiled his boyish smile, and said: "I'm a salesman, may I come in?" She put the coffee pot on, and he explained why she should join his church. He had done his homework well. He pointed out that the best amateur photography lab in town was in the church basement, and her younger son was very involved in photography. He pointed out that most of her older boy's friends were active in the church youth group. He pointed out that her husband sometimes attended a political discussion group which met at the church, and so on. She became embarrassed, and finally said, "But I can't join your church because I don't believe in God." He replied, "Bless you my child, neither do I; that is the biggest reason you belong in my church!" *
This minister let the cat out of the bag; the church had become eminently successful by abandoning religion.

The member of such a church may be a "believer," but on examination his beliefs turn out to have very little content. It doesn't matter much what the priest, rabbi, or minister may be saying, the member of the congregation hears about the same thing. There is a God who is a good guy, but he is not all-powerful.† Gone is the God of Wrath, the Stern Patriarch of the Hebrews, the Demanding Moralist of the Puritan, the Complex Creator and Law Giver of St. Thomas; what remains is a sort of benevolent well-wisher. At times the image of God seems indistinguishable from that of Dwight Eisenhower. The

---

* He went on to say that he did believe in "goodness" and that if some of the older parishioners wanted to call goodness "God," he saw no reason to antagonize them by refusing to use the words with which they were comfortable. But this qualification was really just a further confession of secularity.

† As a matter of fact, some of the ineffectualness which characterizes the middle-class husband and father—the Dagwood Bumstead syndrome—has been transferred to the image of the deity.

primary activity of God is to love the individual—the adjusted American who has trouble loving himself. Mother loved me, but she died; my wife loved me, but she's leaving, yet Jesus loves me, that I know. And all that God asks of man is that he behave himself. God's commands turn out to be identical to those of the neighbors and of the local police. Be respectable and neat, cheat a little on your income tax if you must, but don't ever get involved with your neighbor's spouse. Immortality is insisted on mostly to evade the fear of death. It is dimly conceived as a little like a retirement village in southern California or central Florida—comfortable but unexciting.

These few ideas summarize the whole remaining content of what passes for the religion of the average American. God may enjoy the World Series, but he certainly doesn't determine its outcome. He is on our side in the Cold War, but it's up to us to win it for Him. His ministers have lots of good ideas, but not all of them are practical in real life.

It was Will Herberg who explained why such an insipid body of belief should be able to survive and prosper. In his *Protestant, Catholic, and Jew,*[3] he pointed out that what Americans really worship is the American Way of Life. Its goodness and importance is the center of their faith. They do not believe in the American Way of Life because it supports their religion, they believe in their religion because it supports the American Way of Life.

The very arguments that are used to defend religion in America illustrate this point. We are told to send our children to Sunday School because Sunday School is believed to reduce delinquency. Thus religion is good because it reduces delinquency—which is bad for the American Way of Life. The slogan "The family that prays together stays together" tells us that religion is good because it reduces divorce —which is contrary to the American Way of Life.*

In exchange for being recognized as a useful adjunct to the American Way of Life, the church has abandoned everything which might conflict with the dominant systems. It used to be that people

---

* Norman Vincent Peale has elaborated these simple messages into many books which tell worried Americans that religion will preserve and protect America, make them happy, guarantee their mental health, and insure their success in business. Fundamentally Peale promises that religion will protect the autosystems and help the individual serve within them. No doubt he is right.

were called upon to choose between the church and biology. But now the minister lectures on evolution and explains that the Bible was written for illiterate Jews who could hardly understand science like his intelligent congregation. It used to be that people made the hard choice between going to the movies and going to heaven; now movies are shown in the church basement. And in that same basement, the Avon lady gets together with the girls' Sunday School class to teach them how to apply the cosmetics that their grandmothers believed were a direct insult to God's handiwork.

As a result, there is very little left to rebel against in the church. Margaret Mead pointed this out in a lecture. Noting that younger people were not as anti-religious as the liberals of her generation believed they should be, she explained that the faith had become so bland that there was nothing left to argue about. The birth control issue, for those raised as Catholics, was about the last remaining point for rebellion. The churches inspire enormous apathy but little opposition.

The Dissenters

Some individuals however, remain interested in religion. They have quite naturally gravitated out of the churches, or to those churches least integrated into the society. For the lower classes this has meant entering the storefront sects, which unfortunately thereby become prosperous enough to begin adapting to the society and abandoning their original adherents. College students interested in religion have formed groups around campus ministers who are themselves on campus because of a distaste for the suburban churches. Several years ago there was the neoorthodox movement which read Søren Kierkegaard rather than Norman Vincent Peale, and St. Augustine rather than Billy Graham.

More recent was the growth of the "Jesus Freaks." In a few ways they resemble the neoorthodox, but they were less intellectual and laid more emphasis on faith, ceremony, proselytizing, and above all, the emotive aspects of religion. It is easy to be cynical about the Jesus Freaks; they found a safe and irreproachable way of thumbing their noses at straight society. It was fun to attend a suburban church in exotic clothes, to sit in the front row and shout "Amen, brother!" and "Glory!" as the minister spoke, to the embarrassed agitation of the congregation.[4] Many of the Jesus Freaks were very superficial.*

But in spite of the frequent superficiality there was a serious side to the Jesus Freaks. They turned Christianity back into the mystery religion that it became in Rome. In Rome, as in the United States today, the official religion had become bland and detached from significant emotional reality. Various sects came into Rome which had no social content and no real theology; they directed themselves to individual ecstatic experience and to the promise of individual immortality through initiation into their ceremonies and redemption by their saviors. There were several of these religions: Mithraism, Magna–Madre, Isis–Osiris, and, of course, Christianity. The Jesus Freaks have returned Christianity to this original form. They are unconcerned with social issues and theology; what matters to them is the emotive experience of the Savior, and His promise of eternal redemption.

A very different group of dissidents have been the priests, rabbis, and ministers who feel that the adapted church is failing to provide the leadership which it should in social reform. They take actions based on moral stands which usually estrange them from their church, and often end them in jail. In the early phase the issue was civil rights, later it was Vietnam. In a very different way from the Jesus Freaks, the rebel priests seek the meaning of their religion, but outside the church.

Certainly the largest group of religious dissenters are those who have looked to the East. One of the few books which you can assume a college audience has read is *Siddhartha*[5] by Hermann Hesse. It is strange that this novel written by a modern Swiss about a religion which evolved thousands of years ago and halfway around the world, should seem so relevant to American youth. And yet it does. The popularity of Alan Watts' writings is another case in point.[6] As Roszak has pointed out, the tendency to look to Eastern religions is a

---

* As were two girl hitchhikers who turned out to be Jesus Freaks. I made some reference to the Lord which they misinterpreted. They therefore asked me if I was saved. I assured them that I was not. They then talked to me of what I was missing, and the terms and language with which they described the "Jesus experience" were indistinguishable from the terms and language with which each new drug experience had been described several years before. Jesus kept them high, made them feel really good, helped them get it all together. I inquired about the Bible, and was told that, yes, they really intended to get into it very soon.

reaction against the overly rational, dehumanized, and objectified world of the technocratic society.[7]

Meanwhile, the church in America has perfected its adaptation to the leading sectors by abandoning its own peculiar qualities. The fate of the church is thus inextricably linked with the fate of the dominant autosystems. It is tolerated—even halfheartedly venerated —because it supports the system. But it suffers the usual problem of parasitism: it lacks the capacity to survive its host.

29   Underneath the Controversies

There were several reasons why the United States pioneered the education of the masses. Unfortunately these several reasons conflict with each other. From these conflicts come the familiar academic controversies. We all know what the philosophy professor thinks of the engineering professor, or what the state legislator thinks of the humanities professor. But don't get bored; there are some new things to fight about.

More than any other industrializing nation, the United States pioneered mass education. Schools were developed in the United States to fulfill three major needs. First, America was a country of immigrants from many different places who moved into a land sparsely inhabited by hunting peoples and took it for their own. But for the United States to come into being, a common culture had to be developed among the immigrants. Americans have talked a lot about the "melting pot" in the belief that there was an equal blending of the cultures of all the immigrants. The truth is that there was no melting pot; rather, schools were created to make synthetic Anglo-Saxons out of the immigrants if possible, and out of their children in any case.[1] The immigrant might live his life in the foreign colony of the big city never learning English or American ways, but the compulsory education law forced his child into the English-speaking, America-preaching school. The success of this school as a means of acculturation can be measured by the prevalence of monolinguality and the homogeneity of values among modern Americans.

The second major function of the school was to provide the necessary training for an industrializing technology. As a minimum, a literate population with rudimentary skills in arithmetic was required. It is hard to imagine that 200 years ago skills now taken for granted were unusual.* Then too, industrialization required spe-

---

* This fact was brought home to me by the mariner's compass which divides the directions by cumbersome names such as Northwest by West Three-

cialized training. To some extent these were skills which the parents simply did not possess—the new skills of the industrial era. But even the skills which the parents had could not easily be transmitted from generation to generation once the family ceased to interact as an economic unit.

The third task set for the educational system was to create the proper electorate for an effective democracy; the heritage of the eighteenth century is again apparent in this hope that universal education would make the electorate informed and rational.

The Familiar Controversies

These three functions of education—Anglo-Saxonizing, developing skills, and creating a rational elaborate—have not proved to be entirely compatible in practice. The first two come in conflict with the third, and the jangling has produced the familiar controversies in education. But as we examine these controversies we should take John Kenneth Galbraith's warning. In *Economics and the Art of Controversy,*[2] he proposes that the amount of controversy generated by an economic issue is inversely proportional to the current importance of that issue. The issues which are *currently* crucial are so unfamiliar, and their possible solutions so unclear, that it is very difficult to have controversy over them. Rather they tend to be resolved in a silent struggle in which none of the parties fully understand the game or the stakes. On the other hand, issues which are older, and already largely settled, are familiar. Everyone knows his own position and also that of his opponents. Such issues are comfortable to debate.

It seems that the same situation exists regarding the familiar controversies in education. Once, they were of real importance. But they are frequently discussed today only because they have been largely settled. For example, the clash between the second and third function, has underlain most curricular disputes over the years, both within the school and between the school and the community. On one side of the controversy are those who lay emphasis on the second function and on the other side those who lay emphasis on the third.

Imagine a meeting of a university curriculum committee as it

Quarters West. The modern practice is to divide the circle into 360 degrees, and give the course as 295°. I had been sailing for some time before I realized that what seemed to me a very awkward older system was actually more useful to a mariner who could not deal with numbers going into the hundreds.

considers the foreign language requirement. On this committee are representatives from all segments of the university including, possibly, the philosophy department and the engineering department. The familiarity of the controversy is proved by the fact that anyone who knows colleges could write the dialogue of the debate.*

In actual fact, the issue has been settled, the peace treaty negotiated, and the borders defined. There are occasional border disputes and violations, but the frontiers are universally recognized. The first two years are the proper province of the liberal educators, and the second two years are the proper province of the vocational educators. In the high schools a different accommodation has been devised. Instead of dividing years, students are divided into a group headed for college who are to be liberally educated, and a group destined to become honest craftsmen who are to be vocationally educated. Whatever the merits of the compromises which have been made, the issue is largely disposed of—although you would never get that impression by listening to the arguments.

Another traditional area of conflict lies between the first function —producing uniform, committed Americans, and the third—producing a rational electorate. To illustrate the familiarity of this controversy imagine a debate between a conservative state legislator and a radical humanities professor over academic freedom. Once again, anyone can write the dialogue.† The argument is loud and angry.

---

* Thus the philosophy professor will suggest that the present language requirement is hardly enough to get the student started in a language. He will point out that no mind which is limited to thinking in an single language can grasp the complexities of the world, the diversities of cultures, or the fundamental nature of human thought. He therefore moves that the language requirement be doubled. At this point the professor of engineering becomes agitated. He points out that he is widely known as a friend of culture, but that the engineering department already requires five years to turn out someone who has even minimal training in his field. Moreover, developments are occurring so rapidly that it will be necessary to reduce or even eliminate the foreign language requirement in order to turn out an engineer who is capable of understanding modern technology. The engineering professor will add that he loves foreign languages, but surely there are better ways of acquiring them than by taking vital time away from engineering courses. Other members of the curriculum committee will join in the debate and can be assigned bits of dialogue according to their departmental affiliation.

† The state legislator will argue that he can see nothing wrong with patriotism, that America is a great nation, and that we will destroy ourselves if we refuse to teach our children the virtues of the American Way. Moreover, the legislator cannot see why the taxpayers should pay admitted subversives to turn children against their parents, their country, and the very values that human experience has proven to be best. The humanities professor will reply that the most important thing about a college is its academic freedom, that it

But this issue too is largely settled. The colleges are allowed to practice academic freedom so long as they do it in a way which is not too
obvious or too offensive to the community. The outside community, in
turn, is supposed to support the college and accept the principle of
academic freedom in the abstract, so long as it is not made too evident
in practice. There are border skirmishes, of course, and occasional
battles but neither side conceives of total victory.

Conflicting Images

The functions which an institutional sector was established to
serve are not necessarily the same as the functions which the various
interested parties come to expect it to serve. This is nowhere more
true than with the educational system. For example, as it becomes an
autosystem, the college comes to have its own views of its function.
It views itself as a device for creating college credits and for arranging these credits into degrees. Faculty, students, and state legislatures
are all viewed as unruly and disrupting influences on the orderly
processes of the registrar's office. The college furiously insists that the
legislature fund increases in its capacity to generate credits and degrees, and resists any faculty proposals which challenge the unit of
credit as the only currency which can buy diplomas. It goes almost
berserk if the students threaten to dump any of its file drawers or to
fold its IBM cards.

The governmental autosystem sees the college primarily as a
source of individuals who are programmed to serve as replacement
components and secondarily as a facility to perform miscellaneous bits
of research. Like the college, it tends to regard any student or faculty
behavior not strictly related to its own ends as unfortunate, and it
views the collegiate autosystem as a rather fussy and impractical
anachronism.

For the faculty, the primary function of the college is to provide
a haven from the American tradition of anti-intellectualism. Those
who enjoy intellectual activity for its own sake have made a hideout
of the colleges. There they enjoy the stimulation of reading, think-

---

must serve as a forum where all viewpoints are expressed, and where the
student is forced to choose among them. He adds that the students have had
quite enough propaganda in favor of patriotism by the time they arrive in
college, and what they need to hear are other viewpoints to start them thinking for themselves.

ing, and talking with colleagues and students. One faculty member summarized this perfectly when he said, "The function of the college is to provide me with students to stimulate my mind. These students appear miraculously in my classes, and after stimulating me, miraculously disappear to make room for new students." To be sure, those who truly enjoy intellectual activity are not the only ones on campus. The campus can also be a haven for incompetence or from the outside world. As the old saying goes: "Those who can, do; those who cannot, teach; and those who cannot teach, teach education." But even though the intellectuals may be a minority, they have dominated the faculty and shaped the college to fit their needs.

The students' view of the function of college has undergone a recent change. The returning veteran in 1945 saw college primarily as a way of entering middle-class and professional vocations. However, there has been a radical shift since then. Today, if anything, the student takes the opposite view. *He does not see the school as a means of entering the society, but rather as a means of avoiding it.* This is obvious from the way in which students no longer hurry to graduate and, in fact, actually avoid graduation. Having unavoidably or inadvertently graduated, they may stay on, auditing courses, working on graduate degrees, or merely living beside the campus to partake of its environment.

There are many reasons for this trend, but all of them are fundamentally related to the alienation of youth. They are not eager to assume the statuses their parents have occupied; they question the desirability of families and the necessity of careers. And if the checks stop coming from home, they can still survive without leaving the campus.* However much the students may complain that their professors are alien to them and do not understand them, they seem to feel that the professors are less alien and more understanding than IBM, the United States Army, or the parental home.

The trend to see the school as a retreat from society is most obvious among college students, but it can also be seen in high school students. I visited a high school in one of the most depressed areas of a large city. Most of the students were almost entirely indifferent

---

* Given a little ingenuity in finding part-time employment making picture frames or culturing sewage samples in the disposal plant, supplemented by a bit of welfare and the continuous wealth dumped into the Safeway garbage cans, and granted a willingness to accept slum housing as a way of life, the student can stay with the campus until time for retirement.

to academic achievement. I watched some really excellent teachers trying every device from mild physical violence to subtle sexual cajolery in the struggle to lure their students into spending ten minutes out of the hour on mathematics. Later, I was amazed to hear the teachers discuss how these very students dreaded being suspended—not because they wanted to learn, but because they had nowhere else they wanted to go.

Neither the government, the college, the professors, nor the students are fully conscious of the functions they expect the colleges to serve. Their expectations are implicit, not explicit. But out of these differences in expectations come the real conflicts which currently wrack the educational sector. Like armies which clash in the night, the participants do not really understand the battle, but struggle desperately in silence or with whatever battle cry they recall from previous struggles.

30   Invasions of the Ghetto

The government, the colleges, the intellectuals, and the youth culture are in a four-way struggle for control of the educational system. But the colleges and the intellectuals are minor factors. Fundamentally, the youth culture is trying to take over the colleges, and the government is trying to destroy the youth culture. The man with the chalk in his hand feels like the man in the hut must have felt when he saw Napolean coming from one direction and Wellington from the other. He doesn't know how the battle will go, but he knows what will happen to him.

In their intellectual ghetto, the professors long ago developed means of enduring the pressures of the autosystems—both internal and external. The college, as an autosystem, tries to subordinate everything else to its own steady state as it produces and totals credit units. The leading autosystems—especially the state—have sought to limit impractical intellectual activity and academic freedom. These pressures from the registrar's office and the State Capitol are familiar, and are dealt with through a combination of compromise, passive resistance, and subterfuge.

Students have traditionally been mere raw material for the college; not the highest grade ore, perhaps, but malleable. However, as youth has come to view the academy as the least objectionable corner of an objectionable society, they have begun to agitate for changes.

Student Demands

The academy has regarded its raw material with a benevolent paternalism. The academician is accustomed to viewing himself as a friend of youth who understands youth's problems. As students demand changes he finds himself under attack from an unexpected and painful direction. His defenses have been developed to cope with the registrar and the state legislature, not with the student body.

Student demands raise new controversies which are of critical importance in the future of the college. As Galbraith suggests, however, the new controversies are too strange and too urgent to lend themselves to the comfortable pattern of routine argument. Like a couple in a disintegrating marriage, the student and the professor find themselves alternating between silent struggle and acrimonious dispute without understanding the real issues which divide them. Such understanding may come only years later when the issues, like the marriage, have long been resolved.*

On the surface, the students are voicing a variety of specific demands. One of them is for "student power."† This is an appealing slogan, but of dubious practicality. In a large university there are likely to be 1,000 faculty members and 20,000 students. In recent years some idealistic administrators have attempted to pass power to

---

* Of course the students are hardly unanimous in their pressures. Many remain docile and apparently content with the status quo. And some, budding intellectuals and faculty members themselves, defend the status quo. But there is nonetheless a surprisingly pervasive trend in the pressures exerted by the students who press for change.

† The idea of student power is not new. In the small universities which existed in the Middle Ages, students had greater power than the faculties. Students could fine faculty for tardy or dull lectures and could dismiss faculty for repeated offenses; whereas the faculty had little power to discipline or dismiss students. But student power has been conspicuously lacking in recent academic history. As a matter of fact, colleges have been extremely authoritarian structures in which even faculty power is a recent innovation.

the faculty, and have found the procedural problems to be enormous. Meaningful faculty power must deeply involve the faculty in the making of decisions. This entails a vast multiplication of committees, and an enormous commitment of faculty time and energy to generate democratically the decisions which were once made rapidly by autocratic administrators. To pass power meaningfully to 20,000 students would require an awesome bureaucratic apparatus, and would impose great demands on the time and energy of students. It seems doubtful that this is what the students really want. I believe that what they want is change, and since they are not getting all of the changes they want, they call for the power to make the changes themselves. But it is change, not power, that they are seeking.

What changes do the students want? A prominent one is that there be less emphasis on competition. Certainly our society has stressed competition excessively, and this excess has been apparent in our colleges. For example, curve grading can become a Roman arena in which students fight each other for survival.* But it is one thing to admit that competition can become excessive or even absurd, and another thing to demand that it be eliminated altogether. No one calls for the elimination of competition in sports. Athletes compete to see who can achieve greater feats with their bodies and seem to enjoy it. It is claimed that the greatest runners cannot run at their best without a near rival to pace them. But although competition of the mind can be just as challenging as competition of the body, it has fallen into disrepute. Undoubtedly this is because grades have been overemphasized until intellectual competition lost the camaraderie and sense of sport which still characterizes some physical competition. But it is the overemphasis and abuse of intellectual competition which is at fault, not competition itself. Behind all the rationalizations of the students, one hears a note of something that resembles laziness.

A related demand is for a complete end to grading. Grades, it is

---

* The story is told of an advanced mathematics class at a great university. The class had nine students enrolled in it, and the professor announced that he graded on a strict curve, and gave 10 percent Fs. The students looked at each other aghast realizing that no matter how hard they all worked, one of them would fail, and that there would come to be the most desperate kind of competition among them. However, on the second day of class they appeared with happy smiles; they had taken up a collection and paid the fees for a tenth student. A skid row derelict now sat comfortably in the front row prepared to receive the F.

contended, serve no real function, do not accurately measure student achievement, and distract enormous amounts of student and faculty time from the process of learning. There is considerable justification for these criticisms. But the contention that the elimination of grades would facilitate the educational process seems doubtful at best.

Nothing happens in a college that cannot happen elsewhere—if the individual is sufficiently motivated. And some, indeed, have preferred to carry on their intellectual activities away from the pressures and constraints of academia. Eric Hoffer is a prime example. But the individual who chooses college is seeking help in his quest. One of the kinds of help which he seeks (consciously or not) is in overcoming his human tendency to procrastinate. The student says, in effect, "I am a normal human being who has a tendency to put things off if he can get away with it. But I really want to do some reading, thinking, and writing. At college, certain pressures will help keep me moving in the direction I have chosen to go. That is partly why I have come to college."

Grades are one of the goads with which the instructor prods the student along the path. It is clear that the student does not want the instructor to use the goad too often or too harshly; but it is by no means certain that he does not want it used at all. The experience in ungraded courses and programs has been that the average students, who wanted to get something from the program but weren't exceptionally motivated, emerged with a sense of frustration. They felt that they did not get as much out of the experience as they would have liked. And it is hardly fair to berate them for lack of self-discipline; most of the faculty members would not have finished the reading by a given date if they had not had to discuss it in class.

Considerable reform of the grading system is clearly needed, and grades need to be understood by both students and faculty as nothing more than a means of discouraging procrastination and of helping the student to judge his individual rate of progress. But the complete elimination of grades would hardly be the unmixed blessing which it might initially seem.

Another student demand is for "relevance." Once again, the slogan is beautiful; who could doubt that college should become relevant? But on closer examination, some problems emerge. To be "relevant" from the student viewpoint, the course must *appear* relevant to the student. Therefore in practice, relevance is determined by the student's familiarity with the course content. It is for this reason that courses which have been designed to be "relevant" tend to degenerate into mere "rap sessions" where students exchange opinions which they had already developed when they entered the course. Such courses end in boredom; the students quickly lose interest in what one described as "exchanges of ignorance."

It is in the very nature of education that a course should be irrelevant to the student at the outset; it should confront him with problems which have not previously concerned him, with conceptual tools which he has not previously grasped, and with areas of thought which he has not pursued. Until the individual comes to recognize the problem, he has no interest in the answer. The task is not to make the curriculum over in the image of the student, but to make the student over in the image of the curriculum. It is not relevance, but meaningfulness and importance which matter, and the student really cannot judge this until he has encountered the curriculum. It is the recent graduate, not the lower-classman, who is in the best position to judge the "relevance" of the curriculum.

Another demand is that education become more personal. One student told me that she was incapable of learning from anyone with whom she was not personally involved. This statement so surprised me that I forgot to inquire just what she meant by "personally involved." Certainly impersonality has no intrinsic merits, and there is far too much of it in modern society. But how personal does an intellectual association have to be? Two people may have an intense intellectual association across thousands of miles, and even across time. My long-term arguments with Sigmund Freud and Karl Marx have been intensely meaningful to me; yet both were long dead when our association began. To insist that intellectual activity always be personal is to cut oneself off from a great deal of possible stimulation.

Within the college there are enormous budgetary problems in making every educational association intimate. But even with an unlimited budget, there can be only a handful of truly great teachers on every campus. To limit their activities to those which can be conducted within an intimate framework is to deprive the vast majority of students of any contact with them. Is it always better to sit in a class of ten with a mediocre instructor than to endure a class of a thousand with a truly great one?

Yet all of the student demands have merit, and the colleges have made many concessions. Students are placed on faculty committees as full voting members. Grade curves rise, curve grading is reduced or eliminated, and pass-fail grading is expanded. New courses and new programs devoted to current issues are established: ethnic studies, environmental studies, and so on. Academic credit is given for off-campus activities. Huge classes are curtailed, and teaching is no longer so subordinated to research in the evaluation of faculty. Experimental programs multiply in which there is more intimate contact between students and faculty.

The Cat Out of the Bag

It was while I was teaching in one such experimental program that a student let the cat out of the bag. I was puzzled why, in a program specifically designed to meet student criticisms and demands, the students were not happy and enthusiastic. If anything, they seemed more restless than in the regular program.

The experimental program was very flexible. Some 20 students were assigned to a professor for the semester; they were his full-time load, and their work with him was normally their entire program. The semester had a general topic assigned to it, and a reading list. Beyond that, the instructor and the students were free to proceed in whatever way they decided was best.

A particular young lady was very upset with me. She wanted to leave campus for the semester, go off to the mountains and commune with nature and learn to relate to people. She felt that doing these things would be much more important to her development just then than remaining on campus, reading the books, writing her papers, and attending our tutorial conferences and seminars. I was inclined to agree with her, and was encouraging her to drop out of school for now and "do her thing." This suggestion made her furious. "You are such a fake!" she said. "You claim this program is designed to fit student needs. You admit it would be good for me to get away from campus for a while. And then you refuse to let me go without dropping out of school!" In vain I argued that the college was only designed to fill her intellectual needs, if any, and that if she wanted to do other things she could hardly expect college credit for them. "You know my mother won't support me if I drop out of school!" she said.

As she stalked out of my office, I realized what was really going on. *What she wanted was for the college to become a place where she could do her thing; and her thing did not include intellectual activity!* She wanted the college for her own ghetto; in order to make it over to fit her, she needed to remove its academic content.

This student was extreme, but the trend is pervasive. Finding college more comfortable than the rest of society, youth wants to make it over in the image of the youth culture, and the youth culture is not intellectual. They may be willing to engage in intellectual activity if it is required in order to remain on campus, and may come to enjoy it, but they will resist it initially if they can.

And so the intellectuals, be they students or faculty, find themselves having to defend their traditional ghetto from an internal attack. They are confused by the attack, and hope to appease it by making compromises on specific issues. But such compromises satisfy no one. The controversy is simply whether the ghetto is to be a home for the intellectuals, or for the adherents of the youth culture.

The Millstones

As the colleges compromise with the demands of the youth culture, the leading autosystems become increasingly uneasy. The government comes to see the college as a center for exotic dress, drugs, sex, pacifism, and downright subversion. The result is a second invasion of the campus, this time by the government. The federal government enters with funds and programs, with undercover agents, and sometimes with troops. State officials intervene directly on campus, closing programs, firing professors, and cutting budgets. These governmental invasions superficially resemble the traditional attack on academic freedom, and the college tends to respond to them as if that was all they were. It tries to lie low and wait for the storm to pass. But it is more serious than the usual wave of repression. The autosystems feel threatened by the youth culture; they see the college as its accomplice, if not as its cause. The attack is in dead earnest.

Probably few modern Americans have seen actual millstones in operation. They are large circular slabs of stone. The lower one is generally fixed, and the upper one rotates. Grain is poured through a hole in the upper stone; it is caught by the lower stone, dragged between them, and pulverized.

Between the invasion of the youth culture and the invasion of the state, the college is caught between two millstones. The traditional retreat where the intellectual students and faculty could play their mental games in peace is in real danger of being pulverized.

Holding the Fort

Are there any solutions? The short-run solution would seem to be to discourage people from going to college who are not interested in intellectual activity. The best way to do this would be to provide them with an alternative haven which was at least as attractive. If there is a draft, it would have the same degree of draft immunity as college. If loans are available to the young, they would have to be available in the new haven as easily as in college. Parents would have to be as accepting of having their children in the new haven as in college, and as willing to contribute to their support there. The young people themselves would have to regard the new haven as being as legitimate a place to be as college.

In other words, it would be necessary to quit penalizing people for leaving college and to give them some other place to go. The communes will provide such a haven for some; they could provide a haven for many more if communes were encouraged by the larger society. Unfortunately such encouragement seems unlikely; the communes themselves are under attack as havens of the youth culture.

Some reduction in the number of anti-intellectual youths who are forced into college may in fact now be occurring, but it seems unlikely that the invasion will be ended. And therefore the invasion of governmental forces will also continue. In the long run, the only possible solution to the problem of the colleges involves the resolution of the conflict between the young and the autosystems. And such a resolution seems likely to occur in only one of two ways: youth must be turned into servo-men who docilely accept the dictates and the values of the autosystems, or the autosystems must be brought under control and forced to serve human ends. The crisis on the college campuses is merely a manifestation of the pervasive crisis in modern society.

Part Nine: The Means of Change

31   Friends of the Autosystem

Those of us who seek change would do well to encourage the virtues of middle Americans to prevail over their vices in the coming crisis. This entails giving dignity to them as human beings rather than pounding on them with sociological clichés. It involves understanding why they are where they are, and what might lead them to be somewhere else.

Despite everything, the majority of Americans still lend support to the autosystems and fear and distrust those who press for change. This majority makes up middle America—usually portrayed as something out of a Sinclair Lewis novel: seeped in hypocrisy, smug, shallow, and vicious. This image is as mythical as the image which many middle Americans have of youth—unwashed weirdos living a life of orgiastic sex under the influence of assorted drugs, taking occasional time out to bomb the Bank of America.

Some Americans do reveal characteristics of the middle American stereotype, just as some youth show characteristics of the youth stereotype. But they show these characteristics as living human beings. I recall an evening spent in middle America. We dined in the family station wagon on McDonald's hamburgers and fries. Back home we watched television and discussed the shows and characters. The children believed in Santa Claus, and their parents believed in keeping Christ in Christmas. The wife had her domain in the kitchen and the husband in the garage. National and international affairs played no role in their lives, and they passively accepted the views and conclusions which were expressed on television. I looked with all my psychological and sociological tools for signs of tarnish in their purity and optimism—for cracks in the picture window or in their marriage, for telltale traces of neurosis and rebellion in their children. Of course I found some of what I was looking for, but on the whole I had to admit that they were probably just about as happy, and just about as unhappy, as the sophisticated and committed people I knew. They were living real lives reasonably adapted to where they were. If there was more to life than they were finding, and if their lives lend passive support to genocide in Asia and racism in America, the problem derived from where they were. They would change if and when their experiences changed. But they had to be included in humanity just as they were now. They had accepted me, a bearded radical professor who arrived driving an antique car, into the human race. Those of us who knew the score were going to have to do at least as well.

The Apathetic

There are many reasons why a majority of Americans support the system. Foremost among these is simple apathy. The average individual in any country is usually nonpolitical for the sensible reason that political issues usually have little *apparent* relation to his daily life. He lives within the system, but his attention is on his direct experiences, not on the framework within which these experiences occur.*

Most individuals, therefore, give apathetic support to the system until it begins to fall apart. Such apathy is pervasive, but unstable. Seven percent unemployment is just another boring statistic on the television news as one waits for the sports report until one finds oneself in that seven percent. Much of the support which the American autosystems now enjoy will disappear rapidly as the problems come home to roost at the individual level.

The Uninformed

Along with apathy, lack of information is a major source of support for the autosystems. Beliefs tend to persevere unless or until they are contradicted. To take a nonpolitical example, most Americans believe that the world is round for exactly the same reasons that their

---

* In Europe I was impressed with how little the life and attitudes of the average Spaniard differed from those of the average Yugoslavian. Both were concerned with getting by, thought about what they would have for dinner, wondered if their wives were still mad at them, and thought more about the pretty girl who walked by than about the government. Yet Spain suffered under a decaying fascist dictatorship and Yugoslavia had a government dedicated to democracy and socialism. The Spaniard may have ignored his government because he felt it was hopeless, and the Yugoslav because he trusted it to look out for his welfare, but both were politically apathetic.

ancestors believed that it was flat: they have been told the shape of the world by persons they trust, and this shape corresponds well to their own experience as travelers and as viewers of photos of the earth taken from the moon. If one denied the roundness of the world, few would become angry, threatened, or upset. At the most, they would be incredulous. But were it possible to present convincing evidence that the world was, say, octagonal, they could accept this view without undue psychic strain. Their belief that the world is round is not functional in their personalities, but merely a part of the heritage they have uncritically accepted. Much of the loyalty to the autosystems in middle America derives from such uncritical beliefs. Such loyalty is also unstable if the individual's uncritical assumptions are contradicted by new direct experiences.

The Servo-Men

But for some, the support of the autosystems is less passive. There are those who proclaim that they love the system. I am willing to admit this as a theoretical possibility, but I suspect real love for the system is rare. An arrangement of statuses, communication channels, information storage and retrieval systems, and so on is not a very suitable love object. Most who proclaim their love for the system do so in an angry and defensive way which suggests motivations other than simple affection.

What motivations lead to proclamations of love for the system? For a few, vested interests may play a role. Certainly a large number of Americans *believe* that they have a vested interest in the system. The fourth assistant to the second vice-president is likely to feel a strong stake in the welfare of the corporation if he thinks he may soon be the third assistant. Throughout American society, individuals are striving for rewards which the system has defined for them. But promotion, wealth, and power are not in and of themselves basic human needs. This is most likely to be seen clearly by those at the top who have little more to expect from the system, and therefore see the limitations of the rewards they have won.* But those in the middle

---

* Thus the *Wall Street Journal* reports a significant trend for individuals to abandon careers in mid-life, not because they have failed, but because they have succeeded. The $50,000 a year executive who takes a $10,000 a year job as a teacher obviously does so because he is seeking other rewards than those which the business world defined for him. See "A Way Out," *Wall Street Journal,* February 18, 1970, p. 1.

level can always hope that the next promotion, the next degree, or the next million will finally fulfill them. One becomes a servo-man by accepting the rewards held out by the system as the goal of life. But if the servo-man gets a glimpse of what he really wants, he may, like Gauguin, desert the system quite abruptly.

The Fearful

Others base their loyalty to the system more on fear than on hope. For them, any change in the system threatens to open a Pandora's Box; among them the call for law and order is most pronounced, and anarchy is just another word for pillage, rape, and murder.

Many of the fears of this group result from simple projection. Those who fear relaxation of control over human behavior are the very people who are most frightened by their inner capacity for violence and deviance. Unable to face their own violent potential, they project it onto others. They then see violence everywhere, and call for rigid controls lest it engulf them. Similarly, those who see a rapist behind every lamp post know exactly what they are looking for. The enormous public interest in a torture murder or sex crime reveals the intensity of the psychological involvement of the American in assault and sexual violence. The system has distorted their own minds into something they cannot cope with, and they call upon the system to protect them from it.*

Those whose loyalty to the system is based on fear may be more firmly wedded to it than those whose loyalty is based on apathy, ignorance, or hope of reward. Fortunately, fear may be somewhat less significant in the loyalty of most middle Americans than the other factors.

---

* One very interesting research project found that there was an inverse correlation between concern over crime in the streets, and the crime rate of the neighborhood in which the individual lived. Those who lived in areas where crime was most unlikely were the most terrified by it. People in high crime neighborhoods had of necessity adapted to an undesirable situation. No doubt they feared crime, but their fear was based on reality. The people in the low crime areas were frightened by a fantasy which was more frightening than reality, and whose origin was necessarily in their own minds.

Vices and Virtues

The middle American, then, is not irrevocably wedded to the system. He will probably transcend it, if his experiences go beyond their present limits. Whatever the implications of his views on ghettos, youth, and welfare may be, in his personal life he is concerned. The same suburbanite who was willing to have every village in Southeast Asia destroyed by bombing will cry out in horror if his neighbor kicks a dog. And this horror is not as hypocritical as it may seem. He opposes pain when he can visualize it readily, but becomes indifferent in situations which pass his immediate experience. Give this American a few hours in a village which was hit by a napalm strike and his attitudes would be transformed—at least as long as he remained in the village. It is not *what* he is, but *where* he is that is the problem.

Middle America has some significant virtues. It took a visiting Russian to clarify one of them for me. I was helping to chaperone a group of Russians around San Francisco during Goldwater's campaign for the presidency. One of the Russians said he felt Goldwater's following revealed some fundamental virtues in the American character. I suspected that his command of English was defective, but he assured me he meant what he had said. He hardly favored a Goldwater victory, but he felt that Goldwater appealed to a healthy mistrust of the state which Americans retained as a heritage of the frontier. As Goldwater called for a reduction in the role of the federal government, he appealed to this fundamental mistrust of the autosystems.

The sympathy of the middle American for the underdog is proverbial and important. Provided the problem falls within their personal sphere of experience, they can be counted on to show sympathy for the sufferings and losses of others. Of course they may have unlimited sympathy for the mistreated wife next door, and none for the much more mistreated ghetto dweller two miles away. But here as elsewhere the problem is the limited nature of their awareness and experience.

The Middle American also has some significant vices. One, which has already been considered at length, is his tendency to attempt existential cop-outs. He has difficulty in assuming responsibility for himself, his life, and his world. It is easy to understand why this is so, given the pressures and confusions which surround him. But the consequences of the flight from responsibility are frightening. The

Vietnam war was a demonstration of the effects of existential cop-outs on a massive scale.

A second major vice, no doubt related to the first, is a tendency to seek quick and easy solutions to all problems. Once a problem finally obtrudes into his awareness, he tends to demand an immediate solution. He wants a pill for every ache. Thus when a social problem is recognized by the middle American, he demands a culprit to blame, and a law to prevent the culprit from doing it again. This approach leads on the one hand to all sorts of needless and senseless efforts to regulate human behavior, and on the other hand to inaction on the real roots of the problem.

When and if we come to a major crisis and the gauges of the autosystems dip deeply into the yellow and toward the red, the apathetic and indifferent will become temporarily involved. If the vices of the middle American prevail, the call will go out for a culprit to blame for the crisis and a means of punishing this culprit. Some simple, neat solution will be sought, and neat, simple solutions usually seem to involve tightening the control of the autosystems over human lives. The result could very well be a functional fascism in America, whether or not there was an overt fascist movement. Hippies, professors, and blacks could serve as scapegoats to explain the national crisis, and armaments and police power could become the proposed cure.

If, on the other hand, the virtues of the middle American prevail, distrust of the state and sympathy for the underdog might well lead to a stance against the autosystems and for mankind.

Reaching Middle America

Middle America is critical to the outcome of the coming crisis, but it can be a long way to reach. Those of us who seek change must accept the human reality of middle Americans and help them to accept our human reality. The middle American has a strong tendency to deal with issues in terms of personalities. He often needs to associate an idea with an individual to whom he can relate comfortably before he can hear that idea.

During the campus protests against the Cambodian invasion of 1970, I decided that I could make the greatest contribution by going off campus and meeting groups that were frankly hostile to the student protest. Together with two students, I met with a number of such groups. We found that the evenings fell into a fairly predictable pattern. In the first hour, the middle Americans had a great deal which they just had to tell us. There were certain views which they held about which they were somewhat defensive and which therefore they had to express forcefully. Thus they would tell us about the domino theory of communist expansion in Southeast Asia and about the negative effects that violent protest had on our cause. Once these views had been expressed and acknowledged, a second phase ensued in which they sought to determine if we really accepted them as human beings, if we understood the problems they faced, and if we gave dignity to how things appeared from their point of view. Housewives would tell us rather sharply that they really did do a lot of hard work, and businessmen would point out that they were not really stupid clods. Once we had granted the requisite assurances that we recognized their human validity, they reciprocated and accepted us. A third stage immediately began in which our views could finally be discussed. However, by this point it was really unnecessary for us to say anything. They already knew our arguments, and would explain them to each other if we kept quiet and gave them a chance. One 70-year-old retired plasterer, who had bored us with a tedious explanation of the domino theory earlier, shouted down the rest of the group and said: "I'll tell you why these kids riot! It's like the blacks. They've got something important to say and there's no other way that people will listen!" It was quite obvious that the careful arguments which we had prepared on campus were of little significance. They needed to broaden their experience to include us, and when they had done that, they were willing to consider the views which they knew all along we represented. They were not converted yet, but they were somewhat opened.

---

32   Friends of Change

The game has been rigged, and lots of people are up tight about it. Those who never had a chance to win want to have one before the game is changed. It is the winners, and most of all the winner's kids, who are finished with this game and are checking to see what we can do next.

Social movements, those maverick social structures which press for change in the autosystems, fall into two broad groups. One group is fundamentally reformist, wanting to restore or improve the existing order. The other group is revolutionary, wanting to force fundamental changes in that order.

The Reformers

The most prominent example of the reformers are blacks. Perhaps one American in six is black, and with each year black militancy increases. White America is only beginning to acknowledge the full extent of the economic exploitation which the blacks have endured for centuries. But economic exploitation does not entirely explain the black revolt, or the revolt would have occurred when the exploitation was at its greatest. When people are exploited past a certain point, they lack time or energy for rebellion and can only struggle to survive.* Partial amelioration of the black condition has thus contributed to the demand for further amelioration. But there is a more important source of rebellion. When the physical needs are at least minimally satisfied (as they presently are among most Americans including blacks), the psychological needs become more significant factors in motivation. Among the psychological needs, the need for self-acceptance is clearly the most fundamental. And it is this need for self-acceptance which is most prominent in the motivations of the blacks today.

The individual who is regarded as inferior by a group which is psychologically important to him inevitably becomes infected with their prejudice. To a greater or lesser degree, he too comes to regard himself as inferior. Of course, feelings of inferiority do not inevitably

---

* It is when conditions have improved just enough to allow a moment for reflection, and a glimpse of the possibility of further improvements, that the exploited begin to make effective demands for change. This period is often called the "era of rising expectations," and in such an era each improvement in conditions is likely to result in increased demands.

lead to a lack of self-acceptance. Inferiority can be the basis for an acceptable self-image, provided the individual feels that it is acceptable to be inferior—that there are positive elements in being what he is. For example, many women in America still feel inferior to men, and simultaneously are self-accepting of themselves (much to the disgust of some of the leaders of women's liberation). They do not feel that women are equal to men, but they feel that it is good to be a woman, and that they are successful women.*

During the period of most rigid segregation, many blacks presumably felt both inferior and acceptable in somewhat the same way. They felt confident that they were good blacks. But such attitudes only exist in the Deep South where segregation and economic exploitation were coupled with acceptance of blacks so long as they remained in the place assigned to them by the white power structure. As the blacks migrated into the Northern urban areas, they met with very different attitudes. The Northerner lacked the intimate experience with blacks which most Southern-born whites experienced as children. Whereas the Southern white always viewed the black with a mixture of love and hate, of fear and envy, the Northern white viewed the black as simply bad. To the Southern white, both black and white had their legitimate (if unequal) place in the world; to the Northern white, it was unfortunate that blacks existed.

Thus the kind of prejudice which the blacks experienced in the North did not leave the opportunity for self-acceptance that they had known in the South. And thus was created a major source of black nationalism and of the call for black power. Asserting that "black is beautiful," holding counterracist attitudes toward whites, and seizing power are all effective devices for establishing self-acceptance.

But if the black people now tend to reject everything white and to insist on the superiority of their own ways and values, they nevertheless are essentially a reformist force in America. The blacks want to have the barriers which have been arbitrarily placed in their paths torn down so that they have an equal chance to share in the benefits of the social order. But by this very demand they accept, at least

* Of course it is unfortunate that any group is taught to regard itself as inferior. My point is merely that it is less difficult to cope with feelings of inferiority if they are not complicated by the further belief that being inferior is bad.

temporarily, the validity of the goals and values of that order.* The black movement will continue as a reformist movement until the idea that black is bad has been permanently erased from the black's own consciousness. And until that time, it will be unrealistic to look to the black movement for support in making fundamental changes in society. Part of the white dues for past racism is the loss of black partners in the present struggle to bring the white-dominated social structure under control.

The various other liberation movements—women's liberation, gay liberation, and so on—are in many ways similar to the black movement. They too are struggling for equality of opportunity; and even more for an equal opportunity for self-acceptance. Technological advances have rendered sexual differences increasingly unimportant in employment and daily living (consider the fork lift and the nursing bottle). As equality becomes increasingly practical, women find inequality increasingly difficult to accept—while still accepting themselves. Similarly, the homosexual, long victimized by self-castigation, comes to realize the validity of his sexual proclivities, and demands his own right to freedom from prejudice and to equal opportunity for self-acceptance.

All of the liberation movements share the essentially reformist character of the black movement. It is not their destiny, as yet, to challenge the society which has denied them.

The Anglo poor form a group which might have challenged the existing order, but has not done so. In fact, they have traditionally taken a conservative political position. The American dream of lucky success seems to play somewhat the same role for the American poor that the national lotteries play for the poor in many countries. No matter how bad your condition may be, there is always the hope that a miracle will occur.

There is a new group of unemployable middle-class poor. The electronics engineer in California in 1970 at first accepted his unemployment stoically. He lived while he could on his savings and by borrowing. When he found himself driven to the welfare office, he

---

* Some blacks, of course, press for more radical changes; but they do not do so as blacks. Dick Gregory showed the two levels of his own consciousness very clearly when he commented that he would fight to force the equal hiring of blacks in war industries just as hard as he would fight to have the war industries closed forever. In the first instance he spoke as a black, in the second as a radical.

entered in a state of shock. Usually he explained to the intake worker that he was "not a welfare type," that he "wasn't a chiseler like most of your cases." Having swallowed his pride and turned to welfare, his next shock was that it was not the bountiful haven that he had assumed. The maximum allotment for him and his family could not even cover the monthly payment on his house.

But with a few notable exceptions, the middle-class unemployables have not become any more radical than the traditional poor. The potentiality that they might call for fundamental change exists, but there is no guarantee that the changes they would seek would be liberal.

The Revolutionaries

It is among its most favored children that the autosystems find their most revolutionary opposition. There are many reasons why this should be so. These young have simply had different life experiences. For one thing, the philosophies of Dewey in the school and of Spock in the home have contributed to a somewhat lower average level of neurosis among the young.* And any reduction in the average level of neurosis can be expected to result in an increasing demand for the restructuring of undesirable institutional structures.

We are seeing the emergence of a distinctive and vigorous youth culture. It is important to recognize that a youth culture is not a normal feature of a society. Margaret Mead noted that in Samoa, adolescence was regarded as an uninteresting and tranquil interlude between childhood and adulthood.[1] Even in America, as long as youth entered the economy through the family, a youth culture was basically impossible. The farmer's son entered adulthood through gradually increasing his participation in the family farm which one day he would inherit. And the situation of the son of the small merchant or craftsman was essentially the same. But today the child enters the economy through high school or college, and this era of schooling is relatively

---

* This may seem a strange assertion since it is notorious that youth today run from sensitivity sessions to encounter groups, from drugs to diets, and from saints to gurus, trying "to get their heads straight." But this quest may be a symptom of health rather than of illness. One of the prominent characteristics of youth today is that they know they have problems. That is a major advance over their parents who by and large believed in their own sanity. Youth today are busily and sometimes successfully coping with problems their parents have yet to acknowledge.

independent of his family. Moreover, the family can neither guarantee nor withhold his economic future. As the life of the child thus diverges from his family, the opportunity for him to develop a distinctive consciousness increases.[2]

As Marx pointed out, ideology reflects the social structure which it explains and justifies. And as that structure changes, so does the ideology. Yet individuals have a tendency to hold to the views of their youth. Thus, if there is no distinctive youth culture to implant ideological changes in the new generation, ideologies can be passed along long after they have ceased to reflect any social reality. But when there is a youth culture which reflects a separate and partially autonomous stage in life, it is possible for ideological change to enter more rapidly. The real meaning of the "generation gap" is simply that ideological changes occur primarily intergenerationally rather than intragenerationally.

The basic characteristics of the youth culture therefore represent ideological adaptations to a technological and affluent society. For example, the concept of "dropping out" is of considerable relevance in a society where automation is rendering careers somewhat unnecessary and sometimes impossible. Dropping out represents an acceptance of, and an ideological justification for, something that is necessarily happening.*

The ideology of the youth culture is the logical outgrowth of the system even though it brings youth into basic conflict with the system. *Youth seeks the ideals appropriate to the new reality at the expense of the old order.* The Summer of Love in the Haight-Ashbury in 1967 was a pivotal event. To the more conscious participants, this represented nothing less than an attempt to transform society by example. They were trying to make fundamental social changes not by organized revolution, but in an anarchistic way peculiarly appropriate to a society already overorganized. By doing his own thing everyone would demonstrate both the possibility and desirability of

---

* In a similar way, the hedonistic emphasis of the youth culture, and its emphasis on immediate experience rather than deferred gratification, are appropriate to a society which can afford enjoyment and does not need to struggle for what it wants. The emphasis on individual creation and handicrafts represents a useful adaptation to an overly mechanized, button-pushing technology. Even the panhandling and hitchhiking facets of the youth culture are appropriate to a society wherein there is enough to go around, and the mendicant is not a drain on scarce resources.

letting people enjoy the freedom that the technology now made possible.

The Summer of Love ended in tragedy and with a certain loss of innocence. The existing society was not radically transformed by handing its servo-men a flower or a joint. The McCarthy campaign for president and the protest over Cambodia represented experiments with more orthodox approaches to social change. They, too, ended in disillusionment.

Such disillusionment seems to have shattered the youth culture into three segments. One group, seemingly reverting to the pattern of the 1930s, calls for discipline and violent revolution. Another much larger group seems disposed to wait for awhile, hoping that the situation will clarify and provide some opportunity for them to implement their ideals. Any social movement which can give them such an opportunity (as Nader's Raiders did to a select few) will find itself with an amazing quantity of talent and enthusiasm on its hands.

A third group, small but of extreme significance, has launched the commune movement. The communes are becoming unconscious experimental laboratories in which new social forms are tested and publicized. They are antitechnocratic, but they use the benefits of the technocracy such as modern medicine and basic labor-saving machinery.* Their life styles involve far less drain on resources than modern suburban living, and yet may be inherently more satisfying. Instead of totally automated thermostatically controlled gas furnaces, they warm themselves with fires built with wood they cut themselves. But they use chainsaws instead of axes to cut the wood. They are experimenting with tightly knit groups based on a kind of commitment which has not been common since the demise of the extended family. They insist that they are *communes,* not *communities,* and call their groupings "families." This is not mere rhetoric. They are experimenting with meaningful use of leisure time and with the use of creative capacity for its own sake rather than for achievement. They are experimenting with sexual freedom outside such traditional concepts as

---

* One is reminded of Arthur Clark's amazing first novel, *Against the Fall of Night* (New York: Gnome Press, 1953), which portrayed a society millions of years hence called Lys in which people lived a free and out-doors life in woodland shacks, but were sustained by incredible and completely automated machinery hidden underground. They did what they found humanly meaningful for themselves, and had the machines do the rest.

guilt, jealousy, and promiscuity. In brief, they are experimenting with means of using technology to facilitate the experience of human values in profound association with other people, and in meaningful contact with nature. Whatever their specific successes and failures, they are trying to find the way to combine the best elements of the technological society with the best elements of simpler and more humanly controlled societies.

The access of youth to the various media of communication is of extreme importance in transmitting the experience of these communes back to the society at large. Books and records play their role, and so do the older intellectuals. The young have the unencumbered enthusiasm to undertake the new and the relevant; the older intellectuals have the background to interpret the meaning and significance of the experiments.*

---

33   Revolution Revisited

Those who dream of revolution seem to miss the point as widely as those who fear it. Revolutions occur when and if the gauges go into the red, and the old order cannot continue. The issue is not whether to have a revolution. The issue is if the gauges go into the red, what kind of a revolution do we want? It is entirely possible that man's last great chance to conquer society will come in the next decade. But will we have done enough homework to take advantage of it?

A Ten-Letter Word

For most of a century, revolution was unthinkable in this country, so hardly anybody thought about it. Then, in the years following

---

* I sat in my son's commune one night and wondered about the distorting effect of my sociological presence. Then I realized that today it would hardly be an authentic commune unless some social scientist at times propped his boots up before its fire. I realized that I was the essential link between that commune and the students in my classes.

World War II, the subject was brought up for considerable discussion, but not by the discontented. Partly out of paranoia and partly for personal political advantage, revolution was presented as the ultimate no-no; it became a ten-letter word at least two-and-a-half times as bad as any four-letter word. Everyone from a latrine orderly to a laboratory assistant was required to vow solemnly that he did not believe in revolution.

Now the discontented are beginning to speak of revolution. Some are drawn to the idea simply because it was so long forbidden. Others turn to revolution out of frustration. After the failure of the Eugene McCarthy campaign a young woman told me: "We *tried* to do it through an election, and they wouldn't let us. So we'll just *have* to do it through revolution!"

Few Americans know anything about revolution, and almost none have had personal experience in a revolution. Many of the young see revolution as a quick, if desperate, road to social change. They have romantic visions of charging across the White House lawn with drawn revolvers while machine guns stutter in the background. The vast majority of Americans, however, still view revolution as a ten-letter word. To them the essence of revolution is change through violence, and they firmly believe that revolution would result in the destruction of everything worthwhile in America. They see revolution as caused by evil conspirators—grubby, angry, misfit geniuses who infiltrate the local grade school and make bombs in basements. They have vague visions that after a revolution those not executed would walk the streets dragging clanking chains and old grandmothers would be forced to work in whorehouses. But mostly their thinking about revolution is limited to the simple belief that it is some unspecified but ultimate horror. They are glad to see the harshest penalties meted out to anyone who suggests violent social change.

Real Revolution

Some facts about revolution are badly needed; the ideas of the conservative majority are as wide of the mark as are those of the revolutionaries. To begin with, revolution is not an easy means of social change. In most eras, it is simply impossible. Try to imagine a revolution in the United States in 1944—or in 1954 for that matter! Revolutions can occur only under quite special circumstances.

Neither is revolution the end of the world. Most countries have lived through various revolutions of one type or other, and not only have they survived to tell about it, in retrospect they find positive values in their revolutions. Both the excessive optimism regarding revolution, and the excessive fear of it are largely products of the American lack of revolutionary experience.

Revolutionaries and those who fear revolution agree that revolutions are caused by conspirators. But no less an authority than Leon Trotsky assures us that a conspiracy can never produce a revolution unless the course of events has made the revolution inevitable.[1] The conspirator, however, becomes so involved in his activities that he fails to understand the social forces underlying the events he believes he is shaping.

Change of government is not a revolution; the coup d'état by which General B drives out General A only to himself be driven out by General C is only an overthrow. Revolution is not even necessarily violent; revolution has occurred without much more violence than occurs on any usual day. And revolutions have been initiated by duly elected governments.

The essence of a revolution is that a fundamental change is more or less rapidly forced upon a social structure. In theoretical terms, a revolution is the reorganization of a social system which occurs when the balance of forces underlying that system collapses. The revolution reorganizes the social structure on the basis of a new balance of forces. It is a qualitative, not merely a quantitative, change.

Revolution occurs because fundamental change becomes necessary. As a system defends its steady state, it is unable to make a fundamental rearrangement in its structure, even when such change becomes necessary for survival. At the lower levels in a hierarchy, revolutionary change may be forced upon the system by higher levels.* But when fundamental change becomes essential in the leading sectors, there is no higher level to force the ossified system to undertake the necessary changes. Instead, they continue trying to deal with the crisis through superficial reforms until the gauges actually go into the red and they are simply unable to continue any longer. Lenin saw this very clearly when he commented that revolution does not occur so long as the old order *can* continue.[2]

---

* Thus, for example, the federal government forced a vital reorganization of the banks in the 1930s which the banks were too ossified to undertake for themselves.

But when the old order cannot continue, one of two things must happen. Either the social system must entirely disintegrate, or it must change its fundamental structure to create a system which *can* function under current conditions. At this point the people may, if given a chance, elect a leader from outside the system who can proceed with the necessary surgery. More probably, the new leadership must be installed by a display of force because the ossified system will not allow change through existing channels. In some instances, massive violence may be necessary, usually because outside forces have lent support to the old order. But the essence of revolution is the reorganization which creates a social system which can operate under conditions the old system could no longer tolerate.

The actions of the conspirators have rather little to do with the *timing* of the revolution. If the gauges are not in the red, a system can survive any amount of conspiracy (as everyone knows who has participated in an unsuccessful office revolt against an unpopular manager). There are always revolutionaries, but only occasional revolutions.

The major functions of revolutionary organizations are somewhat different than what the revolutionaries—or the reactionaries—usually believe. The movement develops the consciousness, abilities, and solidarity of those who will ultimately direct social changes. Within revolutionary organizations, the embryos of future governments can be seen. When and if the gauges go into the red, these movements are available to initiate action. But despite their own opinions, the revolutionaries have little capacity to push the gauges into the red. And if the gauges go into the red, power will be more or less thrust upon someone.

As in Country X, by the time of the revolution nearly everyone is opposed to the status quo; as it falls apart, few hands reach out to steady it. The actual overthrow of the old government is usually rapid and not particularly bloody (unless there is outside interference). The real struggle comes after the overthrow. Those who were united in opposition to the old order discover they have nothing else in common and that they want very different kinds of changes.

A period of post-revolutionary struggle now follows until one group is able to achieve consistent control and begin the process of reorganization. This period may be longer or shorter, and more or less violent, depending on the situation. It may last a decade, as it did in Mexico from 1910 to 1920, or it may be as short as a few months, as it was in Cuba. Most of the destruction and bloodshed of a revolution occurs during this period. Millions died in Russia, and the economy was devastated. It is clearly desirable that this period be as short as possible.

One factor which shortens the period of post-revolutionary struggle is a popular and charismatic leader—for example, Fidel Castro or Marshal Tito. Such a leader provides a focal point for popular support which would otherwise be scattered among warring factions. The lack of such a leader was prominent in the Mexican revolution.*

But the mere presence of a strong leader is not enough to guarantee a short period of post-revolutionary struggle. Lenin had as much charisma as Castro or Tito. The leader must also advocate changes which can create a system whose gauges will stay green in the existing situation. Lenin's (and Stalin's) efforts to force collectivization on a peasantry who wanted only land reform were disastrous misreadings of the potentialities of Russia at that time. Tito and Ho Chi Minh initially made the same mistake, but both recognized it in time to change to policies which were practical under the existing conditions. *Some* system will emerge ultimately, but if the leadership attempts the unacceptable or the impossible, there may be a long period of suffering.

Even in a time of revolution, only certain changes are possible. But the range of possible changes is greater in a time of revolution than in any other time. Since the institutional structure *will* be changed, the probability of any particular change is increased. *It is of extreme importance that the revolutionaries do their homework well before the revolution.* If they focus their attention on the *ends* of their revolution (instead of only on the *means*), they will perform a great service by mapping out the possibilities which will come to exist after the collapse of the present structure. By such mapping they can facilitate a more or less conscious choice of the next era. The revolutionaries need to read, to talk, to argue, and to publish. Through such means, a practical consensus can be approximated among the conscious and the concerned. Such a consensus would enormously shorten the period of post-revolutionary struggle and

---

* Apart from Emiliano Zapata who was and remained a regional, not a national, leader.

make it much more probable that the revolution would make worthwhile changes.

The Gauges in the United States

What are the prospects for an American revolution? At the moment of this writing they are nil; the system is functioning, and the gauges are out of the red. But what about the future? If the gauges of one of the leading autosystems move into the red, revolutionary change will become not possible but inevitable. Is this likely to happen? It may. The autosystem which seems weakest at present is the economy. Automation is destroying the distributive system, and while specific predictions are difficult, there seems to be a significant probability of a major economic collapse before, say, 1980. Such a collapse will be forestalled by every means available *within* the system, so if it comes at all the system will have no further cures to try. Of the three scenarios we imagined in Chapter 17, one involved considerable violence, and two (including the most probable) involved only minor violence. But all involved a fundamental change in the economic institution and hence sweeping changes in all other sectors as well.

An American revolution might be achieved by election, although the remaining servo-men would probably attempt to overthrow such an electoral victory. Or the revolution might occur when elections had been suspended and would thus necessarily involve violent seizure of power. *In either case the actual violence and destruction might be minimal, provided the revolutionary homework had been well done and had established exciting and practical blueprints to show to the apathetic as they awakened and demanded change.*

Tightening and Loosening

It is possible we are closer to a revolution than we dream, but there is no inherent magic in revolution. Few revolutions have achieved much of what was hoped of them, or even much of what they might reasonably have achieved. Usually revolutions have ended by creating another system, which, while perhaps an improvement over the old, soon began oppressing humanity in its own way.

The tendency to think in the traditional terms of left and right may be a big obstacle to a *useful* revolution in this country. These terms are meaningful in underdeveloped countries such as Country X; when the problem is land reform, the issues are clear cut. But when the problem is alienation and automation, the issues are clouded.* The Soviet Union is left, and the United States is right; but what choice shall we make between them in the coming crisis? Left governments have been just as oppressive as right governments, and there seems to be little point in wasting a revolution trying to turn the United States into a Soviet Union or vice versa. The issues which confront the people of the advanced countries are fundamentally different. The distinction between "tightening" and "loosening" may be much more meaningful for us than right and left.

Thus there are those who stand for tightening—for increasing the control of systems over human lives, for developing autosystems at the expense of autonomy. Some of these are on the left, and some are on the right; the implications of their policies are much the same. Ultimately the tighteners seek a situation in which everything not required is forbidden, and everything not forbidden is required. In contrast, there are those who stand for loosening—for the development of human autonomy at the expense of the efficiency and stability of the autosystems. There are abundant historical examples to guide our thinking about left- and right-wing policies. But there is nearly a total lack of precedents for the loosening revolution which is needed in the technologically advanced countries.

Assigning the Homework

I am arguing that the fundamental task of the American revolutionary today is not to plan how to surround the White House with tanks or how to induce the Marine Corps to attack the Army. The revolutionary is largely wasting his time learning how to blow up power poles. The urgent task is to devise means of using a revolution-

---

* When I had been living for some months in a peasant village, my thinking was very different than it is now. I remember writing to a friend that the only possible solution to present problems lay on the left. And my friend wrote back, "Fine! But which way is left?" And standing on the dusty road I crumpled his letter in anger for it seemed cheap sophistry. I knew perfectly well which way left was: left meant giving land to the villagers, and right meant keeping it from them. It was that simple. But when my first wave of anger had passed I remembered that there were no peasants back in the United States, and that my simple definitions of right and left were meaningless there.

ary situation, if and when one comes along, to achieve a loosening effect on society. This approach is opposite to traditional revolutionary thinking which stresses organization, discipline, and control as its objective.

Now is the period in which the homework must be done for such a revolution, and this book represents my efforts to contribute to that homework. If we do our homework well, we may not only bring off the next revolutionary change with minimal bloodshed and suffering, but we may also participate in the historical turning point wherein humanity began to conquer the social system which had been running amuck so long.

---

34   Insistent Humanism

Men have sought utopia by attempting to design an ideal society. But any social structure will ultimately generate its own interests and will oppress humanity in order to pursue them—unless men refuse to allow such oppression. Thus, building utopia is, primarily, a matter of establishing and maintaining autonomous human control over the social system. To conquer society, humanism must become insistent.

A Bevy of Futures

From the perspective of the present we can easily imagine at least four unpleasant futures. Our technological society may destroy itself through war, pollution, or a combination of the two. It is easy to accept Nevil Shute's prophecy in *On The Beach*[1] that the last remnants of humanity may await certain death from the radiation created by a futile nuclear war. Or, if the destruction were less than total, war or the destruction of resources could easily force the abandonment of industrial societies and a reversion to an agrarian society along the lines of traditional China. Such a reversion would be in line with Harrison Brown's prediction in *The Challenge of Man's Future*[2] that industrial society will destroy itself and that humanity will find it impossible to industrialize a second time. A reversion to an agrarian society is certainly preferable to annihilation, but the lot of the man in the hut was not altogether enviable.

If the autosystems do not thus destroy themselves, they seem likely to perfect their control over humanity. It is easy to imagine a vicious and all-powerful autosystem such as George Orwell described in *1984*.[3] But it may be even easier to imagine a benevolent but all-powerful autosystem such as Huxley portrayed in *Brave New World*,[4] wherein men are reduced to ant-like automatons beguiled by infantile pleasures. Whether the human anthill is vicious or benevolent, humanity loses out.

Yet the very plausibility of these unpleasant futures may help us to avoid them. They are all consequences of the actions of unrestrained autosystems, and there is a healthy mistrust of social systems in the air today. The technological society, by providing education, affluence, and leisure, seems to have weakened the loyalty of its human components. Moreover, if the potential crisis in the social structure materializes, men will have a chance to make revolutionary changes.

A Philosophy

Unfortunately, there is no permanent solution to the problem of autosystems; the only solution is permanent vigilance. And for men to maintain such vigilance, it is not enough that they understand the origins and nature of their conflict with the social order. Such understanding is essential. But they must also see the meaning and purpose of their lives in distinctly human terms. They must be able to evaluate their lives in terms of their real needs, not in the arbitrary definitions of a social order.* In short, they must have a philosophy in terms of which they can accept or reject the trends they observe in their society. I like to think of such a philosophy as "insistent humanism":

---

* Some will argue that since man is socialized in society, he in fact needs what he has learned to need. Such radical relativism is simply untrue. Man's physical needs are largely determined by biology, and his psychological needs are largely determined by the process (not the content) of socialization. (See *The Adjusted American* [New York: Harper & Row, Publishers, 1966], chapter 3.) Humanistically, the society is good insofar as it fulfills these needs, and bad insofar as it does not. Even with those needs that are entirely learned, it is possible to judge how well the social order fulfills the needs which it has created, and whether those needs clash with more fundamental facets of man.

humanism because it is based on the universalities of the human condition rather than on the specifics of a social system, and *insistent* because it must be continually asserted to counteract the indoctrinating effects of the autosystems. The core of insistent humanism can be expressed very simply: *in the long run, people matter and systems per se do not.*

In order to arrive at a real humanism, men must learn to affirm themselves and their natures. Such affirmation involves a number of specific points.

1. *Saying Yes to Life.* Nietzsche is probably one of the most misunderstood modern philosophers,* but his fundamental message is crucial. He demanded that mankind learn to say yes to life. In *Thus Spake Zarathustra,* the prophet travels through loneliness, ambiguity, temptation, and betrayal, but he is able to affirm them all, to choose them all. "For the game of creation, my brothers, a sacred 'yes' is needed; the spirit now wills his own will, and he who had been lost to the world now conquers his own world." [5] And again: "Only where the state ends, there begins the human being who is not superfluous." [6] This is humanism at its purest.

2. *Keeping Good Faith.* Jean-Paul Sartre's concept of "good faith" is in some ways an extension of Nietzsche's "Yes to life." Sartre recognizes that men are often tempted to turn from an affirmation of the human situation into what he terms "bad faith" and what I have termed "existential cop-outs." By refusing to assume responsibility for their own existence, and by attributing to their lives external obstacles, commitments, or dogmas, they attempt to evade their humanness. To live in good faith is to affirm all the pain and ambiguity of life as well as all its joy and exultation, to "dig" it all and to accept responsibility for it all. The commitment to maintain good faith is an essential element in any truly human set of values.†

3. *Autonomy.* In order to be able to live in good faith, the

---

* The educated individual usually vaguely recalls from his history of philosophy only that Nietzsche was a forerunner of fascism, and that he died insane. The former is false, the latter irrelevant. Until disease destroyed his mind, he was scrupulously sane.

† One curiosity of recent years had been the appeal of Ayn Rand's novels to many people who are repelled by her social and economic stance somewhere to the right of Daddy Warbucks. I believe that the secret of her appeal is that her heroes do live in good faith and accept responsibility for themselves and their world. (This is a rarity among the antiheroes of modern literature.) And in so doing, they find Nietzsche's joyous affirmation of life. See especially her *Atlas Shrugged* (New York: New American Library, 1960).

individual must know how to choose his behavior in the light of a real understanding of his needs. A man can hardly lead a joyously affirming life if he misunderstands what he is seeking. Yet the present society provides the individual with a poor understanding of his psychological needs, and many of the behaviors which he learns lead away from fulfillment rather than toward it. As a result, enormous amounts of energy are wasted, and enormous frustration is engendered. But the man who has been adjusted to his social system cannot but conform to the pattern, however unrewarding, just as his anomic brother cannot but rebel against it, even when rebellion is needless. The autonomous man who understands his needs and the ways in which they can be fulfilled can choose the best and leave the rest out of his social heritage. He, alone, is able to lead a fully human life.[7]

Moreover, the autonomous individual is largely immune to manipulation. Advertising—political or commercial—promises to reduce social unacceptability or increase social acceptability so the individual can fulfill his "need" to be liked and admired by others. The individual who has learned to pursue self-acceptance directly, instead of seeking it indirectly through popularity, is not easily forced to use deodorant X, to drink brand Y, or to vote for candidate Z.[8]

4. *Sexuality.*   Despite all the talk about enlightenment and the sexual revolution, America remains a profoundly antisexual culture. Insistent humanism must affirm the fundamentally sexual nature of men and women. A great advantage of technocratic society is that it can free human energies from productive tasks and make them available for sexuality in all its overt and covert manifestations. But at present, enormous amounts of this available energy are wasted in inhibitions, repressions, fantasies, and discussions.

Moreover, much of the sexual activity which does occur is so scheduled, sanitized, and rationalized, that it becomes fundamentally antihuman. This point is pathetically illustrated by a device advertised in many catalogs of household gadgets. It consists of two little night lights, either one of which can be plugged into a handy electric outlet. One of them lights up to say "Not Tonight, Please" and the other lights up to say "Tonight's the Night."

To be human, we must recapture our sexuality from the constraints within which the social system has channeled it; we must make real what is now only fantasy.

5. *Sensuality.*   Shielded by their technology from the world and by learned inhibitions from their experience, Americans are an

amazingly unsensuous people. They have to take sensitivity training merely to learn the sensations of running their fingers over different types of materials. Probably one of the reasons for the great popularity of marijuana is that it seems to blot out more complex trains of thought and leave the mind free to rediscover the rich data supplied to the brain by the senses.

Insistent humanism necessarily opposes the repression of sensuality involved in the constant strictures of "don't touch," "don't get it on your hands," "don't put that in your mouth," "that's a bad smell," "that feels icky," and so on, endlessly. It supports the cultivation of all the senses. The sense of touch can probably provide much more human fulfillment than the average promotion, as men who learn to disentangle their values from those of the social system come to realize. And the man with a rich sexual and sensual life finds it much easier to retain his autonomy.

6. *Communication.*   Insistent humanism requires open channels of communication between human beings. I am mindful of Tom Lehrer's complaint regarding those who talk constantly about their inability to communicate; he suggested that the least those who cannot communicate can do is to shut up! But there *is* a great lack of communication among Americans. In part, since they have learned to misunderstand themselves, they can hardly communicate to others what they themselves do not know. But there are also an enormous number of taboos which complicate communication. To communicate we use many levels—the words chosen, their intonation and cadence, the body language as we speak, the circumstances in which we choose to speak, and the things we leave unsaid. Thus, depending on all these factors, the phrase, "Come and see me," can mean anything from an offer of hospitality, a sexual solicitation, or even a curt dismissal of the other person. It is no wonder that the messages often come through garbled. To grasp the extent of our socially sanctioned hypocrisy, imagine that a freak virus sweeps through the nation which leaves us telepathic and unable to prevent the direct and literal communication of what is in our conscious minds. Imagine a scenario of life under those conditions! Yet real humanism demands precisely such real communication.

7. *Self-Utilization.*   Insistent humanism necessarily emphasizes the creative use of all capacities. But it must also stress the separation of creativity from the cultural concept of achievement. One of the tragedies of American culture is that the adult is convinced

that he should not do anything that he cannot do well. Give an adult paints and his response will usually be, "But I can't paint!" The child looks at paints and yells: "Hey, gimme those!" He knows he can paint, and he will paint: the paper, the wall, and the dog if he can catch it.* Within broad limits, everyone can do everything—and should.

8. *Inaction.*   Insistent humanism must also help people to avoid becoming so overcommitted that there is no time for doing nothing. Of course to do nothing for an extended period is unhuman, but so is turning every minute to some distinct end. Recently I decided to eat out because it was quite late and I didn't want to take time to shop, cook, and do the dishes—I had writing to do that evening. The nearest place for a quick meal was a beer and sandwich joint where students and street people congregate. As I ate, I was enviously impressed with all the people who somehow had time merely to sit and do nothing. And through that envy I realized just how hungry I was just then for time in which to do nothing. I had again violated my own humanity by overcommitting myself. To be really human there must be time just to *be*.

9. *The Categorical Imperative.*   Insistent humanism must always keep the individual as its central concern. Immanuel Kant formulated what he called the "categorical imperative" which he felt must lie at the heart of any ethical system: *Treat every human being, including yourself, as an end in itself and not as means.* Kant had in mind that this dictum should govern interpersonal relationships, and it should. But it is even more urgent to force the autosystems to treat human beings only as ends in themselves and never as means. The autosystems necessarily regard the human components within them as a means to the fulfillment of the system's functions—to the military, the individual soldier is the means to win a battle. Humanity must recognize this inherent tendency, and guard against it. *Men must treat themselves and each other as ends and never as means, and they must treat their society only as a means and never as an end. And they*

---

* Several years ago a student loaned me a painting which she had done in response to my encouragement. Objectively, it was an unattractive overlay of many colors which in blurred confusion tended to merge into mud brown. She explained that for years she had wanted to do a painting, but had been afraid. She had, however, imagined how her painting would look, and this painting looked rather like that. She had no illusions about artistic quality, but she was delighted with having done the painting and paid me the compliment of assuming that I could share her delight.

*must never allow the society to treat men as a means, but only as an end.**

Autonomous Men and Servo-Men

In one sense, the coming struggle will be between the autonomous men and the servo-men; between those who consciously serve their own human interests and those who have been deceived into thinking that they are serving their interests when they are serving those of the autosystems. But in a broader sense, there can be no such conflict. The servo-man has what Marx called a "false consciousness." The autonomous must continually bear in mind that the conflict is not based on a clash of interests between men, but between men and the social order. The servo-man is not the enemy, but only a prisoner, and the struggle is unlikely to end well if he is treated as an enemy. One of the major goals of insistent humanism must be to reach the servo-men and convince them of their own humanity.

And despite the disasters which loom on the horizon, men probably have a better chance of building a utopia today than ever before. The enormous technological forces make possible the true liberation of mankind, and recent events and experiences are showing the necessity—and the possibility—of subordinating these forces to human interests. This chance is also very possibly our last one. There really does seem to be a forced choice between utopia and doomsday.

---

* Thus the current demands for Saturday and night classes, and for year-round school years, are an entirely plausible effort by the autosystems to increase the efficiency of their operations. Students and faculty, after all, are seen simply as a means of producing units of credit and turning them into degrees. The effort by a system to increase efficiency is proper, but only so long as it does not interfere with human values. When it does, it must be laughingly and firmly resisted. The task of the social system is to be efficient so that mankind does not need to be. In terms of insistent humanism, the educational system exists for the convenience of students and professors; they must never be used for the convenience of the system.

Epilogue

On the Proper Use of Sloth, Apathy, and Indolence

Most reformers have demanded that humanity march uphill toward their reforms. And when mankind has refused to do so, the reformers have become embittered or vindictive. But, like water, mankind prefers to flow downhill. Men make good use of water flowing downhill, and they could also make good use of sloth, apathy, and indolence. All that is necessary is to arrange things so that the desired objective lies downhill from mankind.

The Principle

It is generally apparent from the experience of daily living that mankind has a tendency to be slothful, apathetic, and indolent. Yet this tendency is one of the least studied of human traits. Few theorists even mention its existence, and most of those who do, mention it merely to deplore it. Very few have attempted to explain why it exists, and almost no one has accepted it as a valid human quality and attempted to put it to good use.

In speaking of sloth, apathy, and indolence, I am not referring to the tendency to put off doing things that one really does not want to do, nor to situations in which an individual projects his desire to do something onto someone else, and then denies that desire in the confused conviction that he is opposing external pressure. Such situations involve resistance more than indolence.

The tendency I am describing is more akin to the physical principle of inertia. People tend to avoid the avoidable, even though to do so may be to their overall disadvantage. That which can be ignored tends to be ignored. That which can be put off, tends to be put off. The body at rest tends to remain at rest, and it usually takes an act of will to start doing even what one really wants to do.*

---

* To bring the matter down to a very personal level, sloth, apathy, and indolence are what keep you sitting uncomfortably in your chair for twenty

It is said that mule trails often mark potential highway routes because a mule will not climb more than a certain grade with a load on his back. Thus mule trails follow the contours necessary to maintain a uniform grade. Like the mule, man will often avoid moving as long as he can and will tend to seek the easiest path when he finally begins to move.

As we all know, water flows downhill. This flow is automatic, requires no supervision, and can be made to serve useful purposes. Water flows uphill only very reluctantly, and requires continual pressure and supervision to do so. The wise man contrives so that the natural downhill flow will serve his purposes.

Mankind also tends to flow downhill. He flows uphill only with considerable pressure and under continual supervision. The wise reformer will attempt to arrange the situation so that the downhill slope leads to the desired reform. He will attempt to make sloth, apathy, and indolence serve the cause of virtue rather than the cause of vice.

The Uphill Reformers

In the past, most reformers have tried to make humanity flow uphill, have demanded that men take action in order to implement reforms. These efforts are rather like trying to nail Jello to the wall, and the reformers have rapidly become frustrated. To vent this frustration, they have berated humanity. If the reformers were also in positions of power, they have often ended by punishing humanity for its refusal to flow uphill.

Take educational reform as an example. For more than two thousand years, students have shown a disinclination to read Plato on their own. Educators, for whatever reasons, have tended to hold the conviction that students should read Plato. In the past this conflict has usually been resolved by coercion; educators have used devices such as examinations to pressure the students. By applying pressure, they have attempted to regrade the terrain so that it would be easier to read Plato than to suffer the consequences of not having read him. Whatever the limitations of this whole procedure may have been, at least everyone knew where he stood.

The modern educational reformer, however, refuses to accept the

---

minutes after it has become obvious that you really want to get up and go to the bathroom.

principle that students, by and large, avoid reading Plato because it is easier to avoid reading him than it is to read him. The reformer claims that it is not sloth, apathy, and indolence which stand between the student and Plato, but rather a bad curriculum. Of course he has designed an ideal curriculum. The nature of this ideal curriculum is predictable—it is the curriculum the reformer would have most enjoyed when he was an undergraduate. But whatever the specifics of the program may be, the educational reformer is confident that students will flow uphill toward Plato if only he is allowed to institute his program. Sooner or later in these uncertain and experimental times, he is given his chance.

With considerable fanfare the new curriculum is launched. After a year has passed, it is discovered, quite predictably, that the students have not read Plato. They have not read Plato for the simple reason (simple, that is, to anyone but an educational reformer) that they did not want to read Plato, and no one made them. If you really want to make students flow uphill toward Plato it is well to remember to bring your switch. Since the students in his program did not read Plato, the reformer must choose between alternative explanations of why they did not. He can denounce his own curriculum, or he can denounce the students—*something* obviously slipped up. Naturally, he will claim that the program is all right, but that the students are bad. If he has become really hostile, he will simply claim that they are evil and have taken advantage of his permissiveness rather than made use of his program. But if he feels qualms about this type of moralizing, he will contend that the students are bad only because they were ruined by the high schools—which, of course, have not adopted his curriculum.

In the end, many educational reformers become extremely punitive toward the students—who would have read Plato without too much complaint if only someone had made it clear to them that they would have to read Plato. And all too often the students themselves become convinced that they are evil; they contritely defend the curriculum and explain that they were simply unworthy of it.

Or take the matter of birth control. In the past, birth control has required humanity to flow uphill. Sloth, apathy, and indolence resulted in pregnancies. Particularly the older methods of contraception such as diaphragms and condoms required rather complex uphill behavior to have the right equipment ready and installed at the right time. Not at all surprisingly, a large number of failures occurred.

Applications of the Principle

Although everyone knows about sloth, apathy, and indolence, it is somehow impolite to discuss it. I am sure that I will be accused of reneging on my humanism by writing these lines. And to propose to make a constructive use of sloth, apathy, and indolence, may seem almost satanic. But why not? There is nothing inherently evil about inertia. It can prevent rash and precipitous action just as readily as it can impede worthy action; it can serve to protect human values quite as much as it can serve to erode them. The principle itself is neutral; it is the use which is made of it that is critical.

Perhaps because of the mental set against it, most actual applications of the principle have been for dubious purposes. It is important to study them, however, if we are to learn to use the principle for better ends. One of the most successful and familiar applications is the book club. Such a club sends to its members each month a little card which says: "Unless you return the attached card by the day before yesterday, we will send you our deluxe leather bound edition of the complete works of Plato." The book club knows full well that the downhill slope is to lose the card, to discover one has no stamp, or to postpone mailing it. Whole libraries of books have been sold by this application of the principle of sloth, apathy, and indolence.

The federal government also recognized the principle in its collection of income taxes. As income taxes went up and up, something obviously had to be done in order to collect them. First, the tax had become so large that it represented more money than the average individual ever had at one time. Second, severing such a large sum from the individual was likely to create considerable resentment. But by establishing payroll deductions, the downhill slope was arranged on the side of paying the taxes—not only without action by the individual, but almost without his knowledge since he had never handled the money which was extracted from him.*

It was noted earlier that the difficulty of amending the Constitution served to restrain the operation of Putney's Law. It prevents

---

* An added touch of genius was to raise the monthly contributions to a sufficient level so that the average taxpayer overpaid his tax and became eligible for a refund. This refund seems like manna from the skies, and makes filing the return a pleasure. The individual who has had 3,000 dollars extracted from him—much of which was used for questionable purposes—is delighted to receive a 30 dollar refund. The slope is beautifully graded!

the American people from voting away the freedoms essential to their democracy as rapidly as they would like to do. This was deliberately arranged by the Founding Fathers. By making the Constitution difficult to amend, and by guaranteeing the basic freedoms in the first ten amendments, they placed sloth, apathy, and indolence on the side of freedom rather than on the side of the tyranny of the majority.

I once applied the principle in an educational experiment by establishing what was, in effect, a study hall. The students were not tested over the assigned readings, but they were required to come together for three hours every morning in a room where quiet was maintained. They could read, write letters, or stare out of the window. The effect was to drive many students to read Plato out of sheer boredom—and because it was so easy to get around to reading. At the end of the semester, the students reported that they had done more reading than usual, and that they were pleased with themselves. They resented the study hall somewhat, but felt it had been effective.*

Potential Applications of the Principle

There are vast areas awaiting the application of the principle of sloth, apathy, and indolence. In any given situation, we need first to admit that humanity will not readily flow uphill. We must then survey the terrain, and by the arrangement of suitable small dams, canals, and ditches, contrive so that the downhill slope leads to the desired reform. Instead of trying to drive humanity uphill and ending in purges, massacres, and tyranny, humanity flows easily and happily downhill and toward the general welfare. There is no coercion involved at all; we have merely admitted that most people will flow downhill and have taken the responsibility for seeing that there is something worthwhile at the bottom.†

---

* And for myself, it was delightful. For the first time in many years, I had a downhill slope toward getting done the reading that I wanted to do. After all, I had to set a good example. Usually something intrudes just when one sits down to read: the dishes get done, the papers get graded, and the phone gets answered. But the reading is skimped.

† It seems to me that the lack of coercion is the essential element in a moral justification of the use of the principle. As long as the slope was there to begin with, and humanity was flowing down it, it can hardly be called immoral to attempt to arrange the situation so it will result in good, not ill. But if the slope is artificially created, then coercion is involved even though it may be invisible in operation, and the project is of doubtful moral stature. The

For example, we are rapidly approaching the day when safe, permanent and reversible contraceptive devices will be available for women which, once installed, require no further action to prevent fertility. For men, too, contraceptives seem likely to become available which will meet the criteria of safely establishing a reversible sterility which continues until counteracted.*

Given these technological developments, the solution to the population problem is at hand. It merely requires the proper application of the principle. All women (and all men, too, when practical) are to have a permanent but reversible contraceptive installed at puberty. This is done as a social ritual just like getting a driver's license at 16 or registering for the draft at 18.

But what about civil liberties? Isn't this proposal a horrendous violation of personal freedom? Not at all. Anyone who wishes can become a conscientious objector. All that is necessary is to obtain Form A at Office B, file it in triplicate at Office C, submit an explanatory essay and schedule an interview in Office D, and, in due time, pick up the Certificate of Exemption in Office F. *All* such requests should be routinely approved, so that anyone who really wanted to (and, admittedly, had the intelligence to be able to file forms) could remain continuously fertile. But the direction of the downhill slope is reversed. Whereas sloth, apathy, and indolence (not to mention ignorance and stupidity) once led to reproduction, they now favor population control.

Any couple who desired to have a child could have their devices removed by filing the proper papers to receive the necessary prescription. Once again, *all* such requests should be routinely approved. The devices would be reinstalled, of course, as a standard part of the postpartum procedures. Anyone who wanted could have children, but it would require deliberate action to do so.

Another urgent area for application of the principle is in the struggle to create an effective democracy. In Chapter 21 I suggested the present form of democracy made a rather unrealistic demand that the voters anticipate the effects of legislation before it is passed, and evaluate leaders before they are in office. Particularly if things are

---

uphill reformers may pervert the principle by attempting to drag humanity to a spot from which their objectives will lie downhill. Perhaps I did that with my study hall.

* For women, intrauterine devices are already satisfactory for many and should shortly be developed to the point of being satisfactory for all.

going relatively smoothly at the moment of the election, sloth, apathy, and indolence militate against an effective democracy. It is all very well to rail against the citizens who are apathetic, but it might be much more useful to accept their apathy and attempt to deal with it. It is when a law is not working well, or when a leader does something unfortunate, that the people can be expected to become involved in the political process. To achieve a working democracy we would do well to create procedures which would capitalize on the moment of their interest. An example would be my suggestion for electronic voting devices in each residence so that any government could be automatically dismissed when its opposition exceeded 50 percent of the population.

In a similar vein, there would be merit in a constitutional requirement that all legislation (except, of course, the Bill of Rights) should automatically expire after ten years. The legislature would be entirely free to reenact any legislation, but it would require action to keep it on the books. And at least once in each decade, every law would have to be reconsidered. Thus the downhill slope would be for legislation quietly to disappear, and the presumption for anarchy would be institutionalized.

In Chapter 13 I suggested that new technological developments should not automatically be implemented, but should be subjected to an evaluation of their probable effects on mankind and his environment. This is also an application of the principle. At present, it takes a deliberate and difficult action to present a technological development—however disastrous its consequences may be. Modern techniques of strip mining are a tragic case in point.

Biodegradable products which require no action for their disposal are another urgent area in which the principle must be applied. The beer can which reverts to basic elements on exposure to sunlight will be a major step toward rescuing the environment from an unfortunate consequence of sloth, apathy, and indolence. Meanwhile, perhaps, the beer cans should be attached to the factories with rubber bands so that when released their return for recycling is automatic.

Potential applications are endless, but my goal is merely to illustrate the principle. Whenever possible, the wise reformer will arrange things so that the downhill slope leads to an improvement of the human condition. And he would do well to remember that the auto-systems may attempt to regrade the slope while mankind is not looking. In the old days, it was difficult to enter into a war because a

Declaration of War required action by both houses of Congress—with due opportunity for debate, delay, and public involvement. It took effort to go to war. But the autosystem has evaded this restraint by adopting the simple expedient of going to war without a declaration. It now takes effort to avoid going to war.

Sloth, apathy, and indolence can be an effective means of protecting human interests from the oppression of the autosystems, but only if *men* so arrange things. Men must never allow themselves to become so indolent that they fail to notice when the autosystems regrade the slopes to serve the interests of the systems in ways harmful to the interests of men.

Notes

Prologue   [1] Cited in J. O. Hertzler, *Social Thought of the Ancient Civilizations* (New York: McGraw-Hill Book Co., 1936), pp. 31–32.   [2] See Arthur Oncken Lovejoy, *The Great Chain of Being* (Cambridge: Harvard University Press, 1936), chapter 10, and J. B. Bury, *The Idea of Progress* (London: Macmillan Co., 1924), chapter 4.   [3] Leon Trotsky, *Literature and Revolution* (Ann Arbor: University of Michigan Press, 1960), pp. 249–251.   [4] Robinson Jeffers, *Be Angry at the Sun* (New York: Random House, 1941), p. 101. [5] Allen Ginsberg, *Howl and Other Poems* (San Francisco: City Lights Pocket Bookshop, n.d.), pp. 9 and 15.   [6] Theodore Roszak, *The Making of a Counter Culture* (Garden City, N.Y.: Doubleday & Co., 1969).   [7] Herbert Marcuse, *Eros and Civilization* (Boston: Beacon Press, 1966).

Chapter 1   [1] Erich Fromm, *Escape from Freedom* (New York: Farrar and Rinehart, 1941).   [2] Jules Feiffer, copyright June 19, 1960, reproduced by permission.   [3] Robert Townsend, *Up the Organization* (New York: Alfred A. Knopf, 1970).   [4] Snell Putney and Gail J. Putney, *The Adjusted American* (New York: Harper & Row, Publishers, 1966).

Chapter 2   [1] For a rigorous, concise introduction to systems theory, see William Ross Ashby, *Design for a Brain* (New York: John Wiley, 1952).

Chapter 4   [1] David Riesman, *The Lonely Crowd* (New Haven: Yale University Press, 1967).

Chapter 5   [1] "Theses on Feuerbach No. 11," in C. W. Mills, *The Marxists* (New York: Dell, 1962), p. 71.   [2] For a similar approach to systemic change which derives from very different points of beginning, see William Ross Ashby, *Design for a Brain* (New York: John Wiley, 1952).

Chapter 6   [1] B. F. Skinner, *Science and Human Behavior* (New York: Macmillan Co., 1953), chapter 6.   [2] C. Wright Mills, *The Causes of World War Three* (New York: Simon and Schuster, 1958).

Chapter 7   [1] Hans Reusch, *Top of the World* (New York: Harper & Row, Publishers, 1951).

Chapter 9   [1] Margaret Mead, "Marriage in Two Steps," in Herbert Otto, ed., *The Family in Search of a Future* (New York: Appleton-Century-Crofts, 1970), chapter 7.

Chapter 10   [1] For an interesting description of a society undergoing a technological transition, see Ralph Linton, "The Tanala, A Hill Tribe of Madagascar," in Abram Kardiner, *The Individual and His Society* (New York: Columbia University Press, 1939).   [2] For a more complete treatment of the urban revolution, see V. Gordon Childe, *Man Makes Himself* (New York: New American Library, 1951), chapters 6–8.

Chapter 11   [1] See Roger Burlingame, *Machines That Built America* (New York: New American Library, 1953), chapter 4.   [2] See Norbert Wiener, *The Human Use of Human Beings* (Garden City, N.Y.: Doubleday & Co., 1954), chapter 9.   [3] Samuel Lilley, *Men, Machines, and History* (New York: International Publishers, 1966), p. 230.   [4] See "Taming the H-Bomb," *Wall Street Journal*, December 3, 1969, p. 1.   [5] Harrison Brown, *The Challenge of Man's Future* (New York: Viking Press, 1957), p. 218.

Notes 229

Chapter 12 [1] See Hans Zinsser, *Rats, Lice, and History* (Boston: Little, Brown and Co., 1935). [2] Harrison Brown, *The Challenge of Man's Future* (New York: Viking Press, 1957), p. 159. [3] *Ibid.*, p. 146. [4] See "A Scientist Comes Up with a 'Perfect Car'; Detroit Just Yawns," *Wall Street Journal,* February 15, 1971, p. 1.

Chapter 14 [1] Thorstein Veblen, *Theory of the Leisure Class* (New York: Macmillan Co., 1912). [2] Joseph Heller, *Catch-22* (New York: Dell, 1965), p. 416. [3] Cyril Northcote Parkinson, *Parkinson's Law and Other Studies in Administration* (Boston: Houghton-Mifflin Co., 1957). [4] Dr. Laurence J. Peter and Raymond Hull, *The Peter Principle* (New York: William Morrow & Co., 1970).

Chapter 18 [1] Cited in J. O. Hertzler, *Social Thought of the Ancient Civilizations* (New York: McGraw-Hill Book Co., 1936), p. 216. [2] Eric Hoffer, *The True Believer* (New York: Harper & Row, Publishers, 1966). [3] Jacques Lowe, *Portrait, The Emergence of John F. Kennedy* (New York: Bramhall House, 1961), p. 217.

Chapter 19 [1] For an excellent discussion of the assumptions of the theory of democracy, see Edward Hallett Carr, *The New Society* (Boston: Beacon Press, 1957), chapter 4.

Chapter 21 [1] Alexis de Tocqueville, *Democracy in America* (New York: Harper & Row, Publishers, 1966). [2] Vance Packard, *The Hidden Persuaders* (New York: David McKay Co., 1958). [3] Peter Kropotkin, *Mutual Aid: A Factor of Evolution* (Boston: Extending Horizons Books, 1955). [4] For an excellent discussion of Yugoslavian socialism, see David Tornquist, *Look East, Look West* (New York: Macmillan Co., 1966). [5] B. F. Skinner, *Walden Two* (New York: Macmillan Co., 1970).

Chapter 23 [1] For an early and influential discussion of strategies in the nuclear age, see Herman Kahn, *On Thermonuclear War* (Princeton: Princeton University Press, 1960), especially chapter 1. [2] Walter Schneir, *Invitation to an Inquest* (Garden City, N.Y.: Doubleday & Co., 1965). [3] For a discussion of overkill, see Ralph E. Lapp, *Kill and Overkill* (New York: Basic Books, 1962).

Chapter 24 [1] See Frantz Fanon, *The Wretched of the Earth* (New York: Grove Press, 1968), especially "The Pitfalls of National Consciousness."

Chapter 25 [1] See Frantz Fanon, "Concerning Violence," in *The Wretched of the Earth* (New York: Grove Press, 1968).

Chapter 26 [1] C. Wright Mills, *The Causes of World War Three* (New York: Simon and Schuster, 1958). [2] See comments by George E. Reedy, quoted by Harvey Wheeler in "Powers of the Presidency," *The Center Magazine,* Vol. IV, No. 1, January/February 1971, p. 9.

Chapter 27 [1] See James MacGregor, "Over the Hill," in *The Wall Street Journal,* November 18, 1969, p. 1. [2] See Warren Hinckle, III, "Guerrillas in the Military," in *Scanlan's Monthly,* Vol. I, No. 8, January 1971, pp. 57–58.

Chapter 28 [1] Dan Golenpaul, ed., *Information Please Almanac, Atlas and Yearbook, 1970* (New York: Simon and Schuster, 1970), p. 446. [2] Russell Middleton and Snell Putney, "Religion, Normative Standards, and Behavior," *Sociometry,* 24 (June 1961), pp. 141–152. [3] Will Herberg, *Protestant, Catholic, and Jew* (Garden City, N.Y.: Anchor Books, 1960). [4] See "Hip Culture Discovers a New Trip: Fervent Foot-Stompin' Religion," *Wall Street Journal,* February 2, 1971, p. 1. [5] Hermann Hesse, *Siddhartha* (New York: New Directions, 1951). [6] For example, Alan Watts, *The Spirit of Zen: A Way of Life, Work, and Art in the Far East* (New York: Grove Press, 1960). [7] See Theodore Roszak, *The Making of a Counter Culture* (Garden City, N.Y.: Doubleday & Co., 1969), chapter 1.

Chapter 29   [1] Will Herberg, *Protestant, Catholic, and Jew* (Garden City, N.Y.: Anchor Books, 1960), chapter 2.   [2] John Kenneth Galbraith, *Economics and the Art of Controversy* (New York: Vintage Books, 1959).

Chapter 32   [1] Margaret Mead, *Coming of Age in Samoa* (New York: William Morrow & Co., 1939).   [2] See Gail Putney Fullerton, *Survival in Marriage* (New York: Holt, Rinehart and Winston, 1972), chapter 10.

Chapter 33   [1] Leon Trotsky, "The Art of Insurrection," in C. W. Mills, *The Marxists* (New York: Dell, 1962), p. 269.   [2] V. I. Lenin, *Left-Wing Communism: An Infantile Disorder* (New York: International, 1940), p. 66.

Chapter 34   [1] Nevil Shute, *On the Beach* (New York: New American Library, 1958).   [2] Harrison Brown, *The Challenge of Man's Future* (New York: Viking Press, 1957), chapter 7.   [3] George Orwell, *1984* (New York: New American Library, 1961).   [4] Aldous Huxley, *Brave New World* (New York: Bantam, 1953).   [5] Walter Kaufman, ed., *The Portable Nietzsche* (New York: Viking Press, 1954), p. 139.   [6] *Ibid.*, p. 163.   [7] See Snell Putney and Gail J. Putney, *The Adjusted American* (New York: Harper & Row, Publishers, 1966), chapter 1.   [8] *Ibid.*, chapter 6.

Index